THOMAS MACDONAGH

The 16LIVES Series

JAMES CONNOLLY Lorcan Collins

MICHAEL MALLIN Brian Hughes

JOSEPH PLUNKETT Honor O Brolchain

EDWARD DALY Helen Litton

SEÁN HEUSTON John Gibney

ROGER CASEMENT Angus Mitchell

SEÁN MACDIARMADA Brian Feeney

THOMAS CLARKE Helen Litton

ÉAMONN CEANNT Mary Gallagher

THOMAS MACDONAGH Shane Kenna

WILLIE PEARSE Roisín Ní Ghairbhí

CON COLBERT John O'Callaghan

JOHN MACBRIDE Donal Fallon

MICHAEL O'HANRAHAN Conor Kostick

THOMAS KENT Meda Ryan

PATRICK PEARSE Ruán O'Donnell

SHANE KENNA – AUTHOR OF 16LIVES: THOMAS MACDONAGH

SHANE KENNA is a Doctor of modern Irish history with an interest in late Victorian and Edwardian Ireland. He has lectured at Trinity College, Dublin and Saor Ollscoil na hÉireann University and has designed modules on Irish history for the American College, Arcadia University. He is the author of *War in The Shadows: The Irish-American Fenians Who Bombed Victorian Britain* (Irish Academic Press, 2013) and has also written for *History Ireland* and the *BBC History Magazine*. His website is www.shanekenna.ie

LORCAN COLLINS – SERIES EDITOR

Lorcan Collins was born and raised in Dublin. A lifelong interest in Irish history led to the foundation of his hugely-popular 1916 Walking Tour in 1996. He co-authored *The Easter Rising: A Guide to Dublin in 1916* (O'Brien Press, 2000) with Conor Kostick. His biography of James Connolly was published in the *16 Lives* series in 2012. He is also a regular contributor to radio, television and historical journals. *16 Lives* is Lorcan's concept and he is co-editor of the series.

DR RUÁN O'DONNELL – SERIES EDITOR

Dr Ruán O'Donnell is a senior lecturer at the University of Limerick. A graduate of University College Dublin and the Australian National University, O'Donnell has published extensively on Irish Republicanism. Titles include *Robert Emmet and the Rising of 1803, The Impact of 1916* (editor), *Special Category, The IRA in English prisons 1968–1978* and *The O'Brien Pocket History of the Irish Famine*. He is a director of the Irish Manuscript Commission and a frequent contributor to the national and international media on the subject of Irish revolutionary history.

16 LIVES

THOMAS MACDONAGH

Shane Kenna

THE O'BRIEN PRESS
DUBLIN

First published 2014 by
The O'Brien Press Ltd,
12 Terenure Road East, Rathgar,
Dublin 6, Ireland.
Tel: +353 1 4923333; Fax: +353 1 4922777
E-mail: books@obrien.ie.
Website: www.obrien.ie
ISBN: 978-1-84717-336-2

8 7 6 5 4 3 2 1
17 16 15 14

All quotations, in English and Irish, have been reproduced with original spelling and punctuation.

Printed and bound by CPI Group (UK) Ltd, Croydon, CR0 4YY
The paper used in this book is produced using pulp from managed forests.

PICTURE CREDITS

The author and publisher thank the following for permission to use photographs and illustrative material: front and back covers courtesy of the MacDonagh family; inside-front cover courtesy of Lorcan Collins.

Picture section 1: p. 1 courtesy of the Pearse Museum Collection; p. 2 (top) courtesy of Blackrock College; p. 2 (bottom), p. 3 (top), p. 4 (top) courtesy of the MacDonagh family; p. 3 (bottom), p. 4 (bottom), p. 5 (both), pp. 6–7, p. 8 (top and bottom right) courtesy of the National Library of Ireland; p. 8 (bottom left) courtesy of Kilmainham Gaol Museum. Picture section 2: p. 1 (top), p. 6 (bottom), p. 8 (bottom) courtesy of the National Library of Ireland; p. 1 (bottom) courtesy of the MacDonagh family; p. 2, p. 3 (both), p. 4 (both) courtesy of Lorcan Collins; p. 5, p. 8 (top) courtesy of the Capuchin Archives; p. 6 (top), p. 8 (top) courtesy of Kilmainham Gaol Museum.

If any involuntary infringement of copyright has occurred, sincere apologies are offered and the owners of such copyright are requested to contact the publisher.

ACKNOWLEDGEMENTS

To write a biography about one of the signatories to the Easter Proclamation is truly an honour, and there are a number of people I would like to thank for their help and advice. Firstly, I would like to thank Lorcan Collins and Ruán O'Donnell for all the support they have given me in writing this book. Their knowledge and sense of history and heritage has been of great encouragement. I would like to thank Lorcan in particular for his friendship and support throughout the years. I am exceeding grateful to The O'Brien Press for giving me the opportunity to write this biography and for their courtesy and professionalism; particular thanks must be extended to Nicola Reddy, Helen Carr and Jonathan Rossney.

I would like to thank Pat Cooke of University College, Dublin for his exceptional knowledge of Thomas MacDonagh and the period from 1913 to 1921; Fr Sean Farragher of Blackrock College for his information about MacDonagh's early years; Caroline Mullan, archivist at Blackrock College; John Kirwan, the archivist of St Kieran's College, Kilkenny; Dr Brian Kirby of the Capuchin Archives; Tommy Doyle, senior archivist at RTÉ; the staff of the National Library Manuscripts Department and the National Archives, London; and Brian Crowley of the Pearse Museum for sharing his wealth of knowledge regarding Scoil Éanna. In the course of my research I had the honour of meeting Loretta Clarke, an inspirational person who greatly aided my work by facilitating a visit to the Jackie Clarke Museum. Particular thanks are also extended to Keith Murphy and the staff at the National Photographic Archive and those who work at the Military Archive in Dublin.

I would like to thank all my friends and family for their unwavering support, especially my mother, Olive, and Edel Quinn. I would like to also thank John Kenna, Gerard Shannon, Paul O'Brien, Aiden Lambert, Lucille Redmond, Muriel McAuley, Barry Kennerk, May Casey, Jim Casey, Anne-Marie McInerney, James Langton and Eamon Murphy (a fountain of knowledge regarding the Easter Rising and the Irish Volunteers!) for their kind support, words of advice and exemplary service.

This book has been written using all available sources related to the life of Thomas MacDonagh, and in the course of my research I have met countless people, so I can only apologise to those whom I have inadvertently forgotten to mention. Each and every one of you has been a great help, and your assistance is greatly appreciated. I hope this book will serve as a fitting testimony to all of the help you have provided.

16LIVES Timeline

1845–51. The Great Hunger in Ireland. One million people die and over the next decades millions more emigrate.

1858, March 17. The Irish Republican Brotherhood, or Fenians, are formed with the express intention of overthrowing British rule in Ireland by whatever means necessary.

1867, February and March. Fenian Uprising.

1870, May. Home Rule movement founded by Isaac Butt, who had previously campaigned for amnesty for Fenian prisoners.

1879–81. The Land War. Violent agrarian agitation against English landlords.

1884, November 1. The Gaelic Athletic Association founded – immediately infiltrated by the Irish Republican Brotherhood (IRB).

1893, July 31. Gaelic League founded by Douglas Hyde and Eoin MacNeill. The *Gaelic Revival*, a period of Irish Nationalism, pride in the language, history, culture and sport.

1900, September. *Cumann na nGaedheal* (Irish Council) founded by Arthur Griffith.

1905–07. *Cumann na nGaedheal*, the Dungannon Clubs and the National Council are amalgamated to form *Sinn Féin* (We Ourselves).

1909, August. Countess Markievicz and Bulmer Hobson organise nationalist youths into *Na Fianna Éireann* (Warriors of Ireland) a kind of boy scout brigade.

1912, April. Asquith introduces the Third Home Rule Bill to the British Parliament. Passed by the Commons and rejected by the Lords, the Bill would have to become law due to the Parliament Act. Home Rule expected to be introduced for Ireland by autumn 1914.

1913, January. Sir Edward Carson and James Craig set up Ulster Volunteer Force (UVF) with the intention of defending Ulster against Home Rule.

1913. Jim Larkin, founder of the Irish Transport and General Workers' Union (ITGWU) calls for a workers' strike for better pay and conditions.

1913, August 31. Jim Larkin speaks at a banned rally on Sackville (O'Connell) Street; Bloody Sunday.

1913, November 23. James Connolly, Jack White and Jim Larkin establish the Irish Citizen Army (ICA) in order to protect strikers.

1913, November 25. The Irish Volunteers founded in Dublin to 'secure the rights and liberties common to all the people of Ireland'.

1914, March 20. Resignations of British officers force British government not to use British army to enforce Home Rule, an event known as the 'Curragh Mutiny'.

1914, April 2. In Dublin, Agnes O'Farrelly, Mary MacSwiney, Countess Markievicz and others establish Cumann na mBan as a women's volunteer force dedicated to establishing Irish freedom and assisting the Irish Volunteers.

1914, April 24. A shipment of 35,000 rifles and five million rounds of ammunition is landed at Larne for the UVF.

1914, July 26. Irish Volunteers unload a shipment of 900 rifles and 45,000 rounds of ammunition shipped from Germany aboard Erskine Childers' yacht, the *Asgard*. British troops fire on crowd on Bachelors Walk, Dublin. Three citizens are killed.

1914, August 4. Britain declares war on Germany. Home Rule for Ireland shelved for the duration of the First World War.

1914, September 9. Meeting held at Gaelic League headquarters between IRB and other extreme republicans. Initial decision made to stage an uprising while Britain is at war.

1914, September. 170,000 leave the Volunteers and form the National Volunteers or Redmondites. Only 11,000 remain as the Irish Volunteers under Eóin Mac-Neill.

1915, May–September. Military Council of the IRB is formed.

1915, August 1. Pearse gives fiery oration at the funeral of Jeremiah O'Donovan Rossa.

1916, January 19–22. James Connolly joins the IRB Military Council, thus ensuring that the ICA shall be involved in the Rising. Rising date confirmed for Easter.

1916, April 20, 4.15pm. *The Aud* arrives at Tralee Bay, laden with 20,000 German rifles for the Rising. Captain Karl Spindler waits in vain for a signal from shore.

1916, April 21, 2.15am. Roger Casement and his two companions go ashore from U-19 and land on Banna Strand. Casement is arrested at McKenna's Fort.

6.30pm. *The Aud* is captured by the British navy and forced to sail towards Cork Harbour.

22 April, 9.30am. *The Aud* is scuttled by her captain off Daunt's Rock.

10pm. Eóin MacNeill as chief-of-staff of the Irish Volunteers issues the countermanding order in Dublin to try to stop the Rising.

1916, April 23, 9am, Easter Sunday. The Military Council meets to discuss the situation, considering MacNeill has placed an advertisement in a Sunday newspaper halting all Volunteer operations. The Rising is put on hold for twenty-four hours. Hundreds of copies of *The Proclamation of the Republic* are printed in Liberty Hall.

1916, April 24, 12 noon, Easter Monday. The Rising begins in Dublin.

16LIVESMAP

REBEL POSITIONS
REBEL HELD AREAS
••• BRITISH CORDON OF TROOPS

FINGLAS ROAD

CABRA ROAD

Phoenix Park

St Brendan's Hospital

NTH BRUNSW'

Magazine Fort

Collins Barracks

FIRST BATTALIO

Heuston Station

James's Gate Brewery

Mendicity Institution

Royal Hospital

JAMES'S ST

Kilmainham Gaol

St James's Hospital (South Dublin Union)

FOURTH BATTALION

SOUTH

CIRCULAR

ROAD

Griffith Barracks

To Kimmage

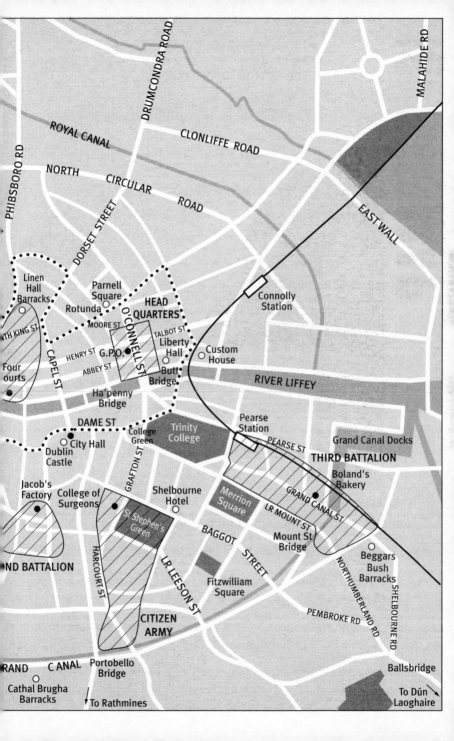

16LIVES – Series Introduction

This book is part of a series called *16 LIVES*, conceived with the objective of recording for posterity the lives of the sixteen men who were executed after the 1916 Easter Rising. Who were these people and what drove them to commit themselves to violent revolution?

The rank and file as well as the leadership were all from diverse backgrounds. Some were privileged and some had no material wealth. Some were highly educated writers, poets or teachers and others had little formal schooling. Their common desire, to set Ireland on the road to national freedom, united them under the one banner of the army of the Irish Republic. They occupied key buildings in Dublin and around Ireland for one week before they were forced to surrender. The leaders were singled out for harsh treatment and all sixteen men were executed for their role in the Rising.

Meticulously researched yet written in an accessible fashion, the *16 LIVES* biographies can be read as individual volumes but together they make a highly collectible series.

Lorcan Collins & Dr Ruán O'Donnell,
16 Lives *Series Editors*

CONTENTS

Introduction   15

Chapter 1: 1878–1901 Beginnings   21

Chapter 2: 1901–1908 'The greatest West Britisher in Ireland'   39

Chapter 3: 1908 'The present state of politics is pitiable'   58

Chapter 4: 1908–1912 'A desert where I could begin again'   85

Chapter 5: 1913–1915 'Dear boy, you'll be shot'   108

Chapter 6: 1913–1914 Troubled times in Ireland   136

Chapter 7: 1914–1915 'The old order changeth'   162

Chapter 8: 1915–1916 'We will have a stir'   181

Chapter 9: 24 April 1916 'Long live the Republic!'   201

Chapter 10: 25–30 April 1916 'Boys, we must give in'   217

Chapter 11: 30 April–3 May 1916 'A great and glorious thing'   239

Chapter 12: 'A loss both to Ireland and to literature'   260

Notes   275

Bibliography   296

Index   300

Introduction

His songs were a little phrase
Of eternal song,
Drowned in the harping of lays
More loud and long.

His deed was a single word,
Called out alone
In the night when no echo stirred
To laughter or moan.

But his songs new souls shall thrill,
The loud harps dumb,
And his deed the echoes fill
When the dawn is come.

(Thomas MacDonagh, 'On a Poet Patriot')

The last man to be invited onto the Military Council of the IRB, the body entrusted with planning the Easter Rising, Thomas MacDonagh was by all accounts a warmhearted, humorous and talkative individual. Originally from Cloughjordan in County Tipperary, he had been brought up in a house full of music, story and prayer. His parents were teachers and his mother a convert to Catholicism, who enshrined in her children a belief in acts of individual charity and morality that would considerably influence his character. During his life he was a schoolmaster, a poet, a theatre manager, an astute literary critic, a supporter of women's rights and the Gaelic League, and a friend to some of the best-known and influential artistic and political figures in literary Dublin. He sought fairer pay and better working conditions for secondary school teachers through the foundation of the ASTI, while his involvement with the Dublin Industrial Peace Committee in 1913 was underlined by a recognisable desire to seek a fair resolution to the Lockout. MacDonagh was sympathetic to the ambitions of the ITGWU, and while not a member of the union and far removed from the realities of its socialist policies, he greatly favoured the workers rather than the employers arising from a sense of justice, fairness and a natural support for the underdog. Finally, he joined the Irish Volunteers out of a sense that nationalist Ireland needed to defend Home Rule. If he had not become involved with the Volunteers and then the IRB, which ultimately led to his execution in May 1916, he could have lived out his life as a well-respected academic. Of particular interest is his final work, *Literature in Ireland*, a detailed study of the development of language in Ireland that, in a remarkable break from the thinking of many Irish nationalists at the time, rejected the assumption that a truly national literature could only be created within the Irish language. His friend Padraic Colum wrote of MacDonagh as:

A poet bent toward abstraction, a scholar with leaning
towards philology – these were the aspects Thomas Mac-
Donagh showed when he expressed himself in letters. But
what was fundamental in him rarely went into what he
wrote. That fundamental thing was an eager search for
something that would have his whole devotion.[1]

This book seeks to examine MacDonagh's place within
the Rising and to portray a man who for too long was overlooked in favour of more celebrated figures. In part, it is
because his role in the rebellion was a minor one, but it is
also because there are no great symbolic tales attached to his
name: he did not read the Proclamation to the Irish people
from the GPO; his garrison at Jacob's Biscuit Factory saw
little action during the Rising; he did not die strapped to
a chair or after marrying his sweetheart in a midnight ceremony; and the famed address he gave during his court-martial is almost certainly an invention. However, his life forms
an interesting story of religious fervour, self-doubt, political
activity, romance, joy and bitter sadness. His execution in
Kilmainham Gaol is punctuated by tragedy: hours before his
death, his desire to see his wife Muriel was thwarted, and
from his final letter it is apparent that he was ultimately a
husband and father concerned for the welfare of his family.

As a leading writer and critic, MacDonagh's work, like
that of Pearse, Plunkett and Connolly, provided a means
through which the 1916 rebellion could not only be justi-

fied but also speak to future generations. However, his works have not been examined as thoroughly as those of his contemporaries: he did not write as prolifically about sacrifice as Pearse and Plunkett, while unlike Connolly he did not leave behind him a defined social policy. Some of his poetry casts the rebel dead of Ireland in a decided romantic light, but this does not equate with an enthusiasm for the blood sacrifice spoken of by his peers. Indeed, Padraic Colum recalled that MacDonagh would have accepted 'reasonable settlement of Irish political conditions from the government of Great Britain.'[2] Lamenting MacDonagh at the time of his death, Colum commented how:

> His country was always in his mind but it did not fill it exclusively, as it might be said to have filled Pearse's mind … I often had a vision of my friend in a Home Rule parliament, working at social and legislative problems and perhaps training himself to become Minister for Education.[3]

His eventual involvement in the Rising seems to have come about as a result of factors beyond his control, in that he became caught up in the excitement surrounding the Irish Volunteers, then in the increasing militarisation of society that followed the outbreak of World War One, and finally in his co-option onto the Military Council of the IRB. The sequence of events that led to him becoming commandant of Jacob's Biscuit Factory was more progressional than premeditated; ten years previously, no one could have predicted that Mr MacDonagh, the well-liked secondary school teacher and part-time poet, would have ended up before a firing squad after being convicted of treason. It is evident, however, that during the Easter Rising and his subsequent court-martial MacDonagh knew he was going to be executed and that he would never see his family again. But, unlike Pearse, he did not fixate on death or indicate that his execution had the power to change the course of Irish history. MacDonagh, in his last words, defined his life in Shakespearian terms, stating, 'in all of my acts – all the acts for which I have been arraigned – I have been actuated by one motive only, the love of my country.'[4] After his execution, *The New York Times* romantically lamented how he had 'gone into battle with a revolver in one hand and a copy of Sophocles in the other.'[5]

Despite the fact that the Easter Rising for which Mac-Donagh was shot belongs to a former century, it still continues to affect the course of Irish life. Reflecting upon the effect of the executions of sixteen men in 1916, using the opportunity of the 97th anniversary of the rebellion, Irish President Michael D Higgins commented how 'the removal of such a strong intellectual core from the definition of independence was the price we paid, a high one, because the succeeding twenties and thirties into the forties are very conservative and very different from either the life-witness or the writings of the people who were the direct participants in the Rising.'[6] This is no more apparent than within the life of Thomas MacDonagh.

Chapter One

1878 – 1901

Beginnings

Thomas Stanislaus MacDonagh was born in Cloughjordan, County Tipperary, on 1 February 1878, the son of Joseph MacDonagh and Mary Parker MacDonagh. Joseph MacDonagh's father was a small farmer and Fenian activist who lived at Kilglass on the Sligo–Roscommon border, and the family claimed to be descendants of the medieval Mac Donnchadha clan of Ballymote Castle, County Sligo. Joseph, born in 1834, was brought up on stories of how the family had defended Ballymote Castle against Sir Richard Bingham in 1586. After the death of his father while he was still young, it would have been expected that Joseph would take over the family farm, but instead he became the protégé of a priest uncle who taught him Latin, classics and a love of literature. Choosing to follow a career in education, Joseph attended the Marlborough Street School in Dublin, where he studied to be a primary teacher and was awarded a First classification from the National Board of Education. In 1867 he took work at Cloghan, County Offaly, where he met and married Mary Louise Parker. Unlike his father, Joseph MacDonagh was decidedly apolitical and wholeheartedly opposed Fenianism. Cynical about political activists, he recalled nationalists, particularly IRB men like his father, as 'great cry and little wool, like the goats of Connacht.'[1]

Mary Louise Parker, born in 1843, was nine years Joseph's junior and came from a relatively prosperous family. Her father was a Unitarian who had moved from England to Dublin when offered well-paid employment as a compositor in Greek for the Trinity College Dublin Press, and Mary Louise grew up in a house filled with music and literature, becoming an excellent pianist and a prolific writer of short stories and amateur poetry. At seventeen she took on teaching as a vocation and taught at Rush and other Dublin schools before taking work in Offaly. Developing an interest in Catholicism, Mary Louise decided to convert in anticipation of her marriage to Joseph.

With the zeal of the convert, Mary Louise was fervently religious and wholeheartedly embraced Roman Catholicism as a standard of living. In an article for *The Catholic Truth Bulletin*, she recommended regular prayer 'for the relief of poor souls in purgatory,' and joining sodalities (lay confraternities) to practice charitable works.[2] Mary Louise believed, however, that pious Catholics needed to be practical about the number of sodalities they joined as this could only undermine their Christian duties. Like her husband, Mary Louise was not a nationalist and held that Ireland was an integral part of the United Kingdom. Moving to Cloughjordan in County Tipperary, a small town with a large Protestant community, the MacDonaghs became the first teachers in the town's new Catholic school, established in 1877 on the initiative of Fr Denis Moloney, the local parish priest. The MacDonaghs were to manage the boys' and girls' school respectively. According to Roche Williams, an historian of Cloughjordan, the school was very cramped and underfunded, with large numbers of students crowded into small rooms.[3] For this work Joseph received £44 while Mary Louise was reasonably in receipt of £32 (including fees). While these salaries were high by Victorian standards, teachers were only paid every quarter year, meaning that in reality the family were not financially secure.

As a strongly Catholic middle-class family, the MacDonaghs were initially put up in Fr Moloney's home until they found more settled accommodation. By the late 19th century the Catholic Church was becoming increasingly influential as a new wave of devotional fervour swept Ireland and revitalised a faith which had long been moribund and suppressed. A new Catholic middle class was increasingly becoming apparent in Irish society, one which tended to adopt Britishness as the norm, into which the MacDonaghs fitted excellently. Unsurprisingly, the MacDonagh house-hold would be one steeped in religious activity, and each evening the family would gather to recite the Rosary. Due to their hard work and sociable nature, they were soon admired throughout the small village, and Mary Louise became well known for giving piano lessons to local children after school. It was apparent that she adored the village, even writing poetry to celebrate it (something she had in common with her son Thomas). Her husband seems to have been known less for his educational abilities and more for his regular bouts of drinking and socialising about the town. All who knew Joseph MacDonagh regarded him as a warm and kind personality with a merry temperament, albeit one prone to overindulgence.

Joseph and Mary Louise had eight children, two of whom died in infancy. Thomas was their fourth. He was preceded by Mary Josephine and Eleanor Louise (sometimes referred to as Nell or Helen) and was followed by John, James and Joseph. Their home, under their mother's influence, was filled with music and learning, and the children were encouraged to expand their knowledge in an idyllic rural environment. They enjoyed 'running little manuscript magazines, playing paper and pencil games and reading improving books'[4] under the tutelage of their parents. John developed a love of singing, while James was encouraged to play clarinet. Thomas, for his part, sang and played the piano. As a child he was 'small, stur-

dily built, with curly brown hair and large grey eyes',[5] pos-
sessing a strong Tipperary accent, a fine sense of mischievous
humour, and a love of ghost stories. His father taught him
a love of the countryside, and he embraced the splendour
of the rural Cloughjordan hinterland, climbing Scott's Hill
and wandering through Knocknacree Wood, which he later
celebrated in a poem called 'Knocknacree':

> *The great wood lies beneath me in the sun!*
> *Through all my days it has been still to me*
> *As to the sailor lad the endless sea,*
> *Or as her cloister to the happy nun;*
> *And so must be until my race is run –*
> *A place of natural childish piety,*
> *Or haven to which I may safely flee*
> *For restful quiet this loud world to shun.*[6]

But as well as a love for literature, music and religion,
Thomas's mother also gave him a strong belief in personal
morality and charity which would considerably influence his
life. As a result, MacDonagh always held that wherever he
saw distress or injustice, he was duty bound to intervene. This
made him decidedly prone to the adoption of causes he saw
to be just in his later life. In a later poem, 'A Rule for Life',
one cannot but see the shadow of his religious mother:

Ne'er regret the evil that thou has not done;
E'er bemoan the good that thou has failed to do;
Manfully finish a good work once begun;
To thy God, to thy country and to thyself be true.[7]

Considering the emphasis on the arts and religion within the MacDonagh household, it came as no surprise that all bar two of the children chose artistic or religious professions in their later life. In 1895 Mary Josephine, the eldest daughter, became a nun with the Religious Sisters of Charity. Eleanor Louise married a policeman, Daniel Bingham, in 1897, and for a time lived in Cloughjordan and then in Clare before emigrating to the US. John had a remarkable operatic voice and trained to be a tenor singer in Italy. He was also an actor and writer, and in 1910 he wrote the script for the motion picture *The Fugitive*, directed by DW Griffith. During the Rising, John left a vivid account of the reality of Easter Week in Jacob's Factory, and eventually became the director of the radio station 2RN, the first one in the independent Irish state. James briefly served in the British Army before joining the London Symphony Orchestra, where he played the cor anglais and oboe. One of his children, Terence, was a founding member of the London Philharmonic Orchestra and was awarded an OBE in 1979. Finally Thomas' youngest brother, Joseph, like John, had hoped to fight in the Easter Rising, and had cycled from Thurles to Dublin to join his brothers at Jacob's, but was unable get past British blockades. Following the rebellion he was elected Sinn Féin MP for Tipperary North in the 1918 general election. He was imprisoned during the election campaign and had previously been on hunger strike with Thomas Ashe in 1917, demanding political status for Republican prisoners. Rejecting the Anglo-Irish Treaty in 1921, Joseph was an active participant within the anti-Treaty IRA and while interned in Mountjoy developed peritonitis, dying on Christmas Day 1922.

However, despite their parents' antipathy to nationalism, it is no surprise that three of the MacDonagh boys eventually became involved in the cause of Irish independence. The Ireland they grew up in was undergoing great social and political change. Since 1 January 1801, Ireland had been a constituent part of the United Kingdom of Great Britain and governed directly by London through an administration operating out of Dublin Castle. Throughout MacDonagh's childhood, the greatest challenge Dublin Castle faced was the question of the land, particularly along the impoverished western coast, where a large tenant farming class was dependent on landlords for their holdings. These farmers' lives were incredibly insecure, as the tenancy system in Ireland was weighted in favour of the landlord, who could increase rent and evict tenants from their farms arbitrarily. In 1878 and 1879 a bad harvest, regarded as the worst on record since the great famine in the 1840s, caused enormous difficulties for farmers, which were further exacerbated by a fall in the price offered for Irish agricultural produce as the market favoured cheaper imports from America, Argentina and Australia. As a result, many farmers were unable to pay their rent and faced eviction, evidenced by the rise in evictions from 406 in 1877 to 1,098 the following year.[8] To defend the rights of the tenant farming class, a Tenants' Defence League was established in Mayo on 26 October 1878, and throughout rural communities across Ireland similar societies emerged. The following year saw the emergence of the Irish National Land League seeking fair rent, fixity of tenure and free sale beneficial to tenant farmers. The ultimate ambition of the movement was to establish peasant proprietorship on the land.

In Charles Stewart Parnell, the Land League had as president an articulate, educated Protestant landlord from County Wicklow who forcibly represented the Irish interest at Westminster. As a member (and later leader) of the Irish Parliamentary Party, he had been elected to the British parliament in 1875, and strongly supported the establishment of a devolved Irish parliament, a policy known as Home Rule. In later years MacDonagh viewed Parnell as a political hero. He described him as an 'austere nationalist'[9] and held him in deep regard as 'a matter of fact politician'.[10] His admiration for Parnell was such that he was outraged when a statue of Parnell that he considered gaudy was unveiled on Sackville Street (now O'Connell Street) in Dublin.[11] Parnell's leadership of the Land League, while calculated to facilitate his rise within Irish politics, took place during what became known as the Land War between 1879 to 1882, a social conflict between landlords, supported by the government, and tenant farmers, organised through the Land League.

In February 1881, the British government introduced a policy of combining conciliation with coercion to deal with the land problem in Ireland. Under conciliation, the Liberal Prime Minister, William Ewart Gladstone, introduced a Land Act on 7 April 1881, which established a Land Court to fix rents at fair prices and allowed for a commission to grant loans of 75 per cent of money needed by farmers to buy out their holdings. Tenants were also to be compensated if they improved their holdings. However, the Act came with a clause asserting that no tenant in arrears could avail of the Land Court and leaseholders were to be excluded until their lease was up for renewal. This meant that the poorer class of farmers, particularly those in the impoverished west, were excluded from its benefits. In effect, the Act was calculated to break the solidarity of the Land League by favouring wealthier farmers. The coercion policy was embodied in the Protection of Person and Property Act, which gave draconian powers to Dublin Castle. Chief Secretary William Forster announced that it would place 'village ruffians and outrage mongers' under lock and key.[12] On 3 February 1881, Michael Davitt, the secretary of the Land League, was arrested, and on the same day, sensing that the government was moving against the Land League, its treasurer, Patrick Egan, made to France with league funds, outside of British jurisdiction.

On 2 March 1881 the coercion bill was passed. Dublin Castle spared little time in using its new powers, with some nine hundred members of the Land League arrested and interned in various prisons as Ireland increasingly descended into anarchy. At Cloughjordan, several Land League activists were arrested, including Michael O'Reilly, secretary of the Cloughjordan Land League, and James M Wall, a journalist with *The Roscommon Herald*. By 13 October 1881 Charles Stewart Parnell had been arrested and lodged in Kilmainham Gaol; within a week of his arrest, the senior Kilmainham prisoners issued a manifesto calling upon tenant farmers to withhold both their rent and the harvest. By 2 May 1882 Parnell had been released from Kilmainham with the understanding that he would use his influence to quell violence in Ireland. In return, the British government would facilitate the entry of tenants in arrears into the land court. This, it was speculated, would facilitate a new era of Irish and British co-operation, signalling an end to the Land War and eventually leading toward a Home Rule parliament. MacDonagh recalled later how the conclusion of the Land War had inspired the Irish nation to 'struggle for legislative freedom and the certainty of triumph and responsibility.'[13]

Within four days of Parnell's release, this new era of co-operation was stymied when a Fenian society calling themselves the Irish National Invincibles assassinated the new Irish Chief Secretary, Lord Frederick Cavendish, and his Undersecretary, Thomas Henry Burke, in Dublin's Phoenix Park. A new round of coercion seemed inevitable and a bill introduced in the aftermath, known as the Crimes Bill, was even more draconian than what had gone before, allowing for special non-jury courts to try cases of treason and murder as well as giving summary powers of arrest and the power to 'proclaim' entire districts. The assassinations, coupled with the experience of coercion, effectively threw the Parnellite-Liberal alliance into disarray. Neither party would co-operate with each other until 1885, dramatically represented by the introduction of the first Home Rule Bill the following year, which provided for a devolved Irish parliament with limited legislative powers. The bill was defeated by 341 votes to 311, with significant numbers of the Prime Minister's Liberal Party voting against their own bill. Despite this defeat, however, Home Rule was now firmly entrenched within the political agenda.

Even as a child, MacDonagh could not have been unaware of the tensions created by all these developments, especially when living in a rural area. But for most of his life, nationalism was to be dominated by constitutional rather than physical-force activism. More radical revolutionary groups, such as the Irish Republican Brotherhood in Ireland and Clan na Gael in the US, who together would plan the Easter Rising, were largely irrelevant and ignored. However, nationalism as a whole suffered a serious blow in 1889 when Parnell was exposed as the lover of a married woman, Katherine O'Shea. The fallout of this scandal was immense, forcing an acrimonious split in the Irish Parliamentary Party and dividing the country into pro- and anti-Parnell factions. Parnell died in 1891, and while the IPP bickered over his legacy, Home Rule became increasingly unlikely. Lamenting his great hero many years later, MacDonagh recalled: 'Parnell exhorted us to national effort, not in terms of hunger and profit, but in terms of tradition and the sacred gift of the ideal for which we have stood against tramplings and settlements these thousand years: "keep the fires of the nation burning."'[14]

In 1892 Joseph and Mary Louise decided that Thomas was to study in Rockwell College, a boarding school in Cashel, County Tipperary, founded in 1864 and administered by the Holy Ghost Fathers. The Holy Ghost Fathers were dedicated to the adoration of the Holy Spirit as well as missionary activity and work with the poor as part of a process of evangelisation. In Ireland they already administered several schools of national repute, including Blackrock and St Mary's College, Dublin. While the reasons for sending Thomas to a boarding school, rather than educating him at Cloughjordan, are not entirely clear, Rockwell College had an excellent reputation;

indeed, the Reverend Nicholas Brennan, President of Rockwell, explained to commissioners investigating intermediate
education how 'the boys who have passed [Rockwell] as a
rule are equal to any of the boys passed through the other
colleges.'[15] The college also housed a Junior Scholasticate for
the training of novice priests, and it can be speculated that
by sending Thomas to Rockwell, Mary Louise was eager for
her son to become a priest within the order.

The culture of Rockwell College was remarkably insular
and conventional, with no nationalist ethos whatsoever. There
was no attempt to teach the Irish language or Irish history.
In terms of sport, the students played rugby and cricket, with
MacDonagh, known to his peers as Tommy, eagerly embracing both. As a student he showed great potential in languages,
particularly Latin and English, excelling as a student in letters
and humanities. He was less gifted in mathematics, however,
and showed a marked inability to grasp algebra.

In 1894 Joseph MacDonagh passed away, leaving his wife
widowed with six children to care for. Thomas was only sixteen years old and, returning to his studies in Rockwell College, he decided to devote his life to missionary work and
prepare for the priesthood. Writing to the Superior General
of the Holy Ghost Fathers in Dublin, he requested entry to
the Junior Scholasticate, stating:

> I like its rules and customs and particularly the great object
> of all its members, and for which it has been founded. I first

learnt of it from some of my friends, and now, having tried by every means in my power to find out to what life I have been called, I have concluded that I have a vocation for this congregation, and a decided taste for the missionary and the religious state. It has always been my wish to become a Priest and now that wish is stronger than ever, and it is to become, not only a Priest, but a missionary and religious.[16]

Accepted for the order, Thomas now moved from the main campus of Rockwell College to the grounds of the Junior Scholasticate, known as the Lake House. Having expressed an interest in missionary rather than diocesan work, Mac-Donagh was enrolled as what the order termed a *surveilliant*; that is, an adolescent boy who shows potential to go further within the Church. However, it was not a commitment to enter the priesthood, nor did it involve taking any vows. On completion, if they so chose, *surveilliants* could continue on to priesthood with the Holy Ghost Fathers. In Ireland the *surveilliant* was called a prefect, and life as a prefect at Rockwell was intense, vigorous and often lonely. Living at the Lake House, mass and private prayer were daily features in his life, as was intensive study regarding Church doctrine on issues of morality, liturgy and philosophy. Prefects were also regarded as part of the clerical administration, with duties in teaching, organising of games and activities in addition to management of the student dorms and study. In 1896 MacDonagh became a junior master, a role which included the instruction of junior students. He seemed to relish being a teacher, and one of his students recalled how he was appreciated by the boys in the class, as MacDonagh, who was quite short, appeared boyish, approachable, and friendly (he always seemed to be smiling, an impression given through a slight prominence in his teeth).[17]

It was around this time that he began to write poetry, and many of the poems written at Rockwell would be used in his first book, *Through The Ivory Gate* (self-published in 1902). It is clear from these and other sources that at some point during his time in Rockwell, his studies and the possibility of being called to the priesthood forced him into a crisis of faith. While evidence remains sparse as to why his vocation was challenged, some of the poems in *Through The Ivory Gate* hint at why he may have experienced doubt toward the Catholic Church and its teachings. Introducing the book, he describes his poetry as 'a struggle of soul from the innocence of Childhood through disillusion, disappointment and ill doubt; and thence through prayer and hope and the pathos of old memories to lasting Trust and Faith.'[18] In essence his first book of poems, if applied to Rockwell College, identifies MacDonagh as a young man struggling to come to terms with Catholic heterodoxy. At the heart of his crisis was an increasing preoccupation with death, as he strongly questioned the central tenet of Christian doctrine: resurrection and the afterlife. These doubts troubled MacDonagh greatly, as without any afterlife there was no hope. Almost mournfully he lamented:

> *Man comes and lives and goes,*
> *Brief houred and frail as they –*
> *And when he's had his day,*
> *Dies – for all time – who knows.*[19]

Why he developed a preoccupation with death in Rockwell College has never been adequately explained; however, one biographer has cited that it may have been due to the death of a friend in the college.[20] This supposition rests in the nature of 'The Dream Tower' section of *Through The Ivory Gate*, when, beginning in Poem Six, MacDonagh wrote about a colleague whom, while initially friendly, grew to be cold and distant. While MacDonagh never mentions his name, he appears to have died while at the Junior Scholasticate and the two were unable to reconcile. With MacDonagh overcome by guilt, he recalled his absent friend taking 'my fairest treasure, my soul's light,'[21] and it was speculated that he wrote 'De Mortuis' in his memory, lamenting:

> *He is dead, my foe – I must be silent now,*
> *Or speak at last whate'er I know of good*
> *In him before whose cold set face I bow*
> *In reverence humble. Once, when he had stood*
> *Long hostile, he said, smilingly – 'Forgive'*
> *For years I have repented that I turned*
> *In scorn away …*[22]

His mood increasingly despondent, MacDonagh visited his friend's grave at Rockwell, recollecting:

There is a green grave in Rockwell's bowers,
Covered with fair and blooming flowers;
In that lowly grave thou liest –
Struck down, when thy hopes were highest,
Of a long and fruitful life,
Spent in holy strife.[23]

As a result of this crisis of conscience, MacDonagh realised that the religious life was something he was not prepared for, although, while rejecting much of the Church's teachings, MacDonagh still retained enough religious belief to avoid the label of atheist. He finally decided he could not remain in Rockwell as a prefect and was not prepared for a vocation. This was an incredibly difficult decision for MacDonagh; through his mother in particular, he had been immersed in Catholicism since his childhood. On 22 June 1901 he wrote to the Order's Superior General asking to be given permission to resign from the Holy Ghost Fathers. In a marked difference from the sixteen-year-old who had written in 1894 of his 'decided taste for the missionary and the religious state'[24], at age twenty-three he now wrote:

Having, after much hesitation and anxious questioning, come to the conclusion that I have no vocation for religious life, with sorrow, I request you to release me from the obligations contracted by me at my reception. [25]

MacDonagh's request was acceded to, but, having resigned from the Holy Ghost Order who administered Rockwell College, it is possible he was made aware that he would need to find employment elsewhere. On the eve of his departure from Rockwell, he wrote 'The Parting':

I found thee when my childhood's home I left,
And grew to love thee fondly through the years
Of blissful quiet in the half lost past –
Tomorrow go I forth of all bereft
But memories deep of thee, and for thee tears –
Tonight I still am thine – this night, the last![26]

It has been claimed that MacDonagh remained teaching at Rockwell for a further two years[27], but this was impossible, as by late 1901, the year he resigned from the Junior Scholasticate, he had had visited Paris for six weeks prior to taking up a new teaching position in Kilkenny. However, while Mac-Donagh's calling was not to a religious life, he remained a vocational individual, and in Kilkenny he would discover a new cause that would consume him utterly: the preservation of the Irish language through the work of the Gaelic League, which would encourage an almost Pauline conversion to the cause of Irish nationalism.

Chapter Two

• • • • • •

1901 – 1908

'The greatest West Britisher in Ireland'

At the turn of the twentieth century Kilkenny was a small city in southeast Ireland dominated by a large Norman castle built in 1195 by the Earl of Pembroke. The town centre was remarkably British, resembling a small town in the English countryside, and was dominated by two cathedrals: St Canice's for the Church of Ireland and St Mary's for Roman Catholicism. In 1904 King Edward VII and Queen Alexandra arrived for a tour of the city, and were greeted by hundreds of well-wishers along heavily bunted and flagged streets. Culturally there was a strong interest in cricket in the city and surrounding area, centred on Mount Juliet in Thomastown to the south of the city. While Irish was spoken in the hinterland, in Kilkenny City the dominant language, associated with privilege, education and business, was English. To speak Irish was to be seen as with backward, poor and superstitious.

Taking a position at St Kieran's Secondary School in September 1901, Thomas MacDonagh taught English and French and fitted well into the community at Kilkenny. He had no interest in the Irish language, and shunned Irish sport and culture. It was evident that he regarded the Irish peasantry, particularly those who spoke Irish, with a certain amount of disdain. His classes at St Kieran's focused almost exclusively on English literature and he had particular respect for Keats and Wordsworth, often becoming totally engrossed in the poetry he read to the class. When the boys played rugby, he was often seen watching, and was fond of playing the sport himself (although many agreed that he was no good at it as he was too gentle). While at St Kieran's, MacDonagh also befriended the pacifist and social reformer Francis Sheehy Skeffington, who had taught there just before MacDonagh took up his post. It has been claimed that MacDonagh and Skeffington lived together at 19 High Street, having rented rooms from the college physician, Dr White. As they taught in the same school, although not at the same time, and both died in the Easter Rising, it's not surprising that some may have believed that they shared rooms, but there is no hard evidence to back this up. A contemporary described them as follows: 'MacDonagh small, stocky, neat, almost dapper, interested in rugby; the other bearded and untidy with a passion for long walks and legendary amongst his students.'[1]

While MacDonagh was settling into Kilkenny, a new movement was gaining momentum across Ireland. Known as cultural nationalism, it was deeply concerned with the influence of British culture in Ireland, believing that the adoption of British manners and customs was detrimental to the national question as it increasingly became hard to distinguish the Irish from the British. Those who adopted British cultural mores were castigated as 'West-Britons' and accused of abandoning Irish culture. Cultural nationalism sought to redefine the Irish nation through the promotion of indigenous Gaelic traditions, with its main emphasis on restoring the Irish language, which had been in decline since the Famine. The first attempt at such a restoration had come from the Society for the Preservation of the Irish Language, founded in 1876. It had sought to have the Irish language taught in Irish schools, but despite their best efforts and the support of the IPP there was little official interest in the scheme, and by 1881 Irish was taught in only a handful of schools. In 1892, addressing the increasing Anglicisation of Ireland, Douglas Hyde delivered a paper to the National Literary Society:

> I have no hesitation at all in saying that every Irish-feeling Irishman, who hates the reproach of West-Britonism, should set himself to encourage the efforts, which are being made to keep alive our once great national tongue. The

losing of it is our greatest blow, and the sorest stroke that the rapid Anglicisation of Ireland has inflicted upon us. In order to de-Anglicise ourselves we must at once arrest the decay of the language. We must bring pressure upon our politicians not to snuff it out by their tacit discouragement merely because they do not happen themselves to understand it. We must arouse some spark of patriotic inspiration among the peasantry who still use the language, and put an end to the shameful state of feeling – a thousand-tongued reproach to our leaders and statesmen – which makes young men and women blush and hang their heads when overheard speaking their own language.[2]

This speech was a rallying call for a new and more vibrant cultural nationalism. Hyde, who was a member of the Society for the Preservation of the Irish Language, viewed the organisation as too elitist and, with two colleagues from the society, Eoin MacNeill and Eugene O'Growney, he established Conradh na Gaeilge (the Gaelic League) in 1893. Organised through a system of branches set up in towns across the country, the League's development was fortuitously timed as the emphasis on cultural nationalism filled the political vacuum within Irish nationalism following the split in the IPP. Many nationalists, disillusioned with the squabbling within the IPP after the Parnell scandal, saw in the League a new means of expression and activism. Seeking to educate the Irish people of the necessity of speaking their own language, the League also trained teachers, known as *timirí*, who facilitated the establishment of branches and travelled throughout the country addressing Irish language conversation classes and training others to teach the language. The League also organised local festivals and concerts highlighting Irish dance, poetry and music, called *feiseanna*. For many of those living in rural towns and the countryside, this often provided a much-needed social outlet. Members of the League were also encouraged to buy only Irish goods and support Irish industry. By 1906, such was the growth of the Gaelic League that 550 branches existed throughout Ireland with an estimated 50,000 members. Seeking to expand its appeal to a wider audience, in 1899 the League founded its own newspaper, *An Claidheamh Soluis* (The Sword of Light), edited by Eoin MacNeill, which was published weekly and appealed to an audience increasingly known as Irish-Irelanders.

In Kilkenny, a branch of the Gaelic League had existed since 1900 and actively organised Irish language classes, which were very popular. By December of that year the branch had at least 103 members, of whom 76 had paid their yearly subscription of five shillings the following year. But despite the progress the Gaelic League had made in Kilkenny City in one year, the branch was crippled by debt and spending far more than it was earning. Its celebration of Irish culture, known as *An Aeridheacht* (the open air entertainment) had been a great success, but the branch had over-spent and the performance needed to be paid for. A series of concerts were organised to make up the deficit, but all were badly attended. This forced an extraordinary general meeting in January 1902 where members seriously considered the possibility of winding down the branch and cutting their losses. In a heated debate the branch was eventually saved by an agreement that all their resources would be placed into a collection run by volunteers and held during Irish Language Week. Thomas MacDonagh is recorded as having donated five shillings, the first time his name appeared on a Gaelic League list.

Shortly after arriving in Kilkenny, MacDonagh had learned of the League meetings in the city, and decided to attend and ridicule the attendees, viewing speakers of Gaelic as a source of amusement. At the meeting, however, he had a radical change of heart and, rather than laughing at the work of the League, he became totally engrossed with the idea of restoring the Irish language. He later told a student that before the meeting he had been 'the greatest West Britisher in Ireland and suppressed the Irish language.'[3] Viewing the restoration of the Irish language as a valuable and worth-while project, MacDonagh, who had arrived in Kilkenny apolitical and troubled with religious doubt, was startled by 'a baptism within nationalism.'[4] He began attending Irish language classes regularly and became a firm proponent of cultural nationalism. As a subscriber to the League's fund collections and an eager collector, MacDonagh was so active that he was elected to the Kilkenny executive branch on 28 April 1902.

Enthused with his new cause, MacDonagh adopted the Irish language and the work of the Gaelic League with an almost religious fervour. Addressing a League gathering in Kilkenny, he commended the organisation for 'doing the work of a messiah.'[5] Describing the Irish language as the nation's soul, MacDonagh passionately emphasised to his audience how 'the Gaelic League was the precursor of a great movement, having for its object an Irish Ireland.'[6] In less than a year, MacDonagh had come to articulate his idea of what the Irish Ireland meant: it was to be Gaelic speaking, embracing the great traditions of Irish culture, and self-sustaining, controlling its own destiny free from British influence. In deference to this, MacDonagh now took to sometimes wearing an Irish kilt, which differed from the Scottish kilt in that it was generally saffron or green and fastened to the shoulder of the jacket with a Tara brooch of silver or copper. The wearing of such a kilt was a bold statement to make, for it visibly demonstrated that the wearer was a proponent of cultural nationalism.

In 1903 MacDonagh became honorary secretary of the Kilkenny branch. This was a time of great development for the League in Kilkenny City as it had successfully negotiated the introduction of Irish prayers into the Capuchin Church at Walkin Street, and through its president, Fr Dollard, had introduced the Rosary in Irish to St Mary's Cathedral. Seeking to expand the League within the wider county, it was agreed that sub-committees would also be established to facilitate the growth of further branches in small townlands and Kilkenny City's suburbs. These branches would provide Irish classes and social outings where financially possible. MacDonagh was given St Patrick's Parish Ward in Kilkenny City and eagerly set about organising a Gaelic League branch within the community. Working tirelessly, he organised an initial meeting attended by over seventy people, but interest dwindled and within a year MacDonagh was forced to close the branch. This failure was repeated throughout the county, as the only real success was at the small village of Johnswell, where a vibrant and well-attended branch was established. Attending an inaugural meeting there on behalf of the city branch, MacDonagh continued his religious theme when describing the Gaelic League. Referencing St John the Baptist, the town's patron saint, he held the League was 'a precursor of great things to follow.'[7]

MacDonagh's prediction of 'great things to follow' did not come to fruition. On a professional and personal level, MacDonagh was having difficulties in St Kieran's College. He had sought to get the school to include Irish as a regular part of its curriculum and wrote to the school's president in support of the initiative. But despite MacDonagh's best efforts, his own school would not embrace Irish. As a senior League activist, this must have been uncomfortable for him. Of equal concern was the increased bickering within the Kilkenny Gaelic League from June 1903 onward. It had failed to expand into different parishes and was becoming reliant on the same individuals rather than recruiting new activists with fresh ideas and enthusiasm. Marked differences of opinion were also becoming noticeable between individual members. Some believed that the League should remain solely a cultural body, committed to revival of the Irish language through teaching and social events, while others argued that it should be more political, intent on national as well as cultural renewal.

This difference of opinion had come from a policy adopted by the Gaelic League executive in Dublin, which stressed that Gaelic League activists should stand for official political positions and it was the duty of members to support their candidacy. At the annual general meeting in June 1903, MacDonagh, in his position as secretary of the branch, condemned two committee members, Alderman James Nolan and Councillor McSweeney, for voting against a Gaelic League activist in a recent municipal election. Despite the fact that he considered Nolan and McSweeney to be good friends, MacDonagh suggested that as they had shown great offence to the Gaelic League and were in violation of its policy, they had affected the prestige of the movement. To all assembled he announced how, as secretary, he would not be doing his duty to the League by 'remaining silent,'[8] as to their behaviour. The meeting became incredibly heated and acrimonious. As a result of the controversy, MacDonagh felt he could no longer remain as branch secretary, and effectively resigned by refusing to stand for re-election to the committee. Disappointed by this, the branch commended him as being:

> Devoted heart and soul to the loftiest ideals of the Gaelic League, unselfish in his motive, kind, tactful, and gentlemanly in his actions towards all, and absolutely fearless in the discharge of the duties which his position, as Secretary or Committee-man, imposed upon him, and we assure him that he carries with him the deep respect and hearty good wishes of every member of the committee.[9]

Receiving this commendation from the branch, MacDonagh was deeply humbled and, in a letter to his friend Dominick Hackett, whom he met through the League in Kilkenny, recalled it as 'a rather high-flown resolution of confidence.'[10]

Through the Gaelic League he was encouraged to visit the Aran Islands off the west coast of Ireland, which were inhabited almost exclusively by native Irish speakers. For members of the League, the Aran Islands represented an ideal:

a strongly Gaelic community almost entirely untouched by British influence and living a simple existence in a wild and beautiful setting. Settling at Inishmaan, the second largest of the three islands, MacDonagh experienced first-hand the traditional way of life of the inhabitants. He was so enchanted by the islands that he would continue to make regular visits in order to improve his Irish. According to his son Donagh, writing in 1945, he was very popular amongst the locals for 'his eager friendship, his exhilarating talk, his archaeological interest, and as the man who introduced the strange song "*Malbrouc se va t'en guerre*" into the islands.'[11]

By the end of April 1903, alongside his Gaelic League activity, MacDonagh had completed and published his second book of poems, *April and May*. As with *Through The Ivory Gate*, many of the selected poems were written during his time at Rockwell College, and he dedicated his new book to his former colleague, Reverend EA Crehan, formerly the Dean of Students there. Although similar in style to his previous collection, it was noticeably less dark and morbid, with MacDonagh asserting how he had hoped that each poem could 'embody the thought of this season, and death in life, and resurrection.' Commenting on his second book, *The Weekly Freeman* welcomed MacDonagh's decision to abandon 'morbid irritability' in favour of an 'irresistible desire to make sweet and pleasant and musical verses.'[12] Considering his new passion for the Irish language, it was not surprising to see that *April and May* included an Irish verse on its title page and made decided appeals to cultural nationalism, including verses celebrating Irish nationalists such as William Rooney, founder of the Celtic Literary Society and co-founder with Arthur Griffith of the nationalist newspaper *The United Irishman*, as well as a poem extolling the virtues of the 1798 rebellion, 'To Ireland'. As with *Through The Ivory Gate*, *April and May* was a commercial failure, and by January 1905 he had only sold sixty-four copies; added to the sales of *Through The Ivory Gate*, MacDonagh's sales totalled only 184 books.[13]

Within two months of the publication of *April and May*, in June 1903, MacDonagh resigned his teaching position in St Kieran's College, finding the environment there incompatible with his newfound nationalism. Coupled with his growing dissatisfaction with the Kilkenny City branch of the Gaelic League, he left Kilkenny and went to Fermoy in County Cork, securing work there at St Colman's College, where he remained until 1908.

At St Colman's College, as elsewhere, MacDonagh quickly gained a reputation as a fine teacher. His students always regarded him as passionate, well-turned-out, and gentle, with a boyish sense of humour. They recalled his tremendous knowledge as well as his tendency to ramble and muse on current affairs or books. St Colman's was far more agreeable for MacDonagh as Irish was part of the curriculum and there was a strong emphasis on the importance of Gaelic games such as hurling and football. He wrote of how 'St Colman's is a very different place from St K's. Gaelic to the spine.'[14] He was thrilled to find that the president of the college, Michael Barrett, was progressive and that its teachers were 'scholars and gentlemen.'[15] As in Kilkenny, MacDonagh sought out the local Gaelic League branch and took an active part in the Mitchelstown organisation, where he came into contact with Padraig MacSuibhne, an Irish language teacher and local activist. Developing a friendship with MacSuibhne, MacDonagh wrote that he had 'never met a Gael like him; he is worth a score of me, a native speaker, a fine teacher and a leader of men.'[16]

MacDonagh continued his study of the Irish language and became proficient to such an extent that he began informal work as a *timirí*. His growing use of the language had been facilitated by regular visits to the Aran Islands, conversational classes in Mitchelstown, and attendance at the Munster Training College, which specialised in teaching through Irish. He found, however, that conversing with fluent speakers was more difficult than teaching his students. Writing to MacSuibhne he explained how each fluent Irish speaker 'idiomatically dumbs me down.'[17] He regularly volunteered his services to facilitate the administrative and social functions of the Mitchelstown League and quickly stood out amongst its membership, rising to become secretary, treasurer, and then vice-president. By 1905 he had attended the annual convention of the Gaelic League where he actively argued for the establishment of an Irish-language university along with financial and administrative reform of the organisation. MacDonagh was also involved in the preparations for festivals celebrating Irish language and culture, particularly the *Feis na Mumhan* (Munster Festival). Although on a journey of self-discovery, he was increasingly burdened by the strain of managing his personal, work and Gaelic League commitments, lamenting how he had a particular 'knack of taking on more work than I ought.'[18]

Around this time, MacDonagh had also been working on a musical cantata in collaboration with the Italian composer Benetto Palmieri, the director of the singing class at the Royal Irish Academy of Music. Based on the escape of the Israelites from Egypt, it was called *The Exodus: A Sacred Cantata*. Submitted to Feis Ceoil, an Irish music festival held in at the Royal University in Dublin, *The Exodus* was first performed on 19 May 1904, featuring a baritone singer accompanied by tenors, sopranos, and a boys' choir drawn from St Mary's College, Dublin. Interestingly, considering MacDonagh's recent past, the boys were all taught by the Holy Ghost Fathers. A resounding success, the cantata was so popular that MacDonagh and Palmieri won first prize at the festival and it was published by Doremi & Co., a London music press, later that year.

After attending the Feis Ceoil, MacDonagh returned to Fermoy, where he continued working on a set of eleven poems called 'The Praises of Beauty', which would eventually form the basis of his third book, *The Golden Joy*. He had been working on these poems since 1903, and they represented an attempt to recapture ground following the failure of *Through The Ivory Gate* and *April and May*. In November 1903 he had sent 'The Praises of Beauty' to Charles Elkin Matthews, a British publisher, but Matthews was not overtly keen and had, according to MacDonagh, set out very strict terms prior to publication. What these terms were remains unknown, but they were clearly unacceptable to MacDonagh, who sent the manuscript to another British publisher, Alfred Nutt. Nutt, who was known for his interest in folklore and Celtic culture, enjoyed the poetry and thought MacDonagh had a graceful style, but he feared his work was not commercially viable. He was only willing to publish if MacDonagh was to bear the brunt of the cost. MacDonagh, having financed his first two books, was unprepared to risk a third, and the manuscript was again returned. Advised by friends to hold back on publication, MacDonagh was eventually successful in 1906 when a Dublin publishing firm, O'Donoghue and Company, published his new book of poems as *The Golden Joy*. Written as a sequel to 'The Dream Tower' in *Through The Ivory Gate*, he wrote in its prologue:

When my first book appeared some friends of mine and

some reviewers said that for all its ending of trust and faith the shadow of the middle gloom remained. I was then working on 'The Praises of Beauty,' and thought for a time to publish it at once – a sequel of joy, as it were to 'Dream Tower'. However, when I had already prepared the book for publication. I considered that it would be wise to wait a little. I have waited through three years of other work, and am now able to join to my book of beauty another choice of poems, which are most of them, Praises of Joy ...[19]

MacDonagh's publisher agreed to print 1,000 copies of his new book of poems and received a retainer of £10 to do so. While *The Golden Joy* was not a commercial success, it was republished in 1908 to generally favourable reviews. *The Tribune*, a London-based newspaper, said it was 'characterised by much beauty of thought and expression, though occasionally the technique is more than a little faulty.'[20] The Dublin-based *Freeman's Journal* believed that MacDonagh's 'verses come straight from the heart,' and 'were never frivolous.'[21] For the British *Daily Chronicle* the book was a terrible letdown as its author, while an Irishman, failed to 'display a great deal of that imagination and emotion which mark the Celt.'[22] Studying these reviews, MacDonagh acknowledged to Dominick Hackett that while his work wasn't received as well as he might have wished, it had established him within the world of poetry. This was certainly not the case and he was undoubtedly exaggerating his artistic appeal to his friend for, as one commentator has noted, MacDonagh 'was still an apprentice insofar as poetry was concerned.'[23]

On top of his teaching, his poetry, his Gaelic League work, and his cantata, since 1904 MacDonagh had been working on a play called *When The Dawn Is Come* about an Irish insurrection led by a council of seven. In his diary he outlined a brief sketch of its plot: '[A] poet[,] a great mind reasoning with little ones. Plotting with Irish rebels, proposes to cheat English by posing as a spy.'[24] MacDonagh had hoped the Abbey Theatre in Dublin, the cultural heart of specifically Irish theatrical work and the headquarters of WB Yeats, would stage his play. At the time, MacDonagh idealised Yeats and had been desirous of capturing his attention and advice. As early as 5 February 1904, he had submitted his play to Fred Ryan, secretary of the Abbey Board, but his proposal was rejected and he was forced to reassess the idea. Working with Padraic Colum, a Longford-born playwright and dramatist, on the narrative, MacDonagh had completed a revised manuscript by 1907, and correspondence indicates that he had made changes to the original script before submission to the Abbey board. Describing the play to Dominick Hackett, MacDonagh explained how it was set fifty years in the future and was 'the story of a young man who has had most to do in getting up the rising.'[25] His protagonist was an Irish rebel poet called Turlough, who in a complicated narrative attempts to trick the British government into believing he was a spy.

Turlough's design, however, is discovered by his comrades, who increasingly believe him to be an informer, forcing a tense confrontation and Turlough's eventual exile and death. After opening correspondence with the Abbey, MacDonagh told friends of how he had met Yeats and won the affection of JM Synge. Synge, however, had certain reservations about *When The Dawn Is Come*, particularly its long speeches and the finale when his main character, Turlough, 'dies in disgrace, having failed to lead his country to freedom.'[26] Desirous to run the play past Yeats and Lady Augusta Gregory, Synge told MacDonagh that he needed to make significant corrections. After reading the play, Yeats agreed with Synge, and felt that while MacDonagh had obvious talent as a poet, he was better suited as a dramatist, with Yeats recommending that he 'write other plays.'[27] Yeats suggested that MacDonagh's ending was too sentimental:

> I am sorry about the delay in sending back your manuscript, but the puzzling nature of it is responsible for that delay. It was read by several of us, and left us so uncertain that we decided to submit it for a final judgement to a reader who reported 'it has real dramatic gifts of characterisation, and arrangement, and general power of building up something that can stand by itself; but the treatment of the hero at the end is so sentimental I hardly see how we can stage it.[28]

Despite Yeats' concerns as to how the play could be staged,

he was clearly interested in it: not only had he taken the time to write to MacDonagh suggesting revisions, he had read the play in its entirety, and by 30 January 1908 he had again written to MacDonagh urging him not to give up, but to rewrite the play and send it to him as soon as possible. Submitting the play to the Abbey board in February, MacDonagh had taken all their suggestions on board and rewritten the ending: Turlough, his protagonist, now returned from exile, albeit disgraced, would reclaim his honour by leading the rebels to victory in battle before his dramatic death from wounds. Synge was reasonably happy and after consulting with Yeats agreed to stage the play at the Abbey:

> We would like to produce your play − possibly this season possibly in the Autumn − but we must be permitted to cut certain passages here and there (not a great deal) according as we feel the necessities of the stage may require.[29]

Having a play produced in Dublin in late 1908 was ideal for MacDonagh, as by November of 1907 he had decided he was going to leave Fermoy. Despite his earlier commendation for the town and his work at St Colman's, he wrote how 'this place now becomes a horror to me.'[30] He had originally set his mind on moving to London, believing that his prospects for work and literary recognition would be greater in the English capital, but instead chose to settle in Dublin and began a new stage of his personal journey that would change his life forever.

Chapter Three

1908

'The present state of politics is pitiable'

Arriving in Dublin in the summer of 1908, MacDonagh settled at 15 Grantham Street near to the South Circular Road. He was starting a new teaching job, as he had been offered a place in Patrick Pearse's new educational venture, Scoil Éanna, but he could also immerse himself within the cultured environs of the capital city, with much greater opportunities for getting a name in literary circles. Furthermore, Dublin was also alive with new political and social developments and MacDonagh, with his customary enthusiasm, threw himself into those causes he felt were worth supporting.

Since 1900 the divided Irish Parliamentary Party had been united under the leadership of John Redmond and had sought to achieve some degree of Irish devolution from

London. However, despite being the third largest party in Westminster, and the only substantial party representing Ireland, this remained a distant aspiration. Internally the IPP was under considerable strain as internal factions and personal rivalries between several leading figures effectively hindered its organisation and electoral strength.[1] This was nowhere more apparent than at the so-called baton convention between 9-10 February 1909, when William O'Brien tried to speak out against Redmond and was continuously heckled and jeered by members of the Ancient Order of Hibernians, many of whom had come from Belfast. It was regarded as 'the stormiest meeting ever held by constitutional nationalists'[2], and as the prestige of the IPP fell, MacDonagh, who increasingly regarded them with disdain, described it in the wake of the baton convention as 'hopelessly degenerate.'[3] He felt that the IPP was in dire need of a strong leader like Parnell, and that Redmond was not up to the challenge.

MacDonagh understood that the party faced almost impossible odds. Firstly, their influence in Parliament was weak as neither the Conservatives, who were in power from 1895 to 1906 and vehemently opposed Home Rule, nor the Liberals, who came to power with a huge majority in 1906, needed the Irish bloc to form a government. As the IPP's power historically came from a minority Liberal Party dependent on their votes to stay in power, this made it difficult for them to affect policy. On top of this, by 1908 both

British parties were also largely disinterested when it came to Ireland. There was a recognition amongst British politicians that the question of Irish Home Rule was dangerous to their ambitions. It was well understood that previous Liberal governments (in 1886 and 1893) had been punished by the electorate after positively embracing the Home Rule question: the most significant casualty being former Prime Minister William Gladstone. There was also the issue of the House of Lords, which could veto any bill passed by the Commons; as the Lords were largely Conservative, they would reject any Home Rule bill by an overwhelming majority.

At the other end of the Irish political spectrum, Fenianism, which advocated the establishment of an Irish Republic by physical force, had been moribund since the Land War of the 1880s. Capturing the decay of Fenianism at the turn of the century, historian Matthew Kelly has asserted that the activities of the Irish Republican Brotherhood were 'consigned to the melancholic bar room reminiscences of the increasingly aged men of '67.'[4] Horrified by the miserable state of Ireland's revolutionary underground, in 1905 a small cabal of revolutionaries living in Belfast decided they had to begin a process of revitalisation. In March 1905 Denis McCullough and John Bulmer Hobson formed the Dungannon Clubs, seeking to promote the concept of an independent Irish Republic. Such clubs were on the surface cultural and commemorative organisations, dedicated to gathering nationalists together for discussion and debate, but they also provided a means of active recruitment for the IRB. The following year McCullough and Hobson made the acquaintance of Seán MacDiarmada, whom Hobson recruited into the IRB. Although initially reluctant, MacDiarmada would soon become one of the most important figures within the IRB revival. Around the same time a new movement, Sinn Féin (Ourselves Alone), had begun to emerge, seeking to challenge the electoral dominance of the IPP. Founded by the journalist Arthur Griffith and led by a national council, Sinn Féin sought economic and cultural self-sufficiency and also represented the growing self-confidence that the Irish cultural revival had encouraged. Officially established on 28 November 1905, the Sinn Féin policy was defined by Griffith as a serious alternative to that of the IPP and decried British governance of Ireland as tyrannical, holding that 'Irish people were a free people, and must continue to possess the rights of a free people.'[5]

Sinn Féin sought to achieve 'a national legislature endowed with the moral authority of the Irish nation,'[6] sitting in Dublin. This national legislature, according to Sinn Féin, could only be formed by passive resistance, with Irish MPs withdrawing from London to Dublin and establishing their own parliament. It condemned the IPP for taking its seats in Westminster, holding that they were making a tactical error in giving recognition to the British claim to make laws for Ireland. Despite its radicalism, however, Sinn Féin was not advocating total separation from Britain. What it had sought was the reestablishment of the former Kingdom of Ireland, which had ceased to exist with the passage of the Irish Act of Union on 1 January 1801, and a restoration of an agreement by the British government, the Renunciation Act of 1783, that the Irish Parliament had the exclusive right to legislate for Ireland. In justification for this strategy, Griffith had pointed to the Austro-Hungarian Empire. In 1867, after Hungarian MPs refused to sit in the Austrian parliament, direct Austrian rule in Hungary became impossible and both countries, although co-operating in matters of finance, taxation and war, were given separate legislatures, armies and institutions of state unified by the common crown. While remaining the emperor of Austria, Franz Josef was recognised only as the King of Hungary. Arthur Griffith and Sinn Féin advocated a similar policy, envisaging the transformation of Ireland and Britain into two separate states united by the one King.

By April 1906 the IRB indicated that it would follow the Sinn Féin programme; however, hardline republicans had a serious problem with the idea of re-establishing the Kingdom of Ireland. Sinn Féin was quickly infiltrated by the IRB, with MacDiarmada, Bulmer Hobson and McCullough bringing in significant numbers of radicalised members. This was partially due to pressure from Irish-America, where the

IRB's sister organisation, Clan na Gael, had been actively pressing for uniting the many advanced Irish nationalist groups, going so far as to threaten the withholding of funding to the IRB unless a unified body was created. This was particularly pressed upon Hobson by Joseph McGarrity, a Clan leader, during an American tour in 1907. By the end of 1907 McCullough, Hobson and MacDiarmada were joined by Thomas James Clarke, who threw himself into the work of reorganisation within the IRB; he commanded respect from the younger generation for having spent fifteen years, often in terrible conditions, in British prisons for his part in the Fenian dynamite campaign in 1883. Despite their disapproval of what they felt were Griffith's passive policies, the IRB subsidised a newspaper, published by Griffith, called *Sinn Féin*. In this endeavour money was again provided by Irish-America through the Clan. As the media organ of the movement, Sinn Féin articulated the strategy of dual monarchy and positioned itself within the sphere of the Irish-Ireland movement. It also supported the cultural revival, arguing for the purchase of Irish goods, as well as support for Irish industry and the Irish language. By 1907, due to pressure from Clan na Gael for the various organisations representing radical nationalism to present a united front, Sinn Féin had merged with the Dungannon Clubs and a smaller organisation, Cumann na nGaedheal, to become a political party.

Despite what he saw as the deplorable state of the IPP,

MacDonagh was initially dismissive of this new initiative. Writing of Sinn Féin, he termed the party name 'a barbarous word,'[7] and doubted the commitment of its members, believing, 'there are very few logical out and out Sinn Féiners.'[8] He believed that the Irish electorate were not tied to any single party and so, while Sinn Féin might initially attract attention, if the IPP could advance their cause within Westminster as they had done under Parnell, 'Sinn Féin would die.'[9] Sinn Féin's first real test came in June 1907, when the IPP MP for North Leitrim, CJ Dolan, frustrated by the inability of the IPP to achieve Home Rule, resigned his seat and defected to Sinn Féin. In the resulting by-election held in February 1908, Dolan was defeated, securing 1,157 votes against the IPP, whose candidate was elected with 3,103 votes. The North Leitrim by-election showed that at this stage Sinn Féin could not count on the support of the Irish people. In 1909, referencing the IPP and Sinn Féin, MacDonagh lamented that 'the present state of politics is pitiable.'[10]

At the same time, the city was being galvanised by the emergence of a new labour movement demanding better conditions for workers. At the turn of the twentieth century, despite its prosperity, Dublin had the worst slums in Europe, with an estimated one-third of its population living in poverty. Most of Dublin's working class lived in overcrowded tenement houses, often with only one toilet per house, meaning that disease spread regularly. Examining the nature of Dublin dwellings, a member of the National Society for the Prevent of Cruelty to Children testified:

> In every house I visited there was something to condemn: bad or narrow or ill kept staircase, congestion and over-crowding, bad air or light, no proper cooking and water accommodation, insufficient lavatory arrangements – one or more of these faults I found in every tenement room I entered ...[11]

Most Irish workers were unskilled, and even when they had work they were trapped by low pay, as union membership was limited to their skilled counterparts. In 1908, however, trade union organiser Jim Larkin arrived in Dublin from Belfast, where he had been involved in the dock workers' strike the previous year. Establishing a new trade union, the Irish Transport and General Workers Union (ITGWU) he had sought to organise and collectively defend the working class. This union was different to any that had come before in that it was specifically Irish orientated and appealed to a general rather than elitist membership. The ITGWU also had a defined political programme centred on the socialist concept of establishing a workers' republic. The new union rapidly spread throughout the country, with branches opening in Belfast, Cork and Limerick. By 1912 it had an estimated 18,000 members. An inspirational orator who was full of energy, Larkin's great strengths as a union leader were his interpersonal skills and his non-elitist personality; unlike other union organisers, he personally related to ordinary workers on an individual basis.

Secondary school teachers like MacDonagh saw the benefit of organising as a union. While they were represented by the Association of Intermediate and University Teachers (AIUT), there was a growing feeling that the AIUT was Dublin-centric and lacked awareness of the conditions affecting its members outside the capital. At the turn of the twentieth century, secondary teachers were casually employed with no security of tenure. By contrast, national school teachers had been unionised since 1868 (in the Irish National Teachers' Organisation) and had successfully lobbied for better pay and working conditions. Although secondary teachers were often university educated, their salaries were relatively low, with men paid £82 and women £48 per annum. By contrast their colleagues in primary education were paid £175 per year, if male, or £56 if female. Hannah Sheehy Skeffington, the wife of MacDonagh's friend Francis, lamented that society was 'seeking to keep the professional out of a living wage.'[12] To rectify the situation, and unhappy with the AIUT, the Association of Secondary Teachers of Ireland was founded at the invitation of St Colman's College, MacDonagh's former employer. Established in Cork on St Patrick's Day 1909, the association had sought to raise the status of secondary teachers and agitate for better pay.

MacDonagh, who had remained in contact with teachers in St Colman's College despite living in Dublin, was a founder member and a good friend of PJ Kennedy, a Gaelic League activist and the first president of the ASTI. The ASTI spread quickly throughout the country and held its first meeting in Dublin in July 1909, seeking to establish professional conditions for teachers.

As well as the political and labour organisations, Dublin was the scene of a vibrant women's movement, which Mac-Donagh also became involved in. Seeking to improve the place of women within society generally, across Britain and Ireland there had been a growing and vibrant movement led by educated liberal thinkers and middle-class political activists who had sought equal voting and social rights with men. These campaigns succeeded in forcing the government to allow women with property to vote in local government elections in 1894, although this only applied to England and Scotland rather than Ireland. Women were, however, still excluded from voting in general elections. Known as 'suffragettes' in Britain, politically active women had utilised a militant campaign of protesting, rallies and lectures. While never as large as their British counterpart, the Irish suffragette movement was just as radical, and within a short space of time there were numerous separate organisations in existence, with membership often based on religion.

In Ireland there was also a thin line between the women's movement and nationalism. In 1900 Maud Gonne had established *Inghinidhe na hÉireann* (Daughters of Ireland) as a dedicated organisation for women nationalists who 'resented being excluded, by reason of their gender, from national organisations'.[13] Gonne argued that it was essential for women to become active in Irish politics as 'without the participation of her women, Mother Ireland was going into battle with one arm tied behind her back.'[14] The organisation was schooled in the belief that women's independence would run parallel to Irish independence. Inghinidhe na hEireann advocated the study of the Irish language and history while discouraging the reading of English newspapers and literature, which they considered to be lowbrow and culturally dangerous. They also established Ireland's first women's newspaper, *Bean na hÉireann* (Women of Ireland), edited by Maud Gonne and Helena Molony. It advocated 'militancy, Irish separatism and feminism.'[15]

By November 1908 the already crowded Irish suffragette scene grew larger with the emergence of the Irish Women's Franchise League (IWFL) founded by Mora Dryhurst and Margaret Cousins and led by Hannah and Francis Sheehy Skeffington. The IWFL's principal aim was to ensure that any future Home Rule Bill would incorporate votes for women. Within a few months of its foundation, one contemporary wrote, 'there can be no doubt that for a society only a few months in existence, this new body has done more propagandist work, has irritated more comfortable people, than many more venerable institutions can boast about.'[16] MacDonagh became a strong advocate of women's rights and regularly attended meetings and political rallies. He also wrote articles in Dublin newspaper *The Leader* in support of suffrage, became a regular subscriber to the IWFL newspaper *The Citizen*, recalling it to be 'a sign of the new times',[17] and also became a speaker on behalf of the IWFL. In 1910 he addressed a meeting on the pros and cons of women's suffrage alongside Francis Sheehy Skeffington at the Ancient Concert Rooms in Dublin.[18] He remained, first and foremost, an Irish-Irelander, however, and took umbrage at the IWFL regularly inviting British suffragettes to Ireland to address their rallies. This was apparent after the appearance of the noted British suffragette Theresa Billington-Greig in the Abbey Theatre on 2 March 1909. To MacDonagh's horror, this unashamed radical and advocate of the rights of the oppressed referenced Britain as 'this country,' and the British parliament as 'our Parliament'.

MacDonagh took to his column in *The Leader* to condemn Billington-Greig's speech, criticising the suffragette for making 'an admirable speech, but English of the English, admirable if to the English. She seemed to have prepared her speech for delivery in some town in the English provinces, and to be ignorant of the fact that in Dublin she was in the capital of another country'.[19] He felt that the IWFL were wrong to invite Billington-Greig to Dublin as 'English-women like Billington-Greig, as utterly English as we should wish Irishwomen to be Irish, can never win for any cause the support and sympathy of more than a fringe of the people in this country.'[20] MacDonagh lamented what he perceived to be a creeping West-Britonism into the IWFL, fearing the league was becoming less radically Irish in its approach and strategy, willing to barter the essence of their Irishness by aligning itself to its British counterpart and focusing on the exertions of British rather than Irish politicians. He suggested it was the duty of members and supporters of the IWFL to keep the movement Irish 'and hold it in Ireland for Ireland.'[21] MacDonagh challenged the IWFL leadership, suggesting:

> I have indicated one great danger that lies ahead of their organisation, West-Britonism. I think the founders of the League feel that there is a danger of some such kind before them, but they do not realise it fully … The League will succeed if it puts before it a definite programme of work in Ireland, and if it stands in Ireland. If it coquets with West Britain and puts forward speakers who will give us talk of 'our army,' and 'our parliament,' and points of debate between Mr. Asquith and others, it cannot grip Irish sentiment or support, as it must do if it is to win here.[22]

MacDonagh's criticism of the IWFL choice to invite Billington-Greig to Dublin was itself criticised. Francis Cruise

O'Brien, a supporter for Home Rule and an advocate of cultural revival, wrote in response, 'I must confess that this objection to everything English amuses me.'[23] O'Brien asserted that while he understood the Irish-Irelander opposition to Billington-Greig, as a leading activist of the suffragette movement she was 'an obvious person to invite.'[24] On behalf of the IWFL, Margaret Garahan answered MacDonagh's criticisms by reaffirming that the IWFL was not being subsumed by its British counterpart, announcing that 'the work of the league will essentially be in Ireland.'[25] The author stressed to MacDonagh that the IWFL was committed to using its resources to achieve 'a passion for freedom among all women – irrespective of creed, religious or political – of our own country'.[26] Garahan, addressing the mindset of Irish-Irelanders, jocularly asked MacDonagh if Billington-Greig should have pretended to be Irish and cited that: 'We did not invite an Englishwoman over here to talk to us as an Irishwoman of Irish conditions of life.'[27]

In September 1908, while all this was going on, MacDonagh was primarily employed in a radical new teaching project, a bilingual school run by Patrick Pearse. On one of his many visits to the Aran Islands he had met Pearse and the two had bonded over their mutual affection for the Irish language. It was evident that MacDonagh held Pearse in high regard and, writing to Padraig MacSuibhne in 1908, he suggested that Pearse had the potential to be 'the greatest of

Irish writers in imagination and power, if not in language.'[28]
Pearse had been seeking to establish a bilingual school since
1905 and had been writing articles in the Gaelic League's
An Claidheamh Soluis eulogising the merits of a system of
education favourable to the Irish language. On a visit to Belgium he had spent considerable time examining bilingualism
in the Belgian education system, and had secured permission from their Ministry of Education to visit some thirty
schools, colleges and universities. Believing a similar system
could work in Ireland, Pearse tried to impress upon senior
Gaelic League members the necessity of a bilingual school,
but while generally favourable of his plans, the organisation
was initially hesitant to support the initiative.

Although unable to get much support from the educational establishment or the Gaelic League, by 1908 Pearse
had secured enough money from some of the most influential families within the Irish revivalist movement to make his
project a reality. Knowing MacDonagh's ability and amiable
temperament, Pearse invited him to be deputy headmaster,
and effectively Pearse's right-hand man. In this role, under
Pearse's direction, MacDonagh was responsible for internal
organisation, administration and the day-to-day working of
the school. Representing the love Pearse and MacDonagh
had for the Aran Islands, they chose to name their bilingual new school institution Scoil Éanna, in deference to St
Enda, the patron saint of the islands. Opening on 8 Sep-

tember 1908, Scoil Éanna was based in Cullenswood House, a former Georgian home in Ranelagh, Pearse had having agreed to an annual lease costing £125. In its first week the school received over forty students, including the children of prominent Irish nationalists like Eoin MacNeill, William Bulfin, and Stephen Gwynn, the IPP MP for Galway City. *An Claidheamh Soluis* enthusiastically described the project as seeking to 'be a nursery of character, intellect, patriotism and virtue, which may eventually exert a benign influence on the private and public life of our country'.[29]

Scoil Éanna was an ambitious project. As well as being Ireland's first bilingual school, it was also the first lay-run Catholic school. Taking its starting point from Irish culture, there was a strong emphasis on the heritage and culture of Ireland, including Irish sports such as hurling and football, Irish history and geography. The very ethos of the school was based on the ancient Gaelic tradition of fostering, when a young boy would be raised, educated and trained by a neighbouring clan. In this case the school favoured, although was not exclusive to, boarders. Each classroom was named after a hero taken from Irish mythology, while the schoolrooms and hallways were adorned with art and sculptures rather than maps and tables. Above the hall doorway in Cullenswood House was written (in Irish) a quote from the Gaelic hero Cúchulainn, reading: 'I care not if I live but one day and one night provided my deeds and my fame live after me.'

The school logo was a Gaelic warrior in traditional clothing holding a sword, while its motto was 'strength in our limbs, truth on our lips and purity in our hearts'. With Pearse and MacDonagh both committed to the revival of the Irish language, it came as no surprise that Gaelic played a prominent role within the curriculum in Scoil Éanna. The emphasis was not on rote learning and it was not confined to the classroom, but became part of the students' overall environment, so that by being immersed in it they would learn to use it every day.

As an institution Scoil Éanna was not profit-driven and was designed to be homely and welcoming, with all students greeted individually by the Pearse family upon arrival. The school fees were relatively modest when compared to similar private institutions, with admissions for day pupils costing £5, £7 and £9 for boys between the ages of ten to over thirteen respectively; for boarding pupils the cost was between 30 and 32 guineas per year. Although the school was described as an institution for Catholic boys, in its first year it had Jewish and Church of Ireland students, with a significant urban and rural mix amongst pupils. Pearse particularly favoured the enrolment of boys from the west of Ireland, especially the islands, who spoke Irish as their everyday language.

From its prospectus Pearse and MacDonagh had set out to achieve a revolutionary style of education that would 'extend the scope and improve the methods of secondary educa-tion'[30] in Ireland. At the time when Scoil Éanna had been established, the Irish education system strongly mirrored its British counterpart and was reliant on a regime of limited curriculum, frequent examination and corporal punishment. Pearse had been savagely critical of that system, describing it as a murder machine, daily undermining the Irish spirit. Unusually for the time, Pearse was reluctant to use corporal punishment as a means of discipline. Pearse and MacDonagh favoured a system seeking to form the characters of its pupils while utilising their skills, imaginations and individual traits as part of the learning process. This learning process was to be aided by pupils taking an interest in extra-curricular activities including the governing of halls and dormitories, the prefecture of games, and nature walks to foster an appre-ciation of their surroundings. This Pearse and MacDonagh had hoped would foster the emergence of a Boy Republic within the school and they enthusiastically supported the development of a council elected by the student body to inculcate a sense of responsibility within the boys.

The school also produced an in-house magazine utilising the talents of students and teaching staff called *An Macaomh*. Published between 1909 to 1913, it included poetry, short stories, history and cultural reviews. Unsurprisingly, Mac-Donagh was a regular contributor. MacDonagh was also committed to teach English and French and thoroughly enjoying the experience, thinking the students 'splendid.'[31] He reported how he had 'the little lads now talking French'[32] on a regular basis and utilised American comic books, in favour of academic textbooks, as a fun means of showing his boys how the English language could be used. External lectures were also provided by recognised and qualified experts seeking to broaden the development of the student and bring a strong degree of respectability to the school. Notable guest lecturers included Padraic Colum, Douglas Hyde, Eoin MacNeill, WB Yeats and Mary Hayden, an Irish historian and women's rights' activist. This also gave Mac-Donagh a chance to mingle with some of Ireland's leading literary figures, which he felt would very beneficial to his career as a writer. By 1909 the school had also published its own bilingual schoolbooks, with MacDonagh commissioned to do three books examining English poems by Irish poets, a story 'in English and Irish atmosphere, and a French text.'[33]

The pairing of Pearse and MacDonagh together as the head- and deputy master respectively was ideal. While both were united by nationalism and their desire to revitalise Irish culture, personally they could not have been more different. In many respects they complemented each other: Pearse, while brilliant and incredibly driven, was burdened by shyness and came across as reserved and socially awkward, in stark contrast to the jocular and easygoing MacDonagh. As well as being responsible for internal administration and the day-to-day working of the school, MacDonagh became the public face of Scoil Éanna, regularly meeting the many high-profile visitors and lecturers. While both men were greatly respected by their pupils, MacDonagh was always their favourite; he had a boyish charm coupled with a strong sense of humour, while his teaching style was unorthodox and strived to help the boys find their own voice and think for themselves. He had a remarkable ability to capture the student's attention and keep them interested, utilising poetry to encourage his charges to strive for excellence and individuality. He had also introduced a system into Scoil Éanna where the teachers would sit with the boys during their meals and talk to them as adults; one student, Milo McGarry, recalled how he was never patronising to the boys and sought to address them as equals.[34] Eulogising his skills as a teacher, one contemporary noted:

> MacDonagh's learning sat lightly on him, and whether his audience was a public meeting, a classroom, or a small gathering of intimate friends, they would often, after leaving his company, realize on reflection how much knowledge he had imparted to them during what seemed to be a light hearted and informal talk.[35]

However, MacDonagh, who was regarded as a great talker, had a noted tendency to get sidetracked, and he was regularly tricked by his students. Sean Dowling, a relative of the Pearses, recalling how 'we used to start him off by asking him a question when he came into the class if we wanted to escape being heard or tasks and he would go off talking and wouldn't stop until the bell rang for the next class.'[36] Another student recalled how 'you could easily put him off the teaching, all you had to do was draw his attention to something that might happen in the paper, and he was off talking about something not connected with the class at all.'[37] Desmond Ryan similarly described how easy it was to sidetrack MacDonagh, who could easily get lost in 'the rich storehouse of his imagination.'[38]

As Scoil Éanna was such a radical project in education it was bound to draw the attention of political activists. One of these was Nora Dryhurst, the suffragette, anarchist and later an Irish Republican, who MacDonagh greatly admired. Lecturing at Scoil Éanna, she had been so impressed by what she had seen that she decided to return with two friends, sisters Muriel and Sidney Gifford. The Giffords were a prosperous middle-class family headed by Frederick (a Catholic lawyer) and Isabella Gifford, two strong-willed Unionists who believed that Ireland's place amongst the nations of the Earth was part of Britain. Isabella was Protestant, and despite her marriage to a Catholic, she was deeply hostile to Roman Catholicism, which she regularly referred to as Papism. Their home was distinctly matriarchal and Isabella was perceived as cold, bigoted and deferent. She instilled into her girls a disbelief of their natural beauty and pronounced her shame at their red hair, forbidding them from leaving the house unless it was hidden under a hat. Despite their mother, the Gifford girls were remarkably stubborn and non-sectarian. Becoming proponents of Irish nationalism, Sidney regularly wrote for *Sinn Féin* under the name John Brennan and saw Sinn Féin as 'setting the country pulsating with new ideas',[39] while Muriel had been heavily involved in volunteer work to help the poor of Dublin city and was a strong supporter of the Irish cultural revival. Their sister Grace, a cartoonist, was equally supportive of the cultural revival and would find fame as the woman given permission to marry Joseph Plunkett just prior to his execution in 1916. By contrast to their rebellious sisters, the Gifford boys were more apolitical. Sidney recalled that they were all of a Unionist persuasion, but this was largely down to the fact that 'they knew that all who did not conform to this political belief were ostracised from the tennis club.'[40]

Meeting MacDonagh, the Gifford girls found a kindred spirit and were enthralled by his charisma and dedication to political causes. Recalling their first meeting in 1908, Sidney remembered how MacDonagh:

> Came racing down the steps of St Enda's with his hands outstretched in welcome. Mrs Dryhurst's introduction was to tell MacDonagh our Christian names and then advise

him to 'fall in love with one of these girls, and marry her', a piece of blatant matchmaking which would have rendered most young girls of that period tongue tied with embarrassment. But MacDonagh, though 'no ladies' man' in the normal sense, accepted the challenge by saying laughingly: that would be easy – the only difficulty would be to decide which one![41]

They regularly attended lectures, rallies and meetings and through MacDonagh met with many figures within the literary and political world. They also enjoyed his boyish sense of humour, particularly alongside the more austere Pearse, who Sidney remembered as 'painfully shy'[42], especially around women. Sidney recalled that MacDonagh was a practical joker and enjoyed playing tricks on Pearse. Coming to Scoil Éanna with her sister on one occasion, they and MacDonagh met Pearse in the Library. In one of her fondest memories, Sidney recalled:

We were all standing in the library talking, when MacDonagh suddenly got me by the arm and said: 'Come outside, I want to talk to you about something.' So I went out, leaving my sister in the room with Pearse. [MacDonagh said:] 'Wait till you see Pearse! Wait till you see Pearse! He won't stay in the room for a minute with her!' and the next thing the door opened and Pearse shot down the passage with his head down like as if he was pursued by devils … it was so funny.[43]

As the friendship between MacDonagh and the Gifford girls blossomed, MacDonagh and Muriel grew close. It was clear there was a mutual attraction between them, but neither acted on their feelings and they would not begin a relationship until 1910.

In the autumn of 1908 MacDonagh was plagued by personal problems. *When The Dawn Is Come*, originally scheduled for May 1908, had been rescheduled for October of the same year. Why the Abbey chose to delay his play has never been adequately explained, and it was first performed in the Abbey Theatre on the evening of 15 October 1908, with two further shows on 16 and 17 October. The cast was headed by famed Abbey actors Joseph Michael Kerrigan and Sara Allgood (who would later find fame alongside Alfred Hitchcock in movies such as *Juno and the Paycock* and *Sabotage*).

Previewing the play, *The Irish Times* speculated that its controversial subject matter (militant Irish nationalism) would cause great excitement.[44] On what should have been one of the proudest nights of his career, MacDonagh was shocked to see that the play had been blighted by poor direction, acting and production, including only three rehearsals. Further complicating matters, one of the actors, Ambrose Power, had refused to learn his lines, which made the third act appear rushed. Many in the audience felt that the set looked haphazard or gaudy, while the costumes provided for the actors were perceived as old fashioned and bizarre, with one reviewer describing the actors as resembling 'the Legion of Frontiersmen'.[45] Another review lamented that the staging was 'simply appalling,' although it did point out that while the play was 'full of the faults of inexperience, [it] held the attention and sympathy of crowded audiences.'[46] Joseph Holloway, an amateur theatre critic was less than favourable to MacDonagh's play, recalling it as 'dull and talky.'[47] The most scathing review came from *The Irish Times,* however:

> It is seldom one has to complain of the acting at the Abbey Theatre, but it must be admitted last night, when Mr. Mac-Donagh's three act tragedy, *When The Dawn Is Come* was produced for the first time, the work of the actors was not in keeping with their reputation. In many cases they forgot their words and had to wait until the prompter came to their aid, while not infrequently whole passages from the dialogue seemed to be omitted.[48]

MacDonagh could only agree with *The Irish Times*, believing that his first play had been 'badly performed', and 'misunderstood.'[49] He blamed the failure largely on the Abbey Theatre and claimed that the Abbey actors were 'very poor; they cannot act well out of peasant plays or plays of middle class Dublin life.'[50] Dejected by the negative response of the media, he decided to rewrite the play and stage it at a later date when he felt it was capable of being performed on 'the stage as I now know the stage.'[51] This was a rather laborious task for MacDonagh, and it was not completed until January 1914.

While he was dealing with this negative criticism of his literary abilities, in November his mother had been taken so ill that she was forced to come to Dublin, where she was taken care of by the Sisters of Charity in the Hospice for the Dying at Harold's Cross. Brought there by MacDonagh, who had taken her from the care of his sister Eleanor at Cloughjordan, Mary Louise had to undergo two very serious operations, which he had described to a friend as 'a matter of life and death.'[52] Meeting his mother in hospital he mournfully explained how 'she is weak; getting no better, everything indicates a fatal end to it.'[53] MacDonagh was forced to juggle his teaching commitments with caring for his dying mother[54] and with the strain taking its toll, he lamented that his life was in 'disarray.'[55] According to MacDonagh, on 26 November 1908, Mary Louise 'died happy and resigned, in her sleep without pain.'[56] Writing to Dominick Hackett, he spoke of how her death had left him emotionally 'crushed.'[57]

Escaping the misery of his mother's death MacDonagh threw himself into his teaching duties at Scoil Éanna and wrote how the school was proving to be a great success.[58] He was, however, disappointed with the standard of some of the students, in particular the Irish-speaking peasant boys from the west, whom Pearse had insisted must attend the school for the benefit of the urban students. To WB Yeats, MacDonagh identified an urban-rural divide and lamented how the western boys were 'too cold, dark and reticent.'[59] He explained to Yeats how he often saw them at Scoil Éanna playing, but 'when no one is looking at them and they are alone or with the Irish-speaking gardener, they are merry, clever and talkative; when they meet an English speaker, or one who has learned Gaelic, they are "stupid". They are a different world.'[60] Aside from this problem, it was evident that Scoil Éanna had become a institutionally a great success, in no small part thanks to MacDonagh.

Chapter Four

1908 – 1912

'A desert where I could begin again'

While teaching at Scoil Éanna, MacDonagh attended University College Dublin (UCD) as a part-time undergraduate student and graduated in 1910, receiving a BA in Irish, French and English. While studying there he had come to know Douglas Hyde, the founder of the Gaelic League, and in a character reference, Hyde stated that Mac-Donagh was a meticulous in his work and had 'not only a good knowledge of classics and Modern Languages and History, but ... is an excellent scholar and speaker as well, and has studied most successfully Modern and Old Irish.'[1] Alongside his scholarly activity, he had also reviewed several books for *The Leader*. Not averse to celebrating his friends, he positively reviewed Padraic Colum's book of poetry, *Wild Earth,* and was full of praise for the artistic work of Grace Gifford and Willie Pearse. MacDonagh was also positively inclined towards literary or artistic work that could be considered distinctly Irish. When JM Synge died in 1909 from Hodgkin's Disease, MacDonagh was given the honour of writing a tribute in *TP's Weekly*. He eulogised Synge's life and work as 'brave and steadfast to his thought.'[2] Defending Synge's play, *The Playboy of the Western World*, which had opened in 1907 and incurred the wrath of many Irish-Irelanders as 'an unmitigated, protracted libel upon Irish peasant men, and worse still upon Irish girlhood,'[3] he claimed people disliked it because the characters resembled them too much. In 1909 MacDonagh celebrated the work of John Cook, who had recently published *The Dublin Book of Irish Verse*, a collection of Irish verses translated into English. Cook's anthology was written at a time when there was immense discussion within literary circles as to whether there was a 'Celtic note' (a distinctive, almost mystical, ambiguity within Irish poetry) inherent within Irish-language writing, an idea suggested by Matthew Arnold in his *On The Study of Celtic Literature*. Irish-Irelanders dismissed Arnold out of hand, and MacDonagh condemned Arnold's theory as 'largely a work of fiction,'[4] amateurishly drawn from poor translations of Irish poetry. By contrast to Arnold, MacDonagh felt that Cook had translated from Irish into English excellently, and thoroughly enjoyed his work. It was apparent that MacDonagh was coming to the conclusion that there was a future for

Irish literature and poetry in English, albeit inspired by Irish folklore and the influence of the Irish language on the way English was spoken in Ireland. Such an idea would prove controversial, as it ran counter to the prevailing notion held by many Irish-Irelanders that authentic Irish literature could only be written in Irish. This was noticeable in his treatment of Cook's work when he commented that Irish poetry, once translated was:

> still often incorrect and slovenly, [and] the work is infrequently wanting in the care that goes to the making of all fine art; but the very carelessness and freshness of the poetry has a winning grace. And it has something more. These poems in English, translated or derived from Irish, are in one way finer than the originals.[5]

Congratulating Cook on his anthology, MacDonagh asserted that from this Celtic note (for want of a better term) would emerge the best new Anglo-Irish poetry.[6] This was the first suggestion that MacDonagh was thinking about refining his literary style and moving toward his celebrated definition of the Irish mode, posthumously published in 1916, whereby Irish literature written in English was inherently based on rhythms of speech native to the Irish language.

It was around this time that we have our first evidence of MacDonagh's romantic relationships. He was introduced to Mary Maguire, a teacher from County Sligo, who spent con-

siderable time with MacDonagh and Padraic Colum. Mac-
Donagh was smitten with Mary, an attractive and vivacious
redhead with a deep interest in Irish literature and poetry.
She was also deeply involved in the women's suffrage movement and with MacDonagh regularly discussed and debated
what she called 'all the books about the position of women,
which corresponded in a way to that of the oppressed races.'[7]
What appealed to MacDonagh about Mary was her intellectual free spirit: a staunch advocate of women's rights, she
was by her own testament 'a university girl who does not
know how to boil water or wash a pocket handkerchief,'[8]
and could not fathom a life 'pottering about a kitchen, planning meals, hanging curtains and so on.'[9] Maguire showed
little interest in MacDonagh as a suitor, however, and despite
several attempts to win her, including a proposal, he was left
dejected. In her autobiography, *Life and The Dream*, although
she doesn't mention MacDonagh by name, she recalled:

> At intervals one or another of my young friends or col-
> leagues would propose to me, but we would laugh it off. I
> had, as far as I remember, no sentimental interest in them,
> only an interest in the causes we were all working for and
> in poems and plays they wrote … One of them, however,
> declined to listen to me and kept assuring me that he was
> the person Heaven had destined me to marry and that I
> could not escape my fate. I always thought, as he was a
> very fine and courageous person, that he would be a nice

man for somebody else to marry, which was what eventually happened – in fact he married before I did. But he made one final determined effort before dropping me. He called at my little flat, armed with an engagement ring, and told me in a very cave-man manner that he had arranged everything, that I was to marry him on a certain date in a certain church and that I had better accept my destiny … the harassing interview ended with tears on both sides with his throwing the ring into the fire and leaving in a high state of emotion.[10]

That this person was MacDonagh is quite possible. Mac-Donagh had married Muriel Gifford before Mary Maguire had married Padraic Colum, and her reference to her suitor as 'a very fine and courageous person', considering his involvement in the later Easter Rising, tends to give credence to this theory. Equally Geraldine Plunkett Dillon had noted that she believed MacDonagh was engaged to Mary Maguire until 'it was decided that he wasn't good enough for her.'[11] Writing a poem in deep melancholy, he lamented:

After a year of love
Death of love in a day;
And I who ever strove
To hold love in sure life
Now let it pass away
With no grief and no strife.[12]

Mary Maguire and Padraic Colum remained firm friends with MacDonagh, with Colum eventually becoming godfather to MacDonagh's future daughter, Barbara. Their friendship was so strong that when the MacDonagh children were left orphaned in 1917 on the death of their mother, the Colums tried to gain custody of them. Heartbroken by Mary's rejection, MacDonagh decided to leave Ireland for a while and, resigning from Scoil Éanna, he went to France, where he stayed for six weeks. Leaving the school left him miserable and he lamented how he would miss Patrick Pearse most of all.[13] Explaining his reasons to Dominick Hackett, he noted that he hoped to find in Paris freedom and solace, 'a desert where I could begin again without shackles.'[14] Settling into the Hotel Jacob at 44 Rue de Jacob in the summer of 1910, he briefly took up painting and improved his command of French.[15] It was recalled that while in Paris, 'he could have passed for a Frenchman and was often mistaken by Parisians for a provincial, by provincials for a Parisian … he talked and joked in the cafés around the Sorbonne, thinking Ireland and himself back into the European tradition.'[16] With Parisian life offering him great solace, he felt he could roam 'silent and free as a hawk in the sky,'[17] and he regularly attended the Comédie Française Theatre and basked within the Luxembourg and Tuileries Gardens. MacDonagh also embraced French literature and philosophy, as well as thoroughly reading Shakespeare, compiling detailed notes of

Hamlet, *Richard III* and *Twelfth Night*, and reading in detail the 1881 publication of Byron's poems, which included a preface by Matthew Arnold.

Returning to Dublin in autumn 1910, he had nothing to do with the decision to relocate Scoil Éanna to the Hermitage in Rathfarnham in September of that year, a move necessitated by its increasing success. However, he did occasionally teach within the school and helped Pearse with the move as much as he could.[18] He moved into the Grange House in Rathfarnham, where he had rented a small gate lodge from David Houston, a Scottish lecturer at the Royal College of Science, Dublin. MacDonagh loved Grange House Lodge and found that his new home was what he had been looking for while in Paris.[19] One biographer noted that in settling into Grange House Lodge, MacDonagh had contradictory motives: 'he sought to continue the life of solitude he had experienced in Paris and at the same time to remain near to the familiar environment'[20] of Scoil Éanna. He lamented his experience with Mary Maguire as 'this crisis of mine last summer',[21] but commented that 'the old things that were mixed up with life in Ireland for me have died and passed, and have left neither desire nor regret,'[22] enabling him to stay. Here one of his contemporaries recalled how MacDonagh had lived a hermit lifestyle to the extent that he became somewhat of a recluse. MacDonagh explains this himself in a letter to Hackett, where he describes Grange House Lodge as the desert he had been looking for and joyously wrote that its owner, Professor Houston, left him to himself and allowed him to avoid 'that worst of all interest in me, a kindly interest.'[23] His isolation within the lodge was incredibly short-lived, however, as MacDonagh, always a sociable individual, soon opened his house to visitors. In particular, his friendship with Houston meant that his home now became the repair of literary Dublin, hosting some of the most distinguished names in Irish literature.[24] Regular visitors included Padraic Colum and James Stephens, who began his career as a poet under the tutelage of George William Russell (Æ), who also occasionally visited. Others who dropped by often included the poets Seamus O'Sullivan and Francis Ledwidge, who had been mentored by Lord Dunsany, an Anglo-Irish writer and patron of the arts. Ledwidge and MacDonagh were similar personalities and enjoyed discussing poetry, song (MacDonagh was fond of humorous Irish song, often singing 'Thank you, Ma'am, says Dan') and literature, with Ledwidge describing MacDonagh as one of his best friends. Through his literary connections he had also made contact with the Belfast poet Padraig Gregory and Standish James O'Grady. Settling into this literary culture, MacDonagh enthusiastically wrote 'I am within striking distance of the life I want.'[25]

In early 1911 Houston had set about establishing a new literary venture. Meeting with Colum, MacDonagh, Mary

Maguire and James Stephens, he announced his intention to publish a intellectual magazine of Irish affairs, culture and literature. Houston hoped that the new monthly magazine, *The Irish Review*, could take the place of the *New Ireland Review,* which had ceased publication in February 1911. MacDonagh was incredibly enthuasiastic about the new venture, which was set up as a cooperative with Colum and Stephens, and was the publication's sub-editor, with Grange House Lodge becoming something of a publication house. Writing to Hackett he described the work as 'hard and ungrateful enough, but worth doing.'[26] Financially backed by Houston, the first edition of *The Irish Review* was published on 1 March 1911 and included contributions from Patrick Pearse, Padraic Colum, Mary Maguire and James Stephens. MacDonagh contributed a poem, 'Catullus to Himself'. Proud of his work on the magazine, MacDonagh believed that *The Irish Review* would 'speak for itself and say something for me too.'[27] Growing in popularity throughout 1911, *The Irish Review* published contributions from WB Yeats, Arthur Griffith and Standish O'Grady. From an early stage, therefore, it was quite apparent that he desired to make the magazine forum for political as well as intellectual debate. As Home Rule had become a real possibility by 1911, MacDonagh believed that the magazine had a role to play in helping to shape the popular mood of the country.

As well as working on *The Irish Review* in 1911, Mac-

Donagh had become involved in a new cause. King George V was scheduled to visit Ireland in July and Dublin was eagerly preparing itself for his arrival. The visit of the King was anathema to radical, or 'advanced', nationalists, however, and in protest they established the United National Societies Committee, which sought to unite nationalist opposition to the visit. Becoming increasingly proactive in political campaigns, MacDonagh joined the committee, and at the Sinn Féin headquarters he worked alongside Seán MacDiarmada, Michael O'Rahilly, Seán Fitzgibbon, Eamon Ceannt and Patrick Pearse. Taking a leading role in the endeavour, he regularly attended meetings and handed out flyers seeking to mobilise popular opposition to the visit. MacDonagh supported an attempt by the committee to force Dublin Corporation to oppose the King's arrival and refuse to present a loyal address to the monarch on behalf of the citizens of Dublin. He was part of a delegation, headed by MacDiarmada, which met the Lord Mayor John J Farrell and tried to gain his support. However, Farrell, a member of the IPP, argued that popular opinion in the city overwhelmingly favoured the visit, and Dublin Corporation's failure to welcome the reigning monarch would not only be an act of ingratitude to the Head of State but also 'a great injury to the cause of Home Rule.'[28] Despite the committee's best intentions thousands turned out to welcome the King to Dublin on 1 July 1911. While Dublin was bedecked in bunting and a sea of Union flags, Eamonn Ceannt and Seán Fitzgibbon had placed a large nationalist banner along the King's route opposite Trinity College, reading 'Thou art not conquered yet, dear land'.[29] Not surprisingly, the Dublin Metropolitan Police tore it down.

The United National Societies Committee were not to be beaten, however, and organised a protest at City Hall, Dublin, on 7 July 1911, where councillors had gathered to debate the royal visit. MacDonagh, the Giffords, Pearse, Ceannt, MacDiarmada and Countess Markievicz, among others, attempted to gain entry to the public gallery during the debate. In anticipation of their arrival, however, City Hall had been locked down by a heavy police presence facing down what one newspaper described as a 'siege'.[30] Uncharacteristically, Pearse tried to break through the police lines and force entry, but MacDonagh persuaded him to remain calm, and 'dragging him away,' he insisted to Pearse that 'if he was arrested it would mean the end of his school.'[31] While he was pleading with his friend, a number of city councillors, including Alderman Thomas Kelly, were assaulted walking into City Hall by the Dublin Metropolitan Police. With several councillors accusing the Lord Mayor of collaborating with 'the hirelings of Dublin Castle,'[32] the debate never took place due to the absence of city councillors who could not gain entry. In an informal meeting several councillors condemned Farrell and repudiated 'the ridiculous claim of the Lord Mayor to represent in any capacity the citizens of Dublin in receiving the King.'[33]

In 1911 MacDonagh had also been working on his second play, *Metempsychosis*, which he completed in November of that year. *Metempsychosis* was remarkably different from *When The Dawn Is Come* in being strictly apolitical. Despite its rather academic sounding name, which drew on the religious notion of the transmigration of the soul, the play was effectively a one-act satire on theosophy, mocking the concept of reincarnation and the transmigration of souls. It centres on the meeting of an unnamed man and the absurdly named Earl Winton Winton de Winton, described as 'voluble, excitable, earnest, visionary, victim of ease and enthusiasm, nearly forty years of age.'[34] It is possible that the play can be seen in the light of a stranger (representing MacDonagh himself) searching for life's meaning and coming up against an individual who, despite a lot of high-sounding talk, was essentially peddling nonsense (and at one stage reveals that he carries a loaded gun at all times so that he can commit suicide when his soul has reached perfection). For one biographer, the character of Winton de Winton was uncomfortably close to Yeats, who similarly was known for his interest in classical and Gaelic metempsychosis, as well as theosophy.[35] Around this time MacDonagh had begun to have doubts about Yeats and was criticising him within his private correspondence. He felt angry with the playwright about how

Thomas MacDonagh aged sixteen.

Above: Thomas MacDonagh (second row, far right) at Rockwell College.

Right: After moving to Kilkenny, Thomas MacDonagh was introduced to nationalism through the Gaelic League. In this photograph he is wearing the Irish kilt, which was thrown over the shoulder and affixed by a Tara brooch.

Right: In December 1911, Thomas MacDonagh was appointed a lecturer of English at University College, Dublin. That same year he was awarded an MA for his thesis 'Thomas Campion and the Art of Poetry'.

Left: Thomas and Muriel Gifford had been introduced in 1908 at Scoil Éanna. They were married in 1912.

Above: Muriel and Thomas MacDonagh with their first child, Donagh.

Left: Their second child, Barbara, was born on 24 March 1915.

Left: Barbara and
Donagh MacDonagh.

Right: Thomas MacDonagh,
Commandant, 2nd Battalion
of the Dublin Brigade of
the Irish Volunteers. This
photograph was taken with
the O'Donovan Rossa
Funeral Committee, 1915.

The funeral of Jeremiah O'Donovan Rossa in 1915. Serving as the Volunteer Acting Commandant General, Thomas MacDonagh was in executive control of all arrangements. MacDonagh wrote about the

Volunteers, 'The Irish Volunteer has taken up in his generation the traditional policy of the Irish people – the policy of physical force. The Irish Volunteer stands pledged to the single service of Ireland in Ireland.'

Above: Thomas and Donagh during the last MacDonagh family holiday in Greystones, Co. Wicklow, in 1915.

Left & above: Thomas, Muriel and Barbara on the same family holiday.

When The Dawn Is Come was treated at the Abbey Theatre, and felt that his handling of Synge's controversial *The Playboy of the Western World* had been to throw 'a whole mist of elf gas around Synge and the Playboy, and [draw] the discussion away from the original wood or frame.'[36] Regarding Yeats as 'a snob' albeit one who could be loved, he argued that Yeats was tainted through his relationship with Lady Gregory 'with that rottenest of taints in Ireland's ground, the ascendency taint.'[37]

Although written in 1911, *Metempsychosis* was first performed by the Theatre of Ireland group on 18, 19 and 20 April 1912. The play was not well received, however, and was regarded to be too intellectual for the average theatregoer. The *Irish Independent* found that it was very difficult to comprehend and far too academic, with the actor playing Winton de Winton sometimes making points by drawing diagrams 'on blackboards that suggested a proposition in Euclid'.[38] It also criticised the play for its use of long-winded and at times incomprehensible speeches, such as Winton de Winton's convoluted explanation of metempsychosis. Having sat bamboozled through the performance, the reviewer commented, 'being an ordinary person, I gave up.'[39] Despite the criticism, however, there were positive aspects to *Metempsychosis*. While the dialogue was incomprehensible and the tone was far from comedic, his skill at writing dialogue showed immense improvement from *When The Dawn*

Is Come. Recognising this, one commentator has correctly noted that there 'enough purely comic lines to make it effective if exploited by talented actors,' especially when combined with comedic improvisation and gestures to highlight how ridiculous the characters actually were.[40]

While living at Grange House Lodge, MacDonagh also met Joseph Mary Plunkett, whose father, George, was a Papal Count with a large property portfolio, as well as being curator of the National Museum in Dublin. Plunkett had been afflicted with tuberculosis since he was young and spent significant parts of his childhood in the Mediterranean along the European and North African coastlines. As a consummate reader with a great interest in science, technology and military affairs, Plunkett wanted to attend UCD and hoped to study Irish to improve his chances of being accepted for a place. His mother, Mary Josephine, placed an advertisement in a newspaper in 1909 seeking an Irish tutor, which MacDonagh answered. On meeting Plunkett the two became great friends. For MacDonagh, Plunkett was outgoing, intellectual and well travelled, and they bonded over the former's growing love for the Irish language and his non-conformity. Both men regularly debated issues of literature and went to the theatre and Gaelic League meetings together. Regarding the two as inseparable, Geraldine Plunkett, Joseph's sister recalled:

It was an instant friendship. They were both poets, loved

theatre, read history, argued fiercely about politics and were full of humour and wit. There were nine years between them but from the beginning it was a deep, personal and important relationship for both. They haunted each other – if [Thomas] didn't come to see Joe, Joe went out to see him.[41]

MacDonagh regularly offered constructively criticism on Plunkett's poetry. This was certainly the case in Plunkett's *The Circle and the Sword*, published in 1911, which carried a dedication to MacDonagh. At the same time MacDonagh was also working on an MA thesis in UCD between 1910 and 1911 on the work of Thomas Campion, a seventeenth century English composer and poet. He had told Dominick Hackett that his desire to complete his MA had been prompted by his 'unexpected success in the BA exam.'[42] Dedicating his dissertation to Professor Robert Donovan, head of the UCD English department, MacDonagh described his thesis as 'a complete treatise on English Metrics and Rhyme, deriving from work, and following my division of English verse into two species of Song-verse and Speech verse.'[43] Receiving a first class honours degree in 27 October 1911, his work was ground-breaking in the way it analysed song verse, pause, rhyme and uniformity. In fact, his MA was so successful that the board of examiners recommended he enlarge the scope of his work and apply for a Doctorate in Literature, but this suggestion was never taken up by MacDonagh.[44] However, within two years of his thesis submission he published his work as an academic book under the title *Thomas Campion and the Art of English Poetry*.

MacDonagh was by now making a name for himself as a poet. In 1910 he published his fourth book of poems, *Songs of Myself*, which had been in the planning since 1908 and represented an attempt by MacDonagh to capture his personality yet 'not to raise up fame for future time; but to lay the ghost of my youth.'[45] It represented a new style in poetry for MacDonagh with its adoption of a motif of journey and discovery. The title of his new book was in deference to the poet Walt Whitman, an American poet remarkable for his use of free verse and controversial subject matter, who had used an almost identical title for one of his poems in 1855. Many of MacDonagh's poems in *Songs of Myself* can easily be related to his youth. One biographer, examining 'In Absence', believes it to reference MacDonagh's experiences at Rockwell and his crisis of faith.[46] While this may be the case, its lonely and melancholic tone, with the continued reference to an absent friend, could also be related to the life-changing experience of his mother's death:

> *Last night I read your letters once again –*
> *Read till the dawn filled all my room with grey;*
> *Then quenched my light and put the leaves away,*
> *And prayed for sleep to ease my heart's great pain.*
> *But ah! that poignant tenderness made vain*

My hope of rest – I could not sleep or pray
For thought of you, and the slow, broadening day
Held me there prisoner of my throbbing brain.[47]

Songs of Myself also included 'John-John', generally regarded as one of his finest poems. 'John-John' depicted the rural phenomenon of the travelling people, who arrived into country towns and pitched their caravans by the sides of roads, offering cheap labour and frequently visiting fairs and markets. Far removed from and suspicious of settled people, they spoke their own language and had their own customs. 'John-John' takes as its (for the time controversial) theme a settled village girl falling in love with and marrying an Irish traveller, John-John, whom she had met at Nenagh Fair, County Tipperary:

I dreamt last night of you, John-John,
And thought you called to me;
And when I woke this morning,
John, yourself I hoped to see;
But I was all alone, John-John,
Though still I heard your call;
I put my boots and bonnet on,
And took my Sunday shawl,
And went full sure to find you, John,
At Nenagh fair.

'John-John' represented MacDonagh's ability to capture the sense of the Irish countryside and deal sympathetically with differing traditions. The poem was a remarkable success and was regarded by *The Irish Times* as having 'an irresistible appeal'.[48] Padraic Colum wrote that 'John-John' was 'a dramatization of the Irish fold mind, but its quaintness of form puts it a place apart' comparing MacDonagh to 'a happy Thomas Hardy'.[49] Of equal note, *Songs of Myself* also included as its final poem 'Envoi', which captured the theme of personal journeying and a desire to lay the ghosts of the past to rest:

> *To lose their sorrow I send them so,*
> *And to lose the joys I hold dear;*
> *Ere I on another journey go*
> *And leave my dead youth here …*
> *And now it is time to start, John-John,*
> *And leave this life behind;*
> *We'll be free on the road that we journey on*
> *Whatever fate we find.*[50]

While at UCD, MacDonagh began a serious relationship with Muriel Gifford. Their relationship was, however, complicated by several problems. Firstly, as he was a Roman Catholic (albeit not practising) and she was Anglican, their relationship had to be hidden from both Muriel's mother and Thomas' sister Mary Josephine, who was a nun and whom he initially feared would be 'troubled' by Muriel's Protestantism.[51] He need not have worried about his sister, however, as Mary Josephine and Muriel became firm friends, the former recalling 'for her I had a sisterly love and affection which she reciprocated.'[52] Muriel's mother, however, was more of a problem: Isabella Gifford was deeply hostile towards Catholicism and Muriel was profoundly fearful that she would see her daughter and Thomas in public.[53] Muriel was also extremely self-conscious (she never regarded herself as naturally pretty) and regularly troubled by jealousy, despite the fact that there is no evidence MacDonagh was ever unfaithful to her. If MacDonagh spent any time around other women, particularly Mary Maguire, she would row with him and write him accusatory letters, then subsequently apologise, finding how she seemed 'to always send [Thomas] horrible loony letters.'[54] On 8 October 1911 she wrote to him complaining about his relationship to her sister Sidney. Fearful that Thomas was beginning to court Sidney, she implored her boyfriend 'for heaven's sake don't make love to John Brennan [Sidney] … You'll break my heart if you fall in love with her.'[55]

Responding to Muriel, MacDonagh wrote her a four-page letter, citing how her complaint had left him very disturbed. Seeking to reassure her, he explained that he liked Sidney as much as all the members of her family (his favourite was Nellie), but his 'liking of them is as different as the spheres from my love for you.'[56] Having convinced Muriel that he was not interested in Sidney, he proposed marriage to her later that month. Overjoyed, Muriel wrote 'how happy I feel – your beautiful ring is like the clasp of your fingers on mine – I can never be lonely now that I have this link connecting you with me.'[57] Despite their engagement in October, Muriel was so nervous of her mother that she did not tell Isabella about the wedding until 22 November. Describing a tense encounter with her mother, Muriel recollected to her fiancé:

> Well darling, I threw the bomb last night when I came in
> … My mother took it very badly – much worse than I
> could have imagined – what about it – I suppose she'll get
> over it sometime. My father kept perfectly silent about the
> whole thing.[58]

Despite her mother's opposition, MacDonagh now became a regular visitor to the Gifford home at Temple Villas in Rathfarnham. Isabella was suspicious of MacDonagh, fearing that her daughter (and any children) would become Catholics. Troubled by the difficulties of mixed marriage in the early twentieth century, MacDonagh frustratingly explained:

> Muriel and I are of the same religion, which is neither
> Catholic or Protestant nor any other form of dogmatic
> creed, neither of us ever go to Church or Chapel, but for
> the sake of several things and people we are willing to con-

form for a marriage ceremony.[59]

Determined that he would not marry Muriel until he secured a permanent job, MacDonagh had been seeking a lecturing position in English at UCD. In December 1911 he got the job, and Thomas and Muriel were married on 3 January 1912 in what was a small and informal wedding in Ranelagh, County Dublin. Writing to Muriel on the eve of the marriage, MacDonagh romantically wrote 'I have lost years and years. Now we'll make up for that … I'll kiss you goodnight in future, always.'[60] Patrick Pearse was to act as witness for the wedding, but for some unknown reason he failed to arrive, so the assembled found a man nearby cutting a large hedge to act as witness. MacDonagh never held a grudge against Pearse for missing his wedding, but often gently teased him for failing to attend, holding that the real reason was because he had grown too plump to fit into the the kilt MacDonagh had requested he wear. MacDonagh was now a changed man: his relationship with Muriel had reinvigorated him, and he no longer needed the desert he had once sought at Grange Lodge. In 'A Song for Muriel', which would later become part of 'The Song of Joy', the contrast with 'Envoi' is unmistakeable:

Now no bitter songs I sing:
Summer follows for me now;
For the Spirit of the Spring

Breathes upon the living bough:
All poor leaves of why and how?Fall before this wonder, dead:
Joy is given to me now?
In the love of her I wed.[61]

Rather than settling into Grange Lodge, the newly married couple rented an apartment in the city centre, settling at No. 32 in fashionable Baggot Street. By November of 1912 Muriel had given birth to their first child, Donagh. Thomas was overjoyed and celebrated the arrival of his first son with a poem entitled 'Wishes For My Son, Born On Saint Cecilia's Day'.

Now, my son, is life for you,
And I wish you joy of it -
Joy of power in all you do,
Deeper passion, better wit
Than I had who had enough,
Quicker life and length thereof,
More of every gift but love.[62]

Donagh MacDonagh was christened a Catholic in the Church of the Three Patrons in Rathgar in South County Dublin. While the christening was taking place, Patrick Pearse happened to arrive in the church to say prayers. Staying for the ceremony, MacDonagh, displaying his sense of humour and remembering Pearse's absence at his wedding, teased his friend with the greeting: 'Well, you got here in time for the christening anyway!'[63]

Chapter Five

• • • • • •

1913 – 1915

'Dear boy, you'll be shot'

In 1913, there were changes at *The Irish Review*. MacDonagh, having secured work at UCD, now took a more relaxed role within the magazine and, while maintaining some interest in its production, became a less frequent contributor. However, despite the cordial relations that had marked the foundation of *The Irish Review* in 1911, David Houston had disagreed with editors Padraic Colum and his wife Mary Maguire on the content of the magazine, and was concerned by the marked inability of Colum to increase its readership. While Colum maintained a high standard of excellence, with regular contributions from well-known literary commentators, *The Irish Review* was steadily losing money and in serious debt. Faced with a bill of £88 per quarter, Houston found the publication was becoming a financial burden, and he was eager to sell it to a reasonable bidder. Colum and Maguire pleaded with Houston to give them time to find a financial backer, and were in talks with several influential figures, including historian Alice Stopford Green and publisher George Roberts. Houston had grown tired of the Colums, however, and found they were 'impossible in matters touching real affairs,'[1] so, eager to find a buyer, MacDonagh arranged a meeting between Houston and Joseph Plunkett.

A deal was agreed whereby Plunkett, if he could raise £200, could purchase the magazine from Houston. The Colums briefly fell out with MacDonagh for arranging the meeting, perceiving it as an attempt by MacDonagh and Plunkett to oust them as editors. Colum believed that MacDonagh, at this point, had little interest in *The Irish Review*, and that Plunkett, due to his poor health, was the wrong man to take control of a magazine, holding 'he is a delicate young man and [may] have to put the whole thing aside on a doctor's order'[2]. He also was afraid that with Plunkett's takeover he would lose his editorial position, which in literary circles could see him branded as a failure. Colum was clearly frustrated with MacDonagh, accusing the latter of treating him with a lack of consideration and compromising his efforts to find a potential buyer. For his part MacDonagh strenuously denied that he had set about to undermine the Colums. For a time there was noticeable tension between all involved, and MacDonagh felt a great deal of regret about how events had unfolded.

By 16 June 1913, the Colums ceased to be editors of *The Irish Review*. Plunkett had raised the £200 from his mother, who was enticed by the idea of her son publishing his own magazine, and so Plunkett's house at 17 Marlborough Road became the new headquarters of *The Irish Review* with Mac-Donagh once again becoming its sub-editor. He also functioned as an ambassador of sorts, regularly meeting with potential contributors and advertisers. Under their stewardship *The Irish Review* became much more politically aware and, while remaining true to its literary values, increasingly began to reflect the great issues affecting the Irish people. This was represented by a change in its mission statement, as described in the magazine's frontispiece. When it had been established, it had sought to be a 'monthly magazine of Irish literature and science', but under Plunkett and MacDonagh *The Irish Review* became 'a monthly magazine of Irish politics, literature and art'. It was inevitable that *The Irish Review* would do this, as by 1913 it was impossible not to be aware of the tide of social and political developments across the country.

Since the beginning of the twentieth century, the prospect of an all-out European war looked increasingly likely. Europe was divided into an alliance system whereby each of the larger countries would come to another's aid if the latter was threatened. Britain, France and Russia were represented by a Triple Entente, while Germany, Austro-Hungry and

Italy were defended by what they termed a Triple Alliance. But throughout the early years of the twentieth century tensions were heightened by an arms and naval race between Britain and Germany, with the Germans hoping to build a fleet to rival the British navy, the world's largest maritime force, and by all the imperial nations seeking to expand their hegemony at the expense of their rivals. Nationalism was also on the rise within Europe, as small countries sought to assert their independence; a particularly problematic region was the Balkans, where Serbian nationalism threatened to plunge the entire region into chaos. It therefore came as no surprise that the first issue of *The Irish Review* in July 1913, edited by Plunkett and MacDonagh, carried an article by Roger Casement entitled 'Ireland, Germany and The Next War'. If Europe was engulfed by a world war, it was likely that Britain would be drawn into the conflict, and Casement's article addressed this possibility. It was also a response to Sir Arthur Conan Doyle, the creator of Sherlock Holmes, who had implored Ireland to support the British war effort. Casement, writing under the alias 'Shan Van Vocht', addressed some provocative themes: that Ireland would have to remain tied with Britain under German rule; a conjectural analysis of a German annexation of the island; and a dismissal of the British perception that German rule would be far worse for Ireland than British governance. Against this, however, he claimed that British defeat to Germany could be beneficial to Ireland, with the emergence of a benign policy of German rule in Ireland, as the Germans would not seek to:

> Impoverish or depress that new won possession, but to enhance its strategic importance by vigorous and wise administration so as to make it the main counterpoise to any possible recovery of British maritime supremacy, so largely due as this was in the past to Great Britain's possession of this island.[3]

Addressing the possibility of annexation, Casement believed that a permanent occupation of Ireland by Germany was unlikely as, coupled with the fall of Britain, 'such a complete change in the political geography of Europe [with] a German owned Ireland could not but provoke universal alarm and a widespread combination to forbid its realisation.'[4] He noted that this 'universal alarm' could be the catalyst for a European solution to the Irish question in the event of a German victory. This solution, Casement predicted, could be rooted in a German defeat of the British navy combined with international pressure (involving American and other powers), making Irish annexation impossible. In this scenario a victorious Germany would seek to maintain its spoils of war through the permanent disabling of Britain's naval supremacy by the creation of an independent Ireland and 'the opening of the seas and their permanent freeing from that overwhelming control Great Britain has exercised.'[5]

Casement asserted that the British position on Ireland was based on the fundamentally arrogant and misguided assumption that Ireland was integrally an part of Great Britain and on a crude belief in the supposed inferiority of the Irish people. However, while the question of a possible war with Germany was occupying people's minds, 1913 was dominated by a far greater social question: the rise of the ITGWU and its growing challenge to the employers.

Since its foundation in 1909 the ITGWU had grown rapidly throughout Ireland. Setting up a headquarters in the former Northumberland Hotel at the corner of Eden Quay and Beresford Place, which they renamed Liberty Hall, the union was ideally positioned in the city centre. Using the policy of sympathetic strikes, the union had secured significant improvements in workers' rights, including wage increases of up to 25 per cent for some of its members. Such was its growing strength that in May 1911 the ITGWU published its own newspaper, *The Irish Worker*, which espoused class struggle, syndicalism and the necessity of workers uniting together in order to secure radical societal change. *The Irish Worker* was also positioned as an alternative newspaper to the right-wing press that dominated the Irish market, such as the nationalist-orientated Freeman's Journal, the populist *Irish Independent* and the pro-Unionist *Irish Times*.

The militant strategy of the ITGWU, coupled with its rapid growth, meant that Irish employers were increasingly frustrated by union organisation amongst their employees. The greatest opponent of the ITGWU was a leading Dublin nationalist and entrepreneurial capitalist, William Martin Murphy. Martin Murphy had been elected to the British parliament as one of the IPP representatives for Dublin in 1885, but in the wake of the Parnell scandal and the subsequent split had become a strong opponent of Charles Stewart Parnell. As Dublin was a stronghold of Parnellite support, Martin Murphy lost his seat in 1892 and left active politics to pursue a career in business. By 1906 he had established the Irish Independent, owned Cleary's department store on Sackville Street, maintained the fashionable Imperial Hotel and was a senior shareholder and chairman in the Dublin United Tramways Company (DUTC). In the latter capacity he had built an outstanding light railway system in Dublin City and overseen the electrification of the trams. Martin Murphy encouraged employers to campaign against the ITGWU, and used his newspaper to criticise Larkin and the workers' movement. He also successfully oversaw the establishment of the Dublin Employers' Federation.

With the employers organising against the growth of the ITGWU, it was inevitable that some form of conflict would emerge, and on Sunday, 19 July 1913, Martin Murphy called a meeting of the DUTC workers where he warned his staff that if they joined the ITGWU or persisted in their membership of the union, they would be dismissed from work with no pay. By 15 August 1913 he had made the same demand of the workers in the *Irish Independent*, dismissing forty men. Having discharged the men from his newspaper, he now found that ITGWU members in press distribution refused to circulate the newspaper in popular outlets, the most important of which was Eason (which distributed the newspaper throughout Ireland). Exasperating his difficulties, newspaper boys refused to sell it on street corners and employees of the DUTC also refused to handle it. Martin Murphy responded by dismissing two hundred tram workers from their jobs. Seeking to undermine Martin Murphy, the ITGWU now initiated a general strike, culminating in the Great Dublin Lockout of 1913, where more than 20,000 workers were locked out of their jobs and replaced by their employers with blackleg labour in a major industrial dispute.

On Sunday, 31 August 1913, Larkin was due to address a rally on Sackville Street. The authorities in Dublin Castle swiftly moved to ban the meeting. However, Larkin was determined to speak and, hiding from police, he stayed overnight in the home of Countess Markievicz. Markievicz had arranged for a friend, Gussie McGrath, to book a room in the Imperial Hotel (ironically, owned by William Martin Murphy) for 31 August, from which he could address the crowd. Getting Larkin into the hotel was, however, logistically difficult as he was incredibly well-known. As a result, MacDonagh's sister-in-law Nellie volunteered to accompany Larkin into the hotel, with the union organiser disguised as a deaf old man and posing as a Protestant clergyman accompanied by his niece. As Larkin drove to the Imperial Hotel, he was followed in a cab by Markievicz, Sidney Gifford and Gussie McGrath, who stopped outside the General Post Office on Sackville Street. They noticed that the street was crowded with police. When Larkin appeared from the window of the Imperial Hotel and began to address the crowd, the police stormed the building and arrested him, while outside they attacked the assembled onlookers with batons, as Sidney Gifford recalled:

> I was standing in the middle of the street when I suddenly realised that police were advancing and closing in on us in a menacing manner from all sides and soon O'Connell Street was covered with prostrate bodies. It was a very terrifying experience. Anybody who moved was beaten flat to the ground. The people fled on all sides and were pursued into the streets by the frenzied police who beat them unmercifully ... [6]

Later known as Bloody Sunday, the ensuing riot resulted in the death a few days later of two workers, James Nolan and John Byrne, while over three hundred people were injured. MacDonagh, speculating that Larkin would speak, had cycled into Sackville Street that morning and was fortunate enough to see the trade unionist emerge onto the balcony, recalling the great excitement as people ran to the hotel exclaiming, 'that's Larkin!'[7] Interested in hearing the speech, MacDonagh saw how within minutes police appeared. Having witnessed Larkin's arrest, he made his way to his bicycle. Testifying to the Askwith Inquiry, set up in 1914 to examine the circumstances which led to the Lockout, MacDonagh recalled:

Nothing occurred until [Larkin] was as far down as Abbey Street or further. I was about to get on my bicycle, then when a man came and told me – 'you had better get out of the way, as there is going to be a baton charge.' When he said that I said 'impossible, there is no crowd to charge.' The police came on after that … they attacked an old woman with a shawl over her head, and batoned her brutally. I saw them baton a small man who had lost his hat, and he was bleeding. I heard the continual rapping of batons. I could not mistake the noise. There is no doubt every policeman had a baton in his hand and was using it.[8]

It was evident that MacDonagh was horrified by the police brutality. A supporter of the ITGWU, although not a member, he was also concerned with the conditions for Dublin's working class. During the Lockout, striking workers were cut off from the salaries and dependent on meagre union remittances. As conditions for the Dublin working class were already among the worst in Europe, the strike only made their situation more difficult as families literally struggled to survive. MacDonagh was further horrified to learn how the Catholic Church actively opposed a union scheme where children of Irish strikers would be sent to Britain and temporarily looked after by British trade unionists. Examining why the Church had prevented starving children from going to England, a perturbed MacDonagh discovered it was because they feared the children would be subject to Protestant or atheist influences. If Irish parents were willing to send their children to families in England in order to survive, MacDonagh concluded it represented absolute desperation on their part and something needed to be done urgently to relieve their distress. Meeting with James Connolly, MacDonagh and Plunkett convinced him to give the workers' side of the story in *The Irish Review*. Eventually published in October 1913 under the heading 'Labour In Dublin', Connolly praised Dublin City for its charitable institutions and sense of community, but condemned 'the perfectly hellish conditions under which its people are housed, and under which its men, women and children labour for a living.'[9] Connolly argued in favour of the sympathetic strike and a betterment of the conditions for the Irish working class, not in only in Dublin, but across the whole country. He asserted that:

> The way out of this deadlock is for all sides to consent to the formation of a conciliation board, before which all disputes must be brought. Let the employers insist upon level-

ling up the conditions of employment to one high standard; treat as an Ishmael any employer who refuses to conform, and leave him unassisted to fight the battle with the Union; let the Union proceed to organise all the workers possible, place all disputes as to wages before the board for discussion, and only resort to a strike when agreement cannot be reached by the board; and as all employers would be interested in bringing in the more obdurate and greedy to reason, strikes would be rare.[10]

As the Lockout continued, a small number of middle-class individuals, including MacDonagh, continued to believe that something needed to be done to bring an end to the dispute. In this endeavour they were led by Thomas Kettle, who had described the industrial conflict as an 'apocalypse of waste, impoverishment and social disorganisation.'[11] Kettle, Professor of Economics in UCD and formerly an IPP MP for East Tyrone, was good friends with MacDonagh. Both men not only worked for the same college, but Kettle had impressed MacDonagh through his editorship of the IPP newspaper, *The Nationalist,* in which Kettle pledged that a Home Rule parliament would support Gaelic League control of Irish education, women's suffrage and industrial self-sufficiency. On 7 October 1913, Kettle established the Industrial Peace Committee as a means to seek a truce between the workers and their employers, and invited MacDonagh to attend. At the inaugural meeting in the Mansion House, Kettle declared that it was the ambition of the committee to galvanise popular opinion in Dublin neither behind the workers or the employers but behind a campaign seeking the end of a 'ruinous campaign'[12]. MacDonagh was elected Honorary Secretary, serving on the committee alongside Joseph Plunkett, Oliver St John Gogarty and the only employer to attend, Edward Lee. Kettle held that the Lockout was counterproductive to all involved, arguing that both workers and bosses were losing money while the daily life of uninvolved parties was increasingly disturbed by the dispute. Kettle commended Larkin and Martin Murphy as two great leaders, describing a paradox where 'capital and labour had [each] found a great leader [and] found it impossible to come to terms.'[13]

By 13 October the Committee had met with the Dublin Trades' Council and had reached an understanding that a temporary truce between employers and workers was possible. To the Dublin Employers' Federation, the committee proposed an intermediary to negotiate with the ITGWU. While the Federation was willing to listen to the Committee's points, their discussions ended with the employers only making a commitment to issue a public statement of their position. In this statement, released to the press in October 1913, the employers' body refused to negotiate with the ITGWU unless the union was reorganised. On behalf of the employers, Charles Coghlan, the Federation secretary, claimed that the ITGWU was not a responsible organisation and that it could not be trusted to keep agreements. MacDonagh now opened formal correspondence on behalf of the committee with the Dublin employers, holding that negotiations remained as necessary as ever between the workers and employers. In this vain, writing a letter to the Employers' Federation, published in *The Freeman's Journal*, he explained:

> Manifestly the time has now come for a conference between the representatives of the employers and those of the workers. The hourly suffering interests of Dublin make such a conference immediately necessary.[14]

The Employers' Federation, however, doggedly stood by their position, refusing to negotiate with the ITGWU. An article in *The Irish Review* by James Bertram, representing the union's view, regarded this position as 'idle sophistry' and announced that 'men are willing to die,'[15] in order to secure their rights within the workplace.

With negotiations deadlocked, Thomas Kettle arranged a meeting between the Committee and the six Home Rule MPs representing Dublin, who made it clear that the Irish Parliamentary Party sided with the employers and would seek to stay above the labour dispute. Only one IPP MP in Dublin, William Field, himself a labour representative, supported the Committee's work. The Industrial Peace Committee continued until November but, failing to facilitate an agreement between employers and workers, was dissolved and replaced by a new organisation called the Dublin Civic League. The Lockout continued into January 1914 but it became increasingly clear that the ITGWU would lose its battle against the Dublin employers. The powerful British union movement also reneged on its support for the Lockout by refusing to strike in sympathy. Many workers were forced to return to work on the basis that they had no further involvement with the ITGWU. Dejected, James Connolly wrote:

> And so, we Irish workers must again go down into hell, bow our backs to the lash of the slave driver, let our hearts be seared by the iron of his hatred and instead of the sacramental wafer of brotherhood and common sacrifice, eat the dust of defeat and betrayal.[16]

Alongside his political activities, 1913 was a year of great literary maturity for Thomas MacDonagh. Since 1911 he had been preoccupied with the idea of a collected edition of new and old poems, using the best works from his less commercially successful publications, *Through The Ivory Gate*, *April and May* and *The Golden Joy*, with some minor edits. This is supported by his decision not to include any poems from his moderately successful *Songs of Myself*. He had also decided to translate poetry directly from the Irish language. Eventually choosing the title *Lyrical Poems,* he published his new book through *The Irish Review* in November 1913, dedicated to Muriel and Donagh.[17] As his own publisher, he had free reign in how *Lyrical Poems* would be structured, making this book of poetry, as one biographer has correctly claimed, 'MacDonagh's real poetic testament.'[18] Clearly excited at the prospect, he wrote to Muriel:

> I have been working – not at exams, as I ought to be, but at a book of poems. I must get that out of the way next by publishing it. I have now put into it all the poems I want published except those in my last book: 8 images, 12 inscriptions, 20 early poems, 4 translations, 6 new poems, 50 poems, 1480 lines, 124 pages.[19]

Lyrical Poems is structured into five sections. This first part deals with the author's journey, a man who has suffered isolation, heartbreak, despair and ultimate triumph through burgeoning contentment. The second section, 'The Book of Images' is a collection of eight mystical poems, culminating in 'The Poet Captain' and 'The Golden Joy' respectively. The third section featured translations of Irish language poems: one such example was the poem 'The Yellow Bittern', by the Fermanagh-born 18th century poet Cathal Buí Mac Guilla Ghunna. Following on from translations Thomas MacDonagh reintroduced earlier poems in his fourth section, including 'Envoi' and 'Of a Poet Patriot'. The final section was called 'Inscriptions' and introduced some new poetry; particularly notable is a remarkably touching poem on father-hood entitled 'Wishes For My Son', in which he writes to his son, 'love I have beyond all men, love that now you share with me.'[20] Also interesting is his poem 'The Song of Joy' which was clearly written about his lost love, Mary Maguire. While the poem describes heartbreak, embarrassment and suffering, MacDonagh concludes by explaining that he is not bitter and has fallen in love again.

Lyrical Poems was reasonably received. The London-based literary magazine *Athenaeum* spoke of *Lyrical Poems* in glowing terms, commending MacDonagh for improving his poetical style and 'freeing himself very largely from the conventional obsessions of the Irish poet, major and minor.'[21] The magazine lauded MacDonagh for being a poet who passionately 'stands on his own feet.'[22] *The Expository Times* recalled his work as 'a fine handsome quarto of Lyrical Poems',[23] while the *Irish Homestead* regarded MacDonagh as 'a rather difficult poet to criticise.'[24] *The Academy* was, however, decidedly critical and wrote 'Mr MacDonagh is quite sure that he is a poet; we are not so sure. Pages of rhyme and pretty thoughts and smooth words do not constitute poetry.'[25] While believing that MacDonagh was capable of good work, *The Academy* found *Lyrical Poems* to be 'dull metal'[26] and lacking inspiration. Around this time, the joy of his new publication was undermined when Muriel, suffering from bouts of depression, suffered 'a nervous breakdown'.[27]

According to MacDonagh, she had been melancholy for six weeks, becoming so bad that she had been put up first in a nursing home and then a convalescent home at Sandycove in County Dublin. The effect was immense on MacDonagh, as caring for Donagh forced him to cancel many of his lectures at UCD, and he feared he was 'leaving his students in the lurch.'[28] But he was also preparing to embark on yet another new venture: with Joseph Plunkett, he intended to establish a new Irish theatre to compete with the Abbey.

On 27 October 1910 *The Irish Times* had advertised the sale of 38½ Hardwicke Street in north inner-city Dublin. A former school, which had once included among its staff MacDonagh's father, Joseph, it was described in the newspaper by the auctioneers, MacArthur's, as 'admirably suited for a lecture hall, public institution, etc., being very spacious and in proximity to the centre of the city.' Believing 38½ Hardwicke Street was being sold at a bargain price, the building was purchased by Countess Plunkett. She did not know what to do with it, however, and it was initially used by the family for social and private entertainments. Showing her interest in the Gaelic Revival, the Countess also rented out a floor of the house to the Dun Emer Guild, a pioneering all-women arts and crafts venture under Evelyn Gleeson. In 1913, however, MacDonagh and Plunkett showed an interest in converting the lofty lecture hall in the house into a theatre. To do so, however, they needed money from Countess Plunkett and, after persuading her of the merits of the venture, she threw her full support behind the renovation. Plunkett's sister Geraldine recalled:

> Ma threw herself into the fun; she was always at her best when she was really busy. She had the stage put back up, very expensive velvet curtains made and got a lot of theatre seats.[29]

MacDonagh and Plunkett were eager to counter the influence of the Abbey Theatre. While recognising that the Abbey was an important part of the Irish literary scene, they felt that that the theatre placed too much emphasis on peasant plays with an exaggerated and stereotypical view of traditional rural Irish life, and a false and pretentious form of what they considered to be Celtic literature and tradition. Logistically, however, what they called the Irish Theatre was a substantial financial and dramatic project, so MacDonagh and Plunkett turned to Edward Martyn for assistance and professional guidance.

Born in 1859, Edward Martyn came from a Catholic Unionist background and was part of the landed gentry, owning Tulira (sometimes spelled Tullira) Castle in County Galway, where he had practiced as a Justice of the Peace. Martyn was well connected within the Irish literary scene, and in 1896 had introduced WB Yeats to Lady Gregory as well as financing the first three seasons of the Irish Literary

Theatre, the precursor of the Abbey. While he had fallen out with Yeats by 1913, he still retained valuable contacts and an established reputation within Irish theatre. Martyn was president of *Na hAisteoirí* (The Actors), an Irish language drama group affiliated with the Gaelic League. For a time he had sat on the executive of the League, and published in 1900 a pamphlet entitled *Ireland's Battle For Her Language*. Martyn was also on intimate terms with Arthur Griffith, having financed Griffith's pamphlet, *The Resurrection of Hungary*, and acted as the nominal president of Sinn Féin until 1908. Famously he had refused to play the British national anthem after a dinner in Tulira Castle, and on revealing himself to be a nationalist, he was forced to resign as Justice of Peace. With Maud Gonne and Countess Markievicz, he had protested Queen Victoria's Irish visit in 1897 and had treated her son Edward VII with equal contempt in 1903 when, as president of the People's Protection Committee, he had sought to lead opposition to the royal visit of that year. Under MacDonagh and Plunkett's plan, Plunkett would provide the hall at Hardwicke Street, MacDonagh would manage the performances, and Martyn would provide the capital. Martyn was reasonably interested as he had long hoped to challenge the dominance of the Abbey. Writing in *The Irish Review* Martyn, describing the project as his own with no reference to MacDonagh and Plunkett, asserted the aim of the Irish Theatre was:

To apply the methods of the Abbey Theatre to an organisation of the most talented amateurs for the encouragement and production of native Irish drama other than the peasant species, and thereby see if, by study and perseverance, we may similarly create a school of young dramatists who will devote themselves to this particular department. I feel that, however, depressed and ruined we may have been by English government and our inept acquiescence by often playing into the hands of the enemy, we have still some inhabitants left in Ireland besides peasants, and that a theatre which only treats of peasant life can never be considered, no matter how good it may be, more than a folk theatre.[30]

Establishing a partnership called the Irish Theatre Company, the trio signed an agreement in June 1914. MacDonagh was to act as managing partner of the Irish Theatre and receive a regular wage of £12.10.0 per month. He could also appoint a secretary, at his own cost, to help assist him in the management of the theatre and the conduct of its business with actors and the general public. This role eventually went to his brother John. Signing the agreement, MacDonagh was aware that in this position he was responsible for the 'rehearsal and production of the plays chosen for production' and 'supplying a company of actors and actresses.'[31] Plunkett was responsible for ticket sales, upkeep, scenery and repair, while Martyn would provide the capital necessary to keep the company financially secure. An ambitious venture, the company hoped to stage fifty performances between September 1914 and June 1915, with the partners agreeing to stage, if possible, five plays per month. In light of their criticisms of the Abbey, the Irish Theatre was determined to stage plays in English which were not peasant dramas, as well as plays in Irish and those translated into English from European playwrights. However, while MacDonagh was responsible for managing the theatre, which included selecting the plays to be performed, the agreement to establish the Irish Theatre left his powers curtailed, as Edward Martyn was determined that half the plays performed by the company had to be written by him, and was so insistent about this that he had a clause inserted into the legal agreement.[32]

Having established the theatre, the company now needed actors, and MacDonagh approached Frank Fay to head a troupe. A founder member of the Abbey, Fay had played Shawn Keogh in the first production of *The Playboy of the Western World;* however, increasingly frustrated by Yeats' style and losing authority in the Abbey, Fay left the company. Part of the reason MacDonagh approached Fay, it seems, was a strategy to obtain for the Irish Theatre playwrights and actors who had fallen foul of the Abbey. The names frequently associated with the Irish Theatre are a veritable who's who of disgruntled Abbey players, including Máire Nic Shiubhlaigh and Una O'Connor. MacDonagh was so eager to get Fay involved with the Irish Theatre that he gave the actor assurances that he could have absolute control over plays that he directed, and he would be allowed to teach acting within the Hardwicke Street premises on a regular basis.[33] According to one author, in approaching Fay 'MacDonagh envisioned an amateur company of young, unspoiled persons, a *tabula rasa* [blank slate] upon which Fay could exercise his gifts.'[34] MacDonagh's proposal interested Fay, as did the offer of a yearly salary of £150. Fay was also negotiating with Plunkett, who found him to be personally dour and lacking in humour, albeit with great enthusiasm and a pronounced knowledge of theatre and acting.[35] Plunkett explained in a letter to MacDonagh how this was not a necessarily a negative trait, but in fact could be of advantage to the burgeoning Irish Theatre as 'at present a high seriousness is undoubtedly required.'[36]

The Irish Theatre eventually staged its first performance on 2 November 1914 as hundreds of theatregoers came to see Edward Martyn's *The Dream Physician* starring Una O'Connor, JM Carre and MacDonagh's brother John. Unfortunately the performance could not be staged in Hardwicke Street due to technical issues and ongoing rewiring, so it was performed in Madame Rock's Little Theatre in Sackville Street. *The Dream Physician*, billed as 'a serious and moving play, lightened by an interlude of comedy ... full of allusions to men and matters connected with the recent developments of politics, literature and art in Ireland'[37] was actually a satire lampooning the playwright George Moore, who had insulted Martyn with his *Hail and Farewell* (alleging that Martyn was a repressed homosexual). Indeed the fourth act of the play was regarded as 'simply an excuse for lambasting George Moore.'[38] Other significant figures satirised included WB Yeats and Lady Gregory, who were portrayed as the characters Brummell and Nurse Fernan respectively. *The Freeman's Journal* found the Irish Theatre's inaugural play was 'a fine drama' but its satire left much to be desired.[39] *The Irish Times* found the play 'wildly improbable,' holding that the performance could not be described as anything more than trivial.[40] Similarly Joseph Holloway, who had been invited to the Theatre by MacDonagh, found the performance 'crude preposterous piffle.'[41] Dublin entertainer Fred Jeffs humorously commented that after the performance the Irish Theatre should rename itself the Libel Theatre.[42]

By January 1915 the Irish Theatre was ready to open in its Hardwicke Street venue, and *The Irish Times* wrote how:

> The little theatre had been considerably renovated recently, and further repairs are in progress. When these are completed it will be fairly comfortable. The gentlemen associated with the management have placed before themselves a high ideal, and even, if they do not fully attain it, they will still have done good work in further literary and dramatic art in Dublin.[43]

The Irish Theatre's 1915 season began on 3 January with MacDonagh opening a night of four short plays, each prefaced by an introduction where he explained the novelties of the presented dramas. The theatre critic 'Jacques' found MacDonagh's lectures rather technical, belabouring and superfluous. The first performance that evening, *The Troth,* was a controversial play written by Rutherford Mayne about a desperate Catholic and Protestant who conspire to assassinate their landlord. Starring Máire Nic Shiubhlaigh, Art Mac an Bhaird and Padraic O Seachain, *The Troth* was performed in an Irish translation by Liam Ó Domhnaill rather than in its original English, and was billed as *Fé Bhrigh na Mionn.* This was followed by an equally controversial play called *The Revolt.* Written in 1870 by the French playwright Auguste Villiers de L'Isle-Adam, it had been banned due to alleged immorality by the French government after only five performances in Paris, a fact that MacDonagh announced to the delight of the assembled audience.[44] The performance, starring Una O'Connor and Frank Fay, was noted as decidedly lacking in immorality and clearly catering to an Irish rather than a Parisian audience. *The Revolt* was followed by a satirical piece, *The Phoenix on the Roof,* written by Eimar O'Duffy, and to close the evening, John MacDonagh performed a version of Chekhov's two-man play, *Swansong,* which, although billed as starring the actor Richard Sheridan, actually included his brother Thomas as the character Nikita. Writing in the *Irish Independent,* 'Jacques' stated, 'The Irish Theatre promises big things for the future. Its friends will hope it makes good.'[45] Joseph Holloway, however, was less than impressed and, examining Thomas MacDonagh, commented how 'he buzzed around … seemingly very busy but actually doing very little.'[46]

MacDonagh had chosen as the highlight of the 1915 season a performance of Anton Chekov's *Uncle Vanya* in June 1915. In choosing this play MacDonagh gave the Irish Theatre the distinction of being the first Irish institution to perform an entire play written by Chekhov. Meeting Joseph Holloway in Dublin, he noted that the performance of *Uncle Vanya* had been long in the planning, and as early as January 1915 he had intended *Swansong* to be an introduction and a prequel of sorts. The staging of *Uncle Vanya* was a risk, however; not only was the play rather avant-garde for an Irish audience, but good summer weather could impact ticket sales and attendance. There was also the consideration that the Irish Theatre was still largely an amateur troupe, but MacDonagh believed that Chekov's play would be easy to rehearse. He was rather devil-may-care in his attitude and, willing to take the risk that the play could flop, he commented to Holloway how 'if twenty true lovers of drama showed up,' he would be happy.[47] MacDonagh had organised a strong cast for the performance, including his brother John, J Anthony Meagher, Seán MacCaoilte, Willie Pearse, Blanaid Salkeld and Maire Nic Shiubhlaigh, amongst others. Opening the play on 28 June, MacDonagh addressed the audience prior to the performance with a rather long lecture. He explained what *Uncle Vanya* was and commented that it was essentially a high-brow production, that the theatre management's objective was artistic, and they were 'not by any means concerned on the subject of public patronage'.[48] In this regard, he informed the audience how it would be almost impossible for them to understand the play unless they had read it beforehand.'[49] One newspaper commented that on the night, 'small as the theatre is, it was not at all fully occupied.'[50]

Uncle Vanya was panned by the critics. For the most part they blamed the hall itself, lamenting its size, darkness and atmosphere. *The Freeman's Journal* described the play as 'post-impressionist,' and questioned how Chekov's masterpiece 'could be done justice in this humble home of drama in Hardwicke Street,'[51] considering the small stage and amateurish costumes and make-up. The newspaper condemned the theatre as 'good enough for a simple fairytale ... but for the adequate interpretation of anything even professing to be a great dramatic inspiration, the surroundings are, to put it very delicately, discouraging.'[52] For the *Irish Independent*, the performance, while supported by a talented company of actors, was broadly 'incomprehensible.'[53] In this the newspaper was supported by *The Freeman's Journal*, which complained the acting as stilted, albeit on account of the lack of stage space. The following January, inspired by the performance, Percy French lampooned the play at the variety show *How Dublin Does It* in a piece called 'Gloom as Done At The Irish Theatre'.

The Irish Theatre at Hardwicke Street lasted six years before it finally closed its doors in 1920. Throughout its existence it remained true to its ideal of staging avant-garde plays written by Irish and European playwrights, including August Strindberg's *Easter* and Henrik Ibsen's *An Enemy of the People*. However, throughout 1915 MacDonagh and Plunkett devoted less and less time to the institution as a result of their increasingly demanding political activities. Their execution in 1916 also impacted both the theatre and Martyn personally, as he had lost two valued friends. Shortly before the Easter Rising, Martyn had his final meeting with MacDonagh in 15 Leinster Street. Recalled by Eoin Lenanne, it was noted that after a long conversation Martyn told MacDonagh, 'Remember, dear boy, you'll be shot and the lot of you will be shot.' Allegedly MacDonagh replied, 'God bless your sense – you don't know everything'. As MacDonagh left, Martyn noted to Lenanne, 'God help that poor man – he'll be shot.'[54]

Chapter Six

1913 – 1914

Troubled times in Ireland

In April 1912, Herbert Asquith, the Liberal prime minister, introduced the third Home Rule Bill. Under Asquith's plan Ireland was to be given a devolved local assembly that consisted of two chambers, a House of Commons with 164 elected representatives and an upper house known as the Senate, comprising of forty nominated members. This parliament would have the power to elect an Irish government, which would run parallel to the abolition of Dublin Castle as the centre of British administration. Despite this revolutionary proposal, however, the Home Rule government would have extremely curtailed powers, with policies relating to taxation, the monarchy, military matters, treason, religion and the army remaining the reserve of Westminster rather than Dublin. There was also a provision within the bill giving authoritative power to the British Privy Council over the implementation of Irish law, meaning that senior

British politicians and lawmakers could block any bill that was passed by the Irish assembly. The bill passed the House of Commons by a slim majority of ten votes. Passed on the House of Lords for consideration, it was defeated by 326 to 69 votes. But as recent changes to Westminster meant that the House of Lords could only postpone the passage of the bill for two years rather than veto it outright, Home Rule for Ireland would become a reality in late 1914. This was a major victory for the IPP, and, twenty-six years since the introduction of the first Home Rule Bill in 1886, nationalist Ireland rejoiced.

All this could only have come about as a result of the political crises which had racked Britain in the previous three years. In 1906 the Liberal Party had entered government with a massive majority, and as this majority meant they were not dependent on the votes of the IPP to stay in power, Home Rule was essentially shelved. But in the budget of 1909, Asquith had sought to introduce unprecedented taxes on the wealthy to fund greater social welfare for the British working classes. Known as the 'People's Budget', the Chancellor of the Exchequer, David Lloyd George, defended it as 'necessary for raising money to wage implacable warfare against poverty and squalidness.'[1] One of the features of the People's Budget was a tax of 6p in the £1 of those earning over £3,000 per year, and a tax on those with annual incomes of over £5,000 as well as a 20 per cent tax on profits accumulated from the sale of land. While the budget received popular support in the House of Commons, the House of Lords, dominated by the Conservative Party, rejected the budget and threw the government's legislative programme into chaos. In the face of an unprecedented constitutional crisis, Asquith's government called a general election for 1910, making the question of the powers of the House of Lords, particularly their powers to veto any bill they disapproved of, a political issue. While the Liberals won the ensuing general election in December 1910, they lost their majority in parliament, returning 275 MPs against 241 Conservatives. The Liberal Party were incredibly fortuitous, however, in that Edward VII had died in May of the same year and been succeeded by his son, George V. This provided an opportunity to appoint a new set of peers of the Upper House, and the new monarch warned the House of Lords that if they did not support the Government's policy to curb their powers dramatically, he would destroy the Conservative majority by appointing a steady number of Liberal Lords to the House. After this intervention from the King, the House of Lords reluctantly facilitated the passage of the Parliament Act in 1911, which meant that the Lords could no longer reject legislation outright, but could only delay it for a period of two years.

Although this was a major victory for the Liberal Party, since the 1910 election it had lost its majority, and therefore needed the support of the eighty-two IPP MPs to remain in government. For the first time since Parnell, the IPP held the balance of power, and they, unsurprisingly, made the introduction of a third Irish Home Rule Bill a condition of their support for the government. Considering the Lords could no longer prevent it, it was now inevitable that Home Rule would be granted by the British parliament. For the IPP and its leader, John Redmond, this was both the justification of over two decades of struggle and the pinnacle of their success and popularity, while Sinn Féin, who once sought to pose a threat to the IPP, were now a much-weakened force. While denouncing Home Rule as an abortion of the national demand, they accepted the inevitability of devolution and began to re-position themselves as a party of opposition in the future parliament.

MacDonagh, for his part, welcomed the the passing of the Home Rule Bill, and wrote to Dominick Hackett about how 'Ireland is all expectancy of Home Rule.'[2] However, the news of a Home Rule parliament for Ireland in the immediate future horrified the largely Protestant Unionist majority in Ulster, who utterly rejected the prospect of Irish self-government, believing themselves to be British and a valued part of the United Kingdom. They feared that a Dublin-based parliament where they would have little influence would lead to Catholic domination of the entire country as well as disenfranchisement from the international markets of the British Empire. This would badly damage the economy of the industrial North, as well as affecting the livelihoods of many Unionists, who dominated industry through sectarian employment and social policies. The opposition of Unionist Ireland to Irish devolution was supported by the Conservative Party, who used it as a means to undermine the Liberal government. In 1911, Andrew Bonar Law, the leader of the Conservative Party, committed himself to the Unionist cause, and the following year he made an extraordinary aggressive speech at Blenheim Palace, holding:

> If an attempt were made, without the clearly expressed will
> of the people of this country and as part of a corrupt parlia-
> mentary bargain, to deprive [Irish Unionists] of their birth
> right, they would be justified in resisting by all means in
> their power, including force.[3]

To the rapturous applause of 13,000 people, the Conservative politician further exclaimed how he could 'imagine no length of resistance to which Ulster can go, which I would not be prepared to support them.'[4] The implication was clear: the leader of the British opposition, while clearly indulging in a bit of theatrical sabre-rattling, was apparently willing to support the use of physical force to prevent implementation of the Home Rule Bill. Many Unionists, seeing Home Rule as illiberal, impractical and an affront to their rights as British subjects, increasingly considered the concept of partition, where the province of Ulster would remain part of Great Britain rather than becoming part of an Irish state. While this appealed to some Unionists, considering Ulster's thriving industry and the large density of Protestants within the province, for others, such as Edward Carson, the concept was appalling. Carson, a Dublin barrister who would become the English Attorney General in 1915, viewed partition as a threat to Southern Protestants and desired that Ireland as a whole remained part of the United Kingdom. Considering that Ulster had the highest proportion of Unionists in Ireland, however, Carson was willing to exploit Ulster Unionist opposition as means of doing so. Carson believed that, considering the power of the Unionist minority in Ireland, the British government would be forced to abandon the legislation for Irish Home Rule. To demonstrate this opposition, Carson organised a series of rallies and parades in the North culminating in Ulster Day, when on 28 September 1912 nearly half of a million people signed a document called the Ulster Solemn League and Covenant, holding:

> Being convinced in our consciences that Home Rule would be disastrous to the material well-being of Ulster as well as of the whole of Ireland, subversive of our civil and religious freedom, destructive of our citizenship and perilous to the unity of the Empire, we, whose names are underwritten, men of Ulster, loyal subjects of his Gracious Majesty King George V, humbly relying on the God whom

our fathers in days of stress and trial confidently trusted, do hereby pledge ourselves in solemn Covenant throughout this our time of threatened calamity to stand by one another in defending for ourselves and our children our cherished position of equal citizenship in the United Kingdom and in using all means which may be found necessary to defeat the present conspiracy to set up a Home Rule Parliament in Ireland. And in the event of such a Parliament being forced upon us we further solemnly and mutually pledge ourselves to refuse to recognise its authority. In sure confidence that God will defend the right we hereto subscribe our names. And further, we individually declare that we have not already signed this Covenant.

By January 1913 Carson, with the support of James Craig and other influential Unionists, established a paramilitary force called the Ulster Volunteer Force to stop Home Rule and defend the position of Ulster as part of the British state. Appointing Sir George Richardson, a retired British Army Officer, as its commander, the UVF was supported by powerful elements within the British establishment and received nearly £1 million to secretly purchase weapons from Germany. This would culminate in the famous Larne gunrunning incident, when the UVF, with the support and knowledge of the British army, smuggled twenty-five thousand rifles and three million rounds of ammunition into Ulster at Larne, Bangor and Donaghadee. These developments were whole-

heartedly supported by the British Conservative Party, with
The Penny Illustrated Paper reporting Bonar Law as exclaiming
'Ulster will never surrender.'[5] FE Smith, who would succeed
Edward Carson as the English Attorney General and later
become Lord Birkenhead, was also a regular participant at
UVF rallies. Speaking at a Conservative meeting in England,
he defended the UVF and the strategy of 'openly arming to
resist'[6] Home Rule. With the support of the Conservatives,
Carson could openly declare:

> We have the declaration of our leader Mr Bonar Law, that
> under existing circumstances we shall be backed up in any
> course we are compelled to take, and we will call upon the
> Unionist Party in England, and there will be no difficulty
> about it, to carry out to the bitter end, the pledge and the
> promise that they have given us, and the government will
> soon find that the quarrel, which looks to them in the dis-
> tance, to be a local one, in a comparatively small part of his
> Majesty's Dominions, will very soon grow until it perme-
> ates into every village and hamlet within the United King-
> dom ... I send our fellow citizens across the sea in other
> parts of the United Kingdom this simple message: 'we are
> preparing and prepared to do our part; we call upon you
> to do yours. We are prepared, as we were always prepared,
> never to betray you; and we call upon you to see that we
> are not betrayed.'[7]

Unionist opposition to Home Rule had reintroduced the threat of violence into Irish politics. The formation of the UVF forced the IRB, whose relevance had waned even further in the light of Home Rule, to consider the establishment of a similar nationalist organisation. According to Owen McGee, John Bulmer Hobson, by now one of the key figures in the Dublin IRB, had recognised the importance of the establishment of the UVF, suggesting that the actions of Ulster Unionism could be used as to persuade the public of the importance of nationalist Ireland arming itself. Since January 1913, the IRB had been training an officer corps at No. 41 Parnell Square, Dublin, with the intention of influencing and controlling the emergence of a similar nationalist volunteer force, which they had predicted would be inspired by the UVF. This work being undertaken by James Stritch and James Boland on behalf of the brotherhood, and the corps were regularly drilled by IRB activists Eamon Martin, Padraig O'Riain and Mick Lonergan of Na Fianna Éireann (a nationalist youth movement similar to the Boy Scouts). As the IRB prepared for the inevitable emergence of a nationalist volunteer force, on 1 November 1913, the Gaelic League's journal, *An Claidheamh Soluis*, published an article written by Eoin McNeill entitled 'The North Began'. It encouraged the establishment of a nationalist volunteer force as 'there is nothing to prevent the other twenty-eight counties from calling into existence citizen forces to hold Ireland for the

Empire. It was precisely with this object that the Volunteers of 1782 were enrolled, and they became the instrument of establishing Irish self government.'[8] MacNeill, originally from County Antrim, was by no means a proponent of violent revolution, and it is clear that he viewed any such volunteer movement primarily as a means of safeguarding Home Rule and counterbalancing the influence of the UVF.

MacDonagh jubilantly supported MacNeill's article and was of the opinion that the UVF and Irish Unionism's response to the passage of Home Rule had, in effect, established a watershed moment in Irish history. He was keenly aware that the British government had not moved to prevent the establishment of the UVF and understood that had an Irish Volunteer Force been established before their Ulster counterpart, the state would have moved to suppress it. In this regard he believed, like MacNeill, that the establishment of the UVF gave nationalist Ireland the cover to establish a similar organisation without British interference. MacDonagh, who knew MacNeill personally, held him in high regard and believed he was the perfect choice to lead a nationalist volunteer force. The IRB also viewed MacNeill as the ideal candidate, largely on the basis of his known moderation and respectability. Of course, their plan was that he would be merely a figurehead while the real power was concentrated behind the scenes in their hands. Bulmer Hobson, very interested by Eoin McNeill's article, arranged a meeting with the assistant editor of *An Claidheamh Soluis*, Michael O'Rahilly, and suggested that McNeill should chair a meeting to establish the force. While the first meeting of what became known as the Volunteer provisional committee was held in Wynn's Hotel on 11 November 1913, the public launch of the Irish Volunteers took place on 25 November in Dublin's Rotunda. Attended by thousands, many of whom enrolled that night, the movement declaring its ambition to 'secure and maintain the rights and liberties common to all the people of Ireland.'[9] From this the Volunteer movement grew with extraordinary speed throughout Ireland; by May 1914 its membership had expanded to 75,000 and showed little signs of slowing down. The new movement was also supported by a national newspaper, *The Irish Volunteer*, which was used as a means to propagate its ideas throughout the country.

While MacDonagh was not present at the Rotunda as he had influenza, in a letter to Dominic Hackett he commended the unifying power of volunteering, feeling that the movement could bring together 'AOH men, Sinn Féiners, Irish freedom men, Parliamentarians, GAA men and University men.'[10] He believed that new movement also provided a civic outlet for the men of Ireland and a means of expressing progressive and positive patriotism. He was so enthused with their establishment that he wrote a poem, 'The Marching Song of The Irish Volunteers', the final verse of which read:

O sacred light of liberty!
O Nation hallowed by thy cause!
We hail the glorious destiny
    That comes with right of native laws.
O God, our comfort in the night,
    Be still our guardian in the day,
And lead Thy people in Thy sight
    To follow still thine ancient way!
For Ireland, for Ireland ... [11]

Despite his inability to attend the founding rally, Mac-Donagh was elected to the provisional committee of the movement, essentially the central executive of the headquarters staff. On 3 December 1913 he enrolled within the Volunteers and became a member of Regiment 1, Company C, 2nd Battalion. Now a senior figure within the Volunteers, MacDonagh was initially closer in his thinking to MacNeill than the IRB. It is apparent from his correspondence that he viewed the Irish Volunteers as a pressure group to force Home Rule rather than for fomenting revolution. In justification of this perspective, he commented to Hackett that the movement was in a position to force the British government to take notice of Irish grievances, and if that failed 'we should be able to get Redmond and the others to withdraw from Westminster and set up a government here.'[12] Interestingly, at no point did MacDonagh advocate violent revolution, a view he shared with most Volunteers. However, as part of his leadership duties meant travelling the country addressing like-minded individuals at rallies of the importance of the Volunteers, he increasingly came into contact with physical-force activists from the IRB, and his attitude appears to have hardened substantially. This was graphically represented in a letter to his friend Dominick Hackett when he commented how 'constitutional politics are no good, we must depend on ourselves and our arms.'[13] Attending a rally in Kilkenny in May 1914 alongside Sir Roger Casement, he advised continual drilling and preparation in the use of arms, advising adherents how 'we have thousands of men old & young, of all classes, of all parties, of all religious denominations, drilling constantly, showing the vigilance ...'[14] A month earlier, at Derry in April, MacDonagh gave a powerful speech in which he again endorsed the use of arms. To rapturous applause, he instructed his audience that nationalist Ireland 'could no longer go untrained in the use of arms and unable to defend their own territories in the case of necessity. It meant that they must have in Ireland a party trained, disciplined and efficient, necessary to secure and maintain the rights and liberties common to all the people of Ireland ... it was time that the Irish people should now be able to enforce their claims if necessary by the use of arms.'[15] Writing to Muriel from the Derry City Hotel, MacDonagh recalled 'the meeting was a great success and I spoke to my perfect satisfaction.'[16]

By mid-1914 the Volunteer movement represented the greatest manifestation of Irish nationalism in the country and was far too big an organisation for the Irish Parliamentary Party to ignore. Despite the fact that they professed to have organised to defend Home Rule, the Volunteers represented a strong challenge to the authority of the IPP. John Redmond, who regarded the Irish Volunteers as 'self elected,' and 'purely provisional,'[17] was determined to bring them under his influence. On 10 June 1914 he demanded that the Volunteer Provisional Committee appoint twenty-five of his supporters to its leadership so as to secure a majority. This would consolidate the power of the IPP over the movement and not allow the emergence of a rival organisation. If the committee refused to concede Redmond's demand, the IPP leader let it be known that he would establish a rival militia, backed by the IPP, a move that would most likely destroy the Volunteers.

After intensive debate, the provisional committee was divided, with the moderates, supported by Bulmer Hobson of the IRB, believing that it was better to accept Redmond's demand than to risk a split and undermine the potential of the Volunteers. Other IRB members of the provisional committee were horrified, both by Redmond's demands, which would massively reduce their influence in the movement, and by what they saw as Hobson's treachery in supporting them, and now sought to exclude him from the revolutionary underground. Those who opposed Redmond's demand were Eamonn Ceannt, MJ Judge, Con Colbert, John Fitzgibbon, Eamonn Martin, Patrick Pearse, Piaras Béaslaí and Seán MacDiarmada. On 17 June 1914 they stated their opposition to Redmond's acquisition of the provisional committee as a 'violation of the general principles which up to the present have carried the Volunteer movement to success.'[18] There is no evidence to suggest that MacDonagh opposed Redmond's demands, and his name is not included amongst the opponents of the Redmondite acquisition. However, MacDonagh regularly worked for the education board as an examiner during the summer; he certainly did so in 1912, 1913, and 1915, and while evidence is patchy for 1914, it can be speculated that he was working as an examiner at the time the meeting took place to decide on Redmond's demands, and was therefore not able to attend. As a result, his opinion on the acquisition of the Volunteers by John Redmond is lost to history.

The following month, in July 1914, the Irish Volunteers were due to receive nine hundred Mauser M1871 rifles and 29,000 rounds of ammunition from Germany. The weapons had been procured by Roger Casement, Alice Stepford Green, Erskine Childers and Mary Spring Rice, and were due to arrive on 26 July aboard Childers' yacht, the *Asgard*, at Howth in north County Dublin. Arriving into Howth Harbour, the *Asgard* was met by hundreds of Volunteer activists who were waiting to spirit away the precious cargo. Mac-Donagh, who was present, recalled:

> Company by company the Volunteers marched at the double up the pier and formed into line. Rifles were passed from hand to hand till all the Volunteers were present and supplied. The remaining rifles and the bulk of the ammunition were put upon motor cars and sent ahead, while the Volunteers reformed in their companies for the return march to Dublin. The whole operation occupied twenty minutes.[19]

MacDonagh was aware that the British could try to prevent the arrival of the guns or strip the volunteers of their weapons. In this event, to avoid bloodshed, the guns handed to individual activists were not loaded and the Volunteers were not given ammunition. However, MacDonagh had speculated in advance of the *Asgard*'s arrival that the British army would not interfere, based on the fact that the state had not interfered with the Unionist gunrunning the previous April, and would now be too embarrassed to take active measures against Irish nationalists. MacDonagh noted in *The Irish Review* that 'the bearing of arms without a licence on the soil of Ireland could be punished only by prosecution in the Courts of Law.'[20] MacDonagh was wrong on this occasion, however, and unlike at Larne it quickly became apparent that the British army were determined to intervene. As the Volunteers left Howth, making their way back to Dublin, they were confronted at Fairview by a column of the King's Own Scottish Borderers under the command of Major Alfred Edward Haig, and several policemen, including the assistant commissioner of the Dublin Metropolitan Police, William Vesey Harrell. What happened next was a stand-off between the Volunteers and the police, supported by the British army. Bulmer Hobson recalling that the tension was palpable as 'soldiers were drawn across the road with fixed bayonets and rifles loaded.'[21]

Hobson addressed the assistant commissioner and demanded he allowed the Volunteer body to pass; Harrell insisted that they stand down at once and surrender their weapons. While refusing to do so, a brief scuffle broke out between the first column of Volunteers and the British Army. Harrell recovered three rifles, while some of the Volunteers received bayonet wounds. A few Volunteers, using revolvers and automatic pistols, opened fire at the police and army. Hobson, supported by MacDonagh and Darrell Figgis, asserted their authority and prevented any more shooting, knowing that further provocation could lead to the army opening fire, thus precipitating a massacre. After the scuffle, the police withdrew to the footpath. To prevent a bloodbath, MacDonagh and Daniel Figgis intervened in Hobson's argument with Harrell. While this was taking place, Hobson used the opportunity to begin dispersing the Volunteers from the rear without Harrell knowing what was happening. Hobson later recalled:

> At this stage Thomas MacDonagh and Darrell Figgis came up and entered into an argument with Mr Harrell. Either of them could have talked him blind; that combined effort was overwhelming. I decided that this colloquy would last for a considerable time, so I ran to the back of the column and ordered the men to disperse across the fields and through the grounds of the Christian Brothers in Marino, to make their way home as quickly as possible and avoid any conflicts or anything which would cause them to lose their rifles. I saw company after company disappear through the hedges and did not return until all but the last company was left when I found Mr. Harrell, looking rather dazed, still listening to Figgis and MacDonagh.[22]

While the Volunteers were surreptitiously dispersing, Harrell continued to demand the surrender of the Volunteers' weapons and insisted to MacDonagh and Figgis that if they were not handed over voluntarily, the British army would forcibly seize them. MacDonagh and Figgis asserted that if the army attempted to take their weapons, ammunition would be distributed amongst their men and the stand-off would only escalate. MacDonagh also pointed out to Harrell that it was not illegal to own a gun, and while it was illegal to have imported guns, it was up to Harrell to prove that the guns did not belong to the men who held them. Against this threat of force, and the impracticability of proving the guns had been imported into Ireland, Harrell eventually backed down and the British army were dismissed. He was also forced to return the three rifles he had captured, as he was forced to recognise that they were seized from the Volunteers illegally. On realising that the body of the Volunteers had dispersed, he tried to intercept them at Marino, but it was all to no avail. Harrell was beaten and believed that 'MacDonagh had cheated him.'[23] MacDonagh triumphantly recalled, with reference to the Celtic king Brian Boru, that 'at Clontarf in 1914, as at Clontarf in 1014, has been won a great national victory. For the Volunteers now: discipline, vigilance, confidence.'[24] As the King's Own Scottish Borderers returned to Dublin empty-handed, news had spread that they were unable to disarm the Volunteers, and at Bachelors Walk, a large gathering had started to jeer them and threw banana skins in their direction. In the official report of the British army, these banana skins became stones; however, 'this does not seem likely as the whole route was paved with large granite setts.'[25] Opening fire on the crowd, the soldiers killed four people and wounded thirty-seven in what became known as the Bachelors Walk massacre. Recalling the scene, an eyewitness reported how:

The Borderers lined up at Lower Liffey Street, the front

rank knelt, took careful aim and opened fired on the crowd. One of the soldiers with a rifle at the ready was seen to pursue a fleeing civilian.[26]

When the soldiers stopped firing, thirty-two civilians were wounded and three – Mary Duffy, Patrick Quinn and teenager James Brennan – had been killed. Their bodies were taken to the Dublin City Morgue, which was besieged by a large crowd. In the aftermath, no member of the British army was ever brought to court-martial and the official explanation given for the incident was that the commanding officer's orders had been misinterpreted. On learning of the Bachelors Walk massacre, MacDonagh was horrified and deeply moved. Like many within the Volunteer leadership he saw the killings as a defining point in the evolution of the Irish Volunteers. The tragedy focused international attention on Ireland and, when coupled with the British response to the Howth gunrunning, effectively exposed British double standards in its dealings with nationalism as compared to Unionism. After the Bachelor's Walk massacre, MacDonagh effectively believed that British control in Ireland was grounded upon military force rather than broad popular consent. It can be concluded that he would have agreed with the *Irish Independent* when it commented:

> Dublin Castle has once more asserted itself. For the Nationalist there is the bullet and the baton; for the Orangemen

there is freedom to do as he pleases amid the enthusiastic plaudits of the Tory Party in Ireland and Great Britain.[27]

As a means of solidarity with the dead and injured, the Volunteer leadership had organised a guard of honour, consisting of 3,000 Volunteers, when Duffy, Quinn and Brennan were to be buried. They had been placed in military formation to line the route for the families of the deceased from the Dublin City Morgue on Ameins Street to the nearby Pro-Cathedral, and would continue on toward Glasnevin Cemetery. The Volunteers were joined by a contingent of James Connolly's Irish Citizen Army, Cumann na mBan (a women's auxiliary to the Irish Volunteers) Na Fianna Éireann and the Irish National Foresters (a nationalist benefits society). Trades and Labour bodies also took part, while Dublin Corporation was represented by the Lord Mayor, Lorcan Sherlock. The bodies of Duffy, Quinn and Brennan were placed in a three separate hearses, with Volunteers marching on either side led by others on horseback. Following the third hearse, which included the remains of James Brennan, members of the Provisional Committee, who had been responsible for the arrangements, including MacDonagh, Eoin MacNeill, Eamonn Ceannt, Seán Fitzgibbon and The O'Rahilly, marched in solemn procession. Behind them stood the main body of the Dublin Volunteers, carrying rifles. Arriving at the cemetery, the armed Volunteers again lined the route to the graveyard in what were described as 'scenes of unprecedented public mourning'[28] and a demonstration that 'the right of Irishmen in the capital to bear arms in public as well as Orangemen in the north was thus asserted.'[29]

Within several days, on 4 August, Britain declared war on Germany and entered the First World War. After Redmond's acquisition of the Volunteers, he had publicly assured the British government that the movement would roll in behind the British war effort. Redmond's reasoning was that by showing the British that nationalist Ireland could be loyal in Britain's hour of need, they would be more favourably disposed toward implementing Home Rule in the face of Unionist and Conservative opposition. Redmond also knew that Carson and the Unionists would support the war, and if the IPP did not do likewise, the government would favour Unionism after the conflict ended, especially as at this stage most believed the war would be over in a matter of months. In any case, Home Rule became law on 18 September 1914, but the British government decided to postpone the implementation of a devolved Irish parliament until the end of the war. With Redmond making such overtures to the British government, however, there was increasing dissension within the Volunteer ranks. Redmond's opponents, especially those linked to the IRB, had no intention of supporting Britain in what they saw as a British war. Indeed, the IRB and its financial backers in the US, Clan na Gael, had decided that Britain's difficulty could become Ireland's opportunity, as the far superior resources of the British army would now be directed to Europe and away from Ireland, establishing the potential for a successful revolution.

Against this background, MacDonagh was given the rather unenviable task of communicating with the media, holding that speculation of an imminent split within the movement was a 'newspaper crisis,'[30] devised by journalists to sell papers. Privately, however, MacDonagh was afraid that Redmond's opponents 'had a whole fight on [their] hands,' and that all 'looked lost.'[31] MacDonagh's worries were only exacerbated when Redmond, speaking to a rally of Volunteers at Woodenbridge, County Wicklow, encouraged enlistment in the British Army:

> The interests of Ireland — of the whole of Ireland — are
> at stake in this war ... [I]t would be a disgrace for ever to
> our country and a reproach to her manhood and a denial
> of the lessons of her history if young Ireland confined their
> efforts to remaining at home to defend the shores of Ireland
> from an unlikely invasion, and to shrinking from the duty
> of proving on the field of battle that gallantry and courage
> which has distinguished our race all through its history.[32]

While Redmond's remarks at Woodenbridge were off the cuff, there was logic to his argument. The IPP leader genuinely believed that if Irishmen joined the British army and proved their worth as loyal and steadfast soldiers in defence of the empire, Britain would hasten to give Ireland Home Rule as a reward. Equally, in Redmond's perspective Irish involvement in the war would create unity between Ulster Unionists and Irish nationalists. Within a couple of days he reiterated his position, holding that the British had given Ireland Home Rule and it was now the duty of the Irish people to 'keep faith with Britain,' and wholeheartedly endorse the spirit of his declaration.[33]

Redmond's call to the Irish Volunteers to join the British army did not have the full support of the Volunteer executive. The Volunteer's chairman, Eoin MacNeill, was horrified by Redmond's endorsement of enlistment within the British Army. Issuing a statement in *The Irish Review*, seeking to prevent a split in the movement, the Provisional Committee asserted that Redmond had 'announced for the Irish Volunteers a policy and programme fundamentally at variance with their own published and accepted aims and pledges … he has declared it to be the duty of the Irish Volunteers to take foreign service under a government which is not Irish.'[34] The statement, signed by MacDonagh as part of the Provisional Committee, called upon the Volunteers to not enlist within the British army as part of the war effort. To reaffirm this, MacDonagh added a supplement called 'Twenty Plain Facts for Irishmen'. The supplement was overtly nationalist and profoundly anti-war, asserting that the Irish nation owed no allegiance to Britain and, placing it within a European context, added that the relationship of Ireland to Britain was similar to that of Belgium to Germany, Poland to Russia and Germany to Austria. Reasserting that the ambition of the Volunteers was to defend the rights and liberties of the Irish nation, MacDonagh finished with the following points:

17. The Irish Volunteers have not been enrolled to defend "England and her Empire," for the defence of which, according to the British proclamation, Your King and Country Needs You, the present war is being waged.

18. No body, committee, or person, has any right or liberty to use or promise to use the efforts of the Irish Volunteers for any purpose other than securing the maintenance of the rights and liberties of the people of Ireland.

19. The Union Jack is the symbol of the Act of Union of 1800, by which the Irish Nation was deprived of her last rights and liberties.

20. The Irish Nation lives.[35]

Despite the best efforts of the Provisional Committee to prevent a split, 170,000 Volunteers answered Redmond's call and became known as the National Volunteers, while 10,000 stayed in Ireland, retaining the name Irish Volunteers. Mac-Donagh lampooned the National Volunteers in verse and sardonically wrote a song to the tune of 'God Save Ireland'. Published in *The Irish Volunteer*, he called his song 'The New

"God Save Ireland"':

Men of Ireland, young men, all
At your king and country's call
Rally round your throne, your empire and your flag;
As your matchless leaders say,
Take the one and nine a day,
Don the khaki of the sionin *and the stag.*

Chorus:
God save Ireland for the empire
God save Ireland all said we
From the base designs of those
Who would free her from her foes
God save Ireland from the woes of liberty.[36]

The following week he again condemned the National Volunteers, and eulogised the work of the Irish Volunteers. Writing a song to the air of 'The White Cockade', published in *The Irish Volunteer*, he announced that Irishmen should take a rifle alongside 'the marshalled manhood of their race,'[37] rather than allow themselves to serve 'in homage to a foreign *Rí* [King]'[38] MacDonagh's earlier suggestion to Dominick Hackett that 'constitutional politics are no good, we must depend on ourselves and our arms,' was increasingly becoming a reality.

Chapter Seven
• • • • • • •

1914 – 1915

'The old order changeth'

With the movement now split, the Provisional Committee organised the first convention of the new Irish Volunteers (as distinct from Redmond's National Volunteers). Taking place in October 1914, it officially repudiated John Redmond and expelled his nominees from the committee. The convention elected a central executive to undertake the day-to-day operation of the Irish Volunteers, and ostensibly to reorganise the movement along militaristic lines. MacDonagh regarded this as 'a refining process,'[1] and was now elected to the central executive alongside Eoin MacNeill, Patrick Pearse, Eamon Martin, Bulmer Hobson, The O'Rahilly, Joseph Plunkett and Éamonn Ceannt, taking on the role of Director of Training. The IRB, which had always sought to use the Irish Volunteers for open rebellion, welcomed this reorganisation. Pearse, Plunkett and Ceannt were all members of the IRB, and Pearse in particular, as the Volunteer's Director of Operations and the individual charged with issuing military orders, had a key role within the central executive. This IRB infiltration meant that there were now two chains of command within the movement: an open one centred on Eoin MacNeill as the Volunteer Chief of Staff, who still believed that the purpose of the Volunteers was to safeguard the implementation of Home Rule, and a secret one run by the IRB with its own separatist agenda. This secret chain of command was further consolidated in May 1915 when the Brotherhood established its own secret military council, consisting of Pearse, Plunkett and Ceannt, whose job was to plan a feasible insurrection and who answered only to IRB leaders Tom Clarke and Seán MacDiarmada.

In late 1914 and early 1915 MacDonagh was not a member of the IRB, and therefore was not privy to the plans of the Military Council. It is apparent, however, that he had some inkling that a rebellion was being planned, and may even have discussed these plans with Plunkett. As Director of Training he was responsible for rallies and general practice, and he took command of the Second Battalion of the Dublin Brigade on 3 December 1914, assisted by First Lieutenant Thomas Slater, Second Lieutenant Bob Price, and Michael O'Hanrahan as the battalion quartermaster. Later that month, on 26 December, he published in *The Irish Volunteer* a song called 'Freedom's Hill – A National Anthem'. Illustrative of his growing Republicanism, and his knowledge of the plans for a rebellion, he celebrated the idea of an independent Ireland, a belief which he described as 'the cause bequeathed from age to age'. He asserted in 'Freedom's Hill' that Ireland would gain her independence through the arms of Irish Volunteers and then the Irish nation could arise and 'salute the sun of victory'.[2] Relishing his Volunteer work, MacDonagh regularly attended drilling at No. 41 Parnell Square and allowed Volunteers to drill in the Irish Theatre when it was not in use. MacDonagh also convinced the Capuchin Friars to allow outdoor drilling and practicing marksmanship in Fr Matthew Park. He had also taken to carrying a revolver and from 1915 onwards stored weapons at his home. Settling into his new role, MacDonagh explained how he felt part of a movement that would see great change for Ireland:

> I work hard every day at Volunteer work. I am a member of the Central Executive of the Headquarters Staff. I am commandant of the second battalion of the Dublin Brigade and senior officer of the Brigade Council. In addition to the work to be done in all these capacities, I am Director General of Training for the whole country and have to keep a staff working to direct that department. But the work, half like that of a cabinet minister, and half like that of a regular military officer, is wonderfully interesting and exhilarating … We have given an ideal and an enthusiasm to the young boys and girls of Ireland, such as you and I did not get. I

have here, in this road, forty boys from ten to sixteen years who would do anything for the country at my bidding. They drill and train three times a week and study Irish and Irish history outside school, and look forward to the time when they may be Irish Volunteers … Ireland is all right.[3]

He regularly produced notes for the training of Volunteers alongside a series of lectures and rallies which he addressed on military themes. According to his son Donagh, by this time he was obsessed with the study of military textbooks, and 'the official publications of the English War Office soon decorated the shelves which had held the works' of English scholars.[4] It was evident that he desired to establish military efficiency and professionalism within the movement, seeing his mission as being 'a very definite thing to do: to train a body of irregular troops to act under the peculiar conditions imposed by the configuration of Ireland.'[5] Seeking to install 'discipline, and sobriety into the Volunteers',[6] MacDonagh was a stickler for punctuality and regularly insisted that Volunteers synchronise their watches and know the times necessary to walk to and from different points of the city. He was also most particular that the Volunteers identified themselves as soldiers and encouraged them to wear uniforms. He insisted upon a programme of regular training, including drilling, scouting, ambushes and fieldwork, often involving two companies of Volunteers in war games, with skirmishing and the seizing of strategic points. This, MacDonagh speculated, would familiarise the Volunteers with discipline, obedience to senior officers, company formation, tracking advance guard and frontal assault strategies. His training style involved 'foot drill, extended order drill, marching, including night marching, scouting and moving across country in small bodies.'[7]

Frank Henderson recalled that MacDonagh was an incredibly good speaker who enthralled his audience. After a recruitment rally at which the Director of Training had spoken, Henderson asserted that if the British 'had a public speaker like MacDonagh on their side they would have thousands of young Irishmen in the British Army.'[8] One of his pupils at a Volunteer lecture, Liam Tannan, recalled him as 'a very good lecturer,'[9] and remembered how he had spoken about the military tactics of the campaign of Xerxes during the Greco-Persian War, including the battle of Thermopylae, where three hundred Spartans defended the Greek city states from Persian attack. His lecture on classical tactics was followed by a talk on the Boer War in South Africa. Volunteer Joseph Lawless, however, found MacDonagh's lectures interesting but rather odd. He remembered that on one occasion MacDonagh, who had a tendency to meander, claimed, 'one could live indefinitely and work hard on a diet of nothing but onions, and he urged all and sundry to sow plenty of onions without delay. What a funny idea, we thought ... perhaps the odour of our combined breath would keep any enemy out of gunshot range.'[10]

MacDonagh regularly published orders in *The Irish Volunteer* calling on regiments to assemble for military training throughout the country, usually on Sundays. He also favoured the establishment of instruction centres and rifle ranges alongside inter-company rifle competitions as a means of 'stimulating healthy rivalry in what is after all the most important part of [Volunteer] training.'[11] Believing that the Volunteers should have a regular sniper division and should be prepared to fight using tactics designed to wear out the enemy, MacDonagh recommended the adoption of sniping as:

> Such tactics as these are most annoying to regular troops. They allow them no rest, inflict considerable losses, and are very damaging to the efficiency of the Army. In Ireland opportunities for adopting such tactics would be abundant, and could be used to the full. Not only do they terrorise the force they are directed against, but they are of the upmost use as training for the soldier practising them.[12]

Lastly, he was desirous of establishing a Volunteer engineering corps to provide engineering services on any future battlefield and assisting a Volunteer infantry brigade. In support of this, he actively proposed the idea amongst the Volunteer executive that the movement recruit amongst the working classes and employ men engaged in engineering and building trades. At Easter 1915, MacDonagh organised a significant training day for the Dublin Brigade whereby Volunteers divided into two opposing forces and were expected to mobilise for attack and defence of a position in North County Dublin. Under MacDonagh's plan, the Volunteers were to be divided into flying columns, with company commanders selecting their best and brightest from each regiment. Patrick Pearse acted as Brigade Commandant General, while MacDonagh, despite organising the event, functioned as Pearse's second-in-command.[13]

While MacDonagh was busily engaged in the reorganisation of the Irish Volunteers, Muriel had been pregnant with their second child. On 24 March 1915 she gave birth to Barbara. MacDonagh adored his new daughter as much as he did his son, and for her part Muriel didn't suffer the bouts of depression and ill-health she had experienced throughout the year after Donagh's birth. By the time of Barbara's birth the family had moved to 29 Oakley Road, Ranelagh, in South Dublin, which one contemporary recalled as 'a home in every sense of the word'[14], and his prominent role within the Volunteers did not prevent him from relishing his role as a new father. Taking the opportunity to thank Muriel for his daughter, he wrote a poem called 'Barbara' to celebrate her life. While the poem, like 'Wishes For My Son' was underlined by the great excitement he felt on the birth of his child, on this occasion he 'contrasted Irish and European civilisation,' and eulogised 'the revival of a national spirit,'[15] and how this was favourable to Barbara's new life.

In addition to his poem 'Barbara', he also produced his third play, *Pagans*, which received its premiere on the evening of 19 April 1915 in the Irish Theatre. For the first time in his literary career, MacDonagh featured ordinary characters with recognisable problems. His protagonists were John and Frances Fitzmaurice, a middle-class married couple, their maid Sarah Churchill, and Helen Noble, an artist and also John's ex-lover. By the standards of the time, *Pagans'* subject matter was quite controversial. As the play opens, Frances sits in a sombre drawing room on the evening of her fifth wedding anniversary, mulling over the failure of her marriage and the whereabouts of her husband, who disappeared three years previously. John is depicted as a bohemian and a free spirit, while Frances is a society woman and conformist. Meeting Helen, who has seen John in Paris, she learns that Helen loved him more and that Frances had been more in love with an ideal image of her husband rather than the real man he was. Returning to his wife, John and Frances discuss their marital problems and how he always loved Helen. As they finally part due to the irreconcilable differences, her husband announces 'now that you have told me to go, I go quite free.'[16] At the very end of the play MacDonagh introduces a veiled reference to nationalism when, as John leaves his wife for the final time, he declares, that 'sooner than you think, politics will be dropped here, and something better will take their place ... You will not know yourself in the Ireland that we shall make here.'[17] Why MacDonagh decided to include a throwaway comment about politics to *Pagans* has never adequately been explained. While one author believes that the change of tone was down to 'MacDonagh's general inability to sustain dramatic narrative and action in prose,'[18] it seems likely that the conclusion of his play, similar to his poem 'Barbara', was influenced by MacDonagh's involvement with the Irish Volunteers. It was becoming apparent that MacDonagh was strongly affected by the excitement and energy of the increasingly militant Volunteer movement and its romantic ideals.

However, despite his involvement within the Volunteers, MacDonagh still insisted that he was decidedly opposed to militarism. This contradiction in his thinking was exposed in May 1915 when he attended a women's anti-war meeting in Dublin inspired by the British government's decision to prevent women from attending an international women's peace conference at The Hague, beginning on 28 April 1915. MacDonagh was scheduled to speak as a representative of the Irish Volunteers alongside Patrick Pearse, but Pearse, who would have been very uncomfortable at a women's gathering, diplomatically excused himself from attending. Addressing the women in his Volunteer uniform, including a Sam Browne belt and revolver, he denounced the European war as unbridled imperialist brutality with ordinary people 'exploited by capitalists and oligarchs for greed and grab.'[19] Commending the women's peace conference at The Hague, he praised their efforts as 'the brightest hopes for European civilisation he had entertained for a long time'.[20] To rapturous applause he exclaimed how 'it was a great thing that representative women in Europe – and women were surer to be right than men - should meet on neutral soil and send out these resolutions … the women and the workers could serve their own cause by serving peace.'[21] Stressing his belief that nationalism and the Volunteers should 'lose no opportunity of pressing for women's rights as citizens,' he announced how if women could take over 'control of the state that would be a revolution which could end war.'[22] Unsurprisingly, the meeting was strongly anti–Redmondite and the assembled women denounced the leader of the IPP in the strongest terms, both for his support of the war and his opposition to women's suffrage. MacDonagh, unable to resist the opportunity of lambasting Redmond, finished his speech by calling upon the women assembled to continue their work and, with sarcastic reference to Redmond and his takeover of the Volunteers, described how 'he had been called a "nobody" [and] "a self elected person" by the greatest man in the country.'[23] MacDonagh attested to the power of believing in one's cause, declaring 'he was believer in the miraculous: let [the women's movement] follow their aspiration, and anything was possible.'[24] Paraphrasing his speech, the *Irish Citizen* recalled that he described himself as:

> One of the founders of the Irish Volunteers, a member of the first Provisional Committee, and now one of the 'quintette' who had been charged with running that organisation. He had devoted a considerable amount of time to the study of military subjects and of military training. It was part of his duty how to instruct men to bayonet their fellow-man; and how to put their foot on his body and pull the bayonet out afterwards. It was disgusting and nobody could hate it more than he did. He was an advocate of peace because everyone was being exploited by the dominant militarism. He had helped to arm tens of thousands of Irishmen for defence; because the only justification for war was to end age-long wars such as that in this country. He hoped that they would not have any war in this country.[25]

The irony of his position, denouncing war while wearing a Volunteer uniform, was not lost to the audience, and the *Irish Citizen* noted that his one apology for 'his share of a different kind of militarism [in Ireland] was that [the Volunteers] were not going to exploit their own people. He hoped – he knew – that they would never be used against their fellow countrymen.'[26] MacDonagh boldly announced that 'he hoped as a Volunteer, that he would have a better opportunity than voting to show that by "people" he meant the women as well as the men of Ireland.'[27] While he received hearty applause for his announcement, not everyone present supported him. The meeting's chairwoman criticised the Volunteers, commenting that Irish militarism could inspire civil war by 'developing the brute in men'.[28] MacDonagh retorted by insisting that the Volunteers had actually prevented civil war between nationalist and unionist, and through their existence, albeit despite the split with the National Volunteers, they had 'prevented attempts to exploit Irishmen' through enlistment in the British army.[29] The chairwoman cut MacDonagh off mid-speech, however, stating it was her belief that 'if the men of Ireland devoted more of their time to loving Ireland, and less to hating England, they would have built up a strong nation. From the congress at The Hague had gone out a strong message, that on love, and not on hate, must the world be constructed.'[30]

Francis Sheehy Skeffington was in attendance that evening and it struck him that MacDonagh was being unusually inconsistent. Like many in the audience he did not fail to see the irony of a senior Volunteer condemning violence in Europe while 'boasting of being one of the creators of a new militarism in Ireland.'[31] Sheehy Skeffington knew MacDonagh well and understood the reasons why he had joined the Volunteers. Like MacDonagh, Sheehy Skeffington had initially believed in the merits of the Volunteers as 'a clean open air movement, which gives the young men of Ireland something better to do than cheer at meetings and pass resolutions. It gives them self respect and reliance.'[32] Indeed, Sheehy Skeffington had thought of joining the movement, particularly after the break with Redmond, whom he disliked. He had changed his mind, however, when the Volunteers made it clear that women would not be allowed membership, and the organisation became more openly militarist in its displays and training. Sheehy Skeffington believed that evening that MacDonagh was not tied to the idea of militarism, but that perhaps he needed to justify it as a member of the Volunteer executive. To convince MacDonagh of the recklessness of his membership, Sheehy Skeffington wrote him an open letter, imploring him to 'think it over, before the militarist current draws you too far from your humanitarian anchorage.'[33] MacDonagh had asserted that the Volunteers had been organised as a militarist body only to defend Irish rights, and potentially prevent war within Ireland by forcing the British government to address Irish concerns. Sheehy Skeffington, however, disagreed completely with MacDonagh on this point, suggesting that the Irish Volunteers were being 'organised to kill,'[34] and eventually they would.

Despite Sheehy Skeffington's appeal, MacDonagh continued to train the Volunteers along military lines and organise recruiting marches as a means of displaying the level of discipline within the Volunteer ranks. This was intended to convince potential recruits, and the British government, that

the movement was 'not a sham.'[35] In a letter to Dominick
Hackett on 19 May 1915 he showed that, as Sheehy Skeffington had feared, he was being swept away by the prevailing
current of militancy. He told his friend how he had come
to believe that Irish independence could only be won by
what he termed 'zealous martyrs ... through peace I hope,
but war if necessary', [36] stating elsewhere that Ireland 'would
become one entire slum unless we go into action.'[37] His
changing attitudes were influenced his association with
Pearse and Plunkett, especially as in April 1915 he had
joined his friends in the Irish Republican Brotherhood.
Throwing himself into the work of the revolutionary movement, MacDonagh's first test as an IRB activist came in June
1915 when he was given the perfect opportunity to show
not only to Ireland, but to the world, that the Volunteers
were a force to be reckoned with.

On 29 June 1915 the veteran Fenian activist Jeremiah
O'Donovan Rossa died at the age of eighty-four in St Vin-
cent's Hospital, Staten Island, New York. O'Donovan Rossa,
jailed in 1865 at the height of the Fenian troubles in Ireland, had been the manager of the Fenian newspaper *The
Irish People,* while his composure at his trial for sedition was
described by one contemporary as 'a defiance of the British
government'.[38] Sentenced to life imprisonment, he had, like
Tom Clarke, suffered inhuman treatment in British prisons.
He was regularly beaten and strip-searched, and often con-

fined to a punishment diet for his inability to abide by prison rules; in one instance, for thirty-five days his hands were cuffed behind his back and he was forced to eat his meals off the floor by prison staff. In 1869 he had been amnestied to America on condition that he would never return to Ireland for the duration of his sentence. Rather than abandon the Fenian cause, however, he championed a bombing campaign in Britain in the 1880s, known as the Fenian dynamite campaign, and survived an assassination attempt in 1885 when an Englishwoman, Yseult Dudley, tried to kill him in New York City.

The day following the announcement of his death, *The Irish Times* announced that 'there was a time in Ireland when his death would have created a sensation, but it is no exaggeration to say that today there are many who had almost forgotten his existence.'[39] O'Donovan Rossa was perhaps one of the most famous Fenians of his generation, and John Devoy, a senior figure in Clan na Geal based in New York, described O'Donovan Rossa's life as 'an epitome of the history of Fenianism.'[40] Devoy was confident that historians of future generations would come to regard O'Donovan Rossa as 'the very incarnation of [the Fenian] spirit.'[41] James Connolly believed O'Donovan Rossa to be 'an unconquerable fighter', [42] Arthur Griffith eulogised him as a man 'whose spirit was the free spirit of the Irish Nation', [43] while O'Donovan Rossa's daughter, Eileen, regarded her father as 'unconquerable'[44] in his spirit. Patrick Pearse similarly regarded O'Donovan Rossa as a revolutionary chieftain, 'a man that to the masses of his countrymen then and since stood most starkly and plainly for the Fenian ideal,'[45] celebrating him as an 'unrepentant Fenian.'[46] Writing of O'Donovan Rossa, MacDonagh also celebrated his life:

Grieve not for him: speak not a word of sorrow;
Although his eyes saw not his country's glory,
The service of his day shall make our morrow:
His name shall be a watchword in our story.

Him England for his love of Ireland hates:
This flesh we bury England's chains have bitten:
That is enough; for our deed he waits;
With Emmet's let his epitaph be written.[47]

O'Donovan Rossa's final wish was to be buried in a humble graveyard alongside his father and other victims of the Great Hunger in Rosscarbery, County Cork. With the permission of his family, however, Clan na Gael and the IRB sought to bury O'Donovan Rossa in Ireland's national graveyard, Glasnevin Cemetery. This endeavour was handled by John Devoy in America and Tom Clarke in Ireland. Both men predicted that the funeral could re-awaken the national spirit of the Irish people, whom they feared were becoming more British than the British themselves. They also hoped to show the strength of advanced nationalism as well as providing a demonstration of the military discipline of the Volunteers. The IRB were determined that the Volunteers were going to provide the funeral procession for the deceased Fenian, and used their influence within the movement to facilitate the establishment of a Volunteer committee to oversee the burial. MacDonagh was made responsible for the preparations and oversaw the planning of a great procession through the streets of Dublin. Tom Clarke handpicked MacDonagh for this task, believing that as an IRB member MacDonagh would arrange the event to provide the maximum benefit for the organisation, and it was recalled that 'for weeks beforehand [MacDonagh's] time was taken up working out the details.'[48] The procession also included members of the GAA, the Irish Citizen Army, and Redmond's National Volunteers, the final time the four organisations would parade together. Serving as the Volunteers' acting commandant general, MacDonagh arranged to have O'Donovan Rossa's remains placed in Dublin's City Hall for three days in a coffin covered by a plate-glass lid with a Volunteer Guard of Honour. Thousands of Irish people came to both pay their respects, and see the military spectacle.

The funeral took place on 1 August 1915 and the cortege left City Hall at 2pm, led by Mrs O'Donovan Rossa and her daughter Eileen. On the morning of the funeral, MacDonagh had gathered his men on Grattan Bridge, and gave orders to Peter Gilligan, an IRB activist and Volunteer officer, to arrange a party to keep a clear passage to facilitate the procession. The cortege took a circuitous and lengthy route through the main streets of the city, escorted by a heavy Irish Volunteer presence, while bands followed playing patriotic songs. Before thousands of onlookers, the military procession to Glasnevin Cemetery was a great show of Irish nationalism and demonstrated the tremendous military discipline of the Irish Volunteers.

Arriving at the cemetery, O'Donovan Rossa was buried beside old Fenians John O'Leary and James Stephens. As the crowds gathered around the grave, Patrick Pearse delivered his now famous graveside oration, openly declaring that the British government had no right to be in Ireland and defined the aim of the Volunteers as achieving 'the freedom of Ireland.' He announced that a new generation had found it necessary to continue the work of Fenian activists like O'Donovan Rossa. Finding his generation 're-baptised in the Fenian faith', which the fallen activist personified, Pearse famously finished his oration by declaring:

Life springs from death; and from the graves of patriot men and women spring living nations. The defenders of this realm have worked well in secret and in the open. They think they have pacified Ireland. They think they have purchased half of us and intimidated the other half. They think they have foreseen everything, think they have provided against everything; but the fools, the fools, the fools! – they have left us our Fenian dead, and while Ireland holds these graves, Ireland unfree shall never be at peace![49]

After Pearse's speech on behalf of the new generation, who would now take on the work of men like O'Donovan Rossa, combined with the professional militaristic display of his funeral procession organised by the Irish Volunteers, the *Irish Independent* prophetically noted: '[T]he old order changeth.'[50]

Chapter Eight

1915 – 1916

'We will have a stir'

In the months following the O'Donovan Rossa's funeral, the Volunteer movement went from strength to strength and the following year held a massive rally at the Mansion House, Dublin, on 30 March 1916. The rally had been inspired by the deportation orders against Volunteers Liam Mellows, Alfred Monaghan and Ernest Blythe issued in late 1915. Further deportation orders were issued against Denis McCollough, president of the IRB Supreme Council, and Herbert Moore Pim, a political activist who wrote regularly for *The Irish Volunteer*. These orders were issued at the behest of Dublin Castle using the Defence of The Realm Act 1914 (DORA), which gave the government extensive wartime powers of arrest, censorship and requisition. At the rally, attended by thousands of Volunteers, resolutions were passed condemning the government for attempting to deport Irishmen who had committed no crime. A Catholic priest, Fr O'Connolly, drew comparisons with the UVF, citing that the men whom the government sought to deport were being punished for activities which it condoned in the North. Eoin MacNeill concurred with Fr O'Connolly and, addressing the crowd, denounced the deportations as a 'terrible outrage' and a 'monstrous proposal', which he feared could lead to unrest and potential trouble.[1]

In January 1916 the executive of the Irish Volunteers had condemned the British government in an article entitled 'Resistance', asserting that 'Irish Volunteers cannot submit to the denial of their personal rights and freedom involved in the new practice of the British government.'[2] In retaliation to the policy of arrest and imprisonment without trial, the Volunteers intensified their activity, suggesting it was 'the duty of every Volunteer company to arm itself here and now.'[3] On 19 February *The Irish Volunteer* denounced DORA as 'a political engine used by politicians for the persecution of those who are not their obsequious and humble servants.'[4] On 26 February the Volunteer executive instructed members how it 'was desirable that all public holidays, such as St Patrick's Day, Easter Sunday, Whit Sunday etc, should be availed of ... for the purpose of field training, concentrations, marches etc.'[5] The executive was desirous that Volunteers show the British government they would not be intimidated and that the upcoming St Patrick's Day parade would be marked by a military display by all company commanders. Around this time, many rank-and-file Volunteers were told to make themselves thoroughly acquainted with Dublin and noticed a sharp rise in training and preparation, with one, Donal O'Hannigan, recalling 'it was becoming apparent things were coming to a head.'[6] Addressing the question of deportations, MacDonagh personally wrote an appeal rejecting DORA called 'Dublin's Reply to Deportation Order' in *The Irish Volunteer*. He condemned the British government and, referencing Bloody Sunday and the Dublin Lockout, claimed that the Volunteers had changed Irish politics forever by '[putting] an end to the old system of ruling Ireland by holding her in subjection by the block-house system of the RIC barracks and the baton charges of the DMP … the men of Dublin will never again run from the baton charges.'[7] Despite the protestations of the Volunteers, however, the men, having refused to leave Ireland, were arrested and interned in Mountjoy Jail.

IRB preparations for a rebellion against British rule were gathering momentum, particularly following the co-option of James Connolly to the IRB Military Council in early 1916. Connolly's increasingly militant language throughout 1915 and early 1916 made the IRB fear that he would use his tiny Irish Citizen Army to launch an insurrection of his own, thus giving Dublin Castle the excuse to deport or imprison Volunteers, suspected IRB men, or anyone else they felt was a threat to the State. By this stage the Military Council had decided that a rebellion was to be held on Easter Sunday 1916 and planned to use the Volunteers as the vanguard. In Dublin, strategic positions were to be taken by the combined force of the Volunteers and the ICA. Central to this was a plan to organise a defensive line at key points around the city. IRB activist Donal O'Hannigan had been instructed to mobilise a force at the historic Hill of Tara and make for Dunshaughlin in County Meath before arriving on Blanchardstown in North Dublin. Here the Volunteers were expected to seize a railway station and disrupt communications between Dublin and the militarily important Athlone, preventing British consolidation within the city. The Volunteers in North Dublin, Wicklow and Kildare were to flank their left and right respectively and form a ring around the city stretching from the north of the city from Swords and Blanchardstown to Tallaght and Lucan in the south. The object of this plan was that a British attack on Dublin City from the rear could be prevented and the consolidation of reinforcements would be severely disrupted. If the rebel forces were unable to hold out against the superior strength of the British, they had planned to make westwards toward the River Shannon, beyond which Volunteers from Cork and Kerry would create a base in southwest Ireland. This base was to be consolidated by a line protecting the River Shannon near Athlone, consisting of Volunteers from Clare, Roscommon and Limerick. This retreat strategy was reliant on the ring surrounding the city, as it was believed the Volunteers maintaining the circle could hold open a line of retreat towards the west, facilitating escape and adopting a strategy of guerrilla attacks on British positions. On behalf of the IRB, Seán MacDiarmada kept the plan for the Easter Rising in a safe in the Volunteer Headquarters on Dawson Street, Dublin.[8] According to O'Hannigan, the plans were 'drawn up by MacDonagh [albeit not yet a member of the Military Council], assisted by Joseph Plunkett.'[9]

The IRB plan was framed with the realities of the First World War. While the IRB had little interest within the actual conflict, those planning the rebellion realised that it offered them a great opportunity. Not only would British resources be turned from Ireland, but there could be potential German support for a rebellion, as the Germans could use a Rising as a means to undermine the British war effort. Through the interventions of Clan na Gael, a clandestine mode of communication was established with the German embassy in Washington, which sent communiqués to Berlin. Key to this relationship were John Devoy in New York and Sir Roger Casement, an Irish-born British diplomat who had become a fervent supporter of Irish independence. Under Devoy's initiative, Casement was given $3,000 and sent to Berlin in October 1914 to secure an official German declaration favourable to Irish independence. Casement was successful in this regard, but his attempt to recruit an Irish Brigade, made up of Irish soldiers from the British army held as prisoners of war in Germany, was largely a failure. Joined by Joseph Plunkett, Casement presented plans for the IRB rebellion to the Germans, which initially envisaged a German invasion supporting a nationwide revolt, with Volunteer companies rebelling in every county in Ireland. Eventually the Germans agreed that they would provide rifles and ammunition to be brought to Ireland aboard a ship called the *Aud,* which was registered as a Norwegian vessel. The Germans hoped that as Norway was neutral, the British would ignore it. The weapons were due to arrive on Good Friday 1916 and would be distributed throughout the Volunteers for action on Easter Sunday. The Military Council had agreed that it would use its influence to secure Volunteer mobilisation for Easter Sunday under the cover of normal manoeuvres. In this vein, *The Irish Volunteer* called on members to assemble on Easter Sunday 'to test mobilisation and equipment'[10] as well as appealing for members to come out and be prepared for active manoeuvres in what was 'to be regarded as more important than the carrying out of an ambitious piece of field work.'[11] The Military Council plan was by now entirely reliant on the arrival of German weapons.

MacDonagh was only co-opted onto the Military Council early in April 1916, and in the history of the Rising it is generally accepted that he was not privy to its planning and organisation. This is despite the fact that two of his most trusted friends, Pearse and Plunkett, had commanding positions overseeing the strategy. This belief that he knew nothing about the insurrection is strengthened by a statement by Aine Ceannt, who was told by her husband Éamonn how MacDonagh had been informed of the plans for the Rising only three weeks beforehand. Éamonn Ceannt recalled how MacDonagh was 'surprised but very enthusiastic.'[12] However, according to MacDonagh's son Donagh, his father was well aware of the plans before his co-option onto the Military Council, which corresponds with the testimony of Donal O'Hannigan, who insisted that MacDonagh had drawn up the plans with Plunkett. While the exact amount of knowledge that MacDonagh possessed before April 1916 may never be known, it would be surprising if Plunkett did not mention the Rising in passing to him, considering their close friendship in addition to their joint interest in military strategy.

A further factor necessitating his co-option so near to the date of the Rising was that as an IRB member, MacDonagh was incredibly important within the Volunteer command structure. He was a Dublin brigade commandant within the Volunteer executive, making a rebellion without his support or knowledge somewhat problematic. Once a member of the Military Council, MacDonagh threw himself into the work for preparation for a rebellion, and must have been struck by its remarkable resemblance to the council of seven which he had described in his play *When The Dawn Is Come*.

MacDonagh's appointment to the Military Council, however, was a calculated risk, as he was chatty, gregarious, and not prone to keeping secrets. In many cases MacDonagh gave glaring hints that something out of the ordinary was being planned. Oscar Traynor, a young Volunteer, recalled how MacDonagh had declared at Fairview on 22 March, weeks before the Rising, that 'there would be something more than manoeuvres,'[13] at Easter. Traynor had left the meeting with the distinct impression that a rebellion was imminent. What MacDonagh did not know, however, was that as he spoke, a British spy, codenamed 'Chalk', was in attendance. Chalk hastily informed his handler how MacDonagh 'addressed the Volunteers and amongst other things said "I am not afraid of what I have to say here. But I won't say anything of importance on the street. I wish to tell all the men here present that when you joined the Irish Volunteers you were made aware that you would have to make sacrifices…"'.[14] Equally, one of his students at UCD recalled:

> I began to realise, with a feeling of foreboding, that something was about to happen for I noticed at times, though only for a few seconds, how abstracted and worried Thomas MacDonagh looked. Suddenly, one day, during a lecture on the Young Ireland poets, he took a large revolver from his pocket and laid it on the desk. 'Ireland can only win freedom by force', he remarked.[15]

Speaking with Kitty O'Doherty, the quartermaster of Cumann na mBan, he bluntly stated that 'within three weeks, we will have a stir.'[16] He told O'Doherty 'that he had been scouting Dublin, and that he had all the maps of the neighbourhood, the hills and everything. We discussed some back lanes and shortcuts and things.'[17] O'Doherty was in no doubt that a rebellion was imminent.

On another occasion, MacDonagh was approached by Volunteer commandant Éamon de Valera, the adjutant general of the Dublin battalion and his second-in-command. De Valera told MacDonagh that men under his command seemed to know more about the movement and its inner counsels than he did. Stressing his concerns to MacDonagh, de Valera explained how he suspected some of the men belonged to the IRB. In a decidedly unconspiratorial fashion, MacDonagh confirmed de Valera's suspicions and told him that that he was himself a member of the IRB. MacDonagh also told de Valera that the men under his command whom he complained of also belonging to the IRB, and if de Valera wished to know more he would have to be sworn into the organisation. De Valera was horrified. As a Catholic, he felt that he could not join a secret society. There was also the practical concern of his position in the Volunteers: in the event of a conflicting order, who should he obey, the Volunteer executive or the IRB? Remarkably, MacDonagh next explained to de Valera that a conflict of interest was impossible as the IRB controlled the Volunteer executive. Taking in this highly sensitive information, de Valera was remarkably close to abandoning the Volunteers, but instead agreed to be sworn into the IRB on the basis that he was not included in their counsels, knew nothing of its members, and did not have to attend its meetings. Swearing him into the movement, MacDonagh agreed to his conditions and stressed to de Valera that his membership of the IRB would not be enforced or impinge upon his Volunteer work. MacDonagh later recalled De Valera fondly, telling Éamonn Ceannt that De Valera would survive the Rising, prophetically holding, 'he will come through, as he always falls on his feet.'[18]

On 16 April, a few days before the Rising, he addressed the Fingal Brigade of the Irish Volunteers alongside IRB activist Michael Staines, and 'without telling them in as many words, [MacDonagh] made it clear that a rising was coming off on Sunday.'[19] This admission was against the general orders of the Military Council and Staines questioned MacDonagh as to the logic of his admission. All MacDonagh could say was 'it takes a professor to say a lot without saying anything.'[20] While MacDonagh understood that the audience he was speaking to were committed to the nationalist cause, his indiscretion in sharing such sensitive information prior to the rebellion had the potential to undermine the entire plan. There is no doubt that had Clarke or MacDiarmada, the professional conspirators, known about this, they would have tried to quell MacDonagh's outspokenness. What MacDonagh did not know, however, was that on the evening of 16 April Chalk was again in attendance. The informer could not believe his luck: a senior figure within the Volunteer executive was openly speaking of an imminent rebellion. On meeting with his handler, the informant mentioned how 'Professor MacDonagh, on issuing orders on Wednesday night last said – we are not going out on Friday but on Sunday. Boys, some of us may never come back – mobilisation orders to be issued in due course.'[21] While Chalk's information gave few specific details, it was important enough to warrant a report being sent to the Detective Department in Dublin Castle. What is surprising, however, is that Dublin Castle did not act on Chalk's information, no doubt due to the slow machinery of the Castle's bureaucracy.

The principal reason for MacDonagh's joining the Military Council, it seems, was his close relationship with Eoin MacNeill, which they wished to utilise in order to influence the Volunteer Chief of Staff, who could potentially cause problems as he was not privy to (and would not have supported) the IRB's plans. It is highly unlikely, however, that MacNeill was unaware that significant numbers of the IRB had infiltrated the Volunteers, or that others within the Volunteer executive, including Pearse and Plunkett, were IRB members. He had earlier arranged a meeting of the Volunteer executive with James Connolly when he learned of the latter's intention to use the ICA for a rebellion, where he told Connolly, in the presence of Pearse, 'that if his men went into it, they would be left alone'[22]; i.e. that the Volunteers wouldn't hinder or, more importantly, help them. When he sought to discover the views of the Volunteer executive on the likelihood of rebellion, he discovered that Pearse, Plunkett and MacDonagh were in favour of insurrection. MacNeill expressed to them his opinion that there could be no rebellion without the popular support of the people, and even with this, any rebellion could only be justified if the British government attempted to suppress the Volunteers, impose conscription in Ireland during the War, or renege on the promise of Home Rule. He furthermore stressed that he could never support rebellion until the Volunteers were fully armed and trained. After this, MacNeill secured a promise from the three that nothing would happen.

But despite this guarantee, the Military Council continued to plot. Through a nationalist official employed at Dublin Castle, Eugene Smith, the Military Council received a coded document purporting to reveal the Castle's intention to suppress the Volunteers, Sinn Féin and the Gaelic League, in addition to the raiding and occupation of a number of properties owned by Irish nationalists. This would run parallel to the arrest of a number of specifically named individuals, including MacNeill himself. Smith had given the document to Joseph Plunkett, who, in order to get MacNeill on side, deliberately doctored it to make it seem more alarming than it actually was. Becoming known as the Castle Document, it was sent to Alderman Thomas Kelly, who read it out during a meeting at Dublin Corporation on Wednesday 19 April. Alleged to come from a sympathiser within the Castle, the document was brought to MacNeill's attention by Dr Seamus O'Kelly who, while not a Volunteer, was connected to the movement and a friend of the Chief of Staff. Considering the draconian powers given to the Castle by DORA, MacNeill was alarmed and ordered Volunteers to be on prepared for a possible stand-off with the British army. He went so far as to instruct the Volunteers to forcibly resist any attempt by the government to 'suppress or disarm'[23] the movement.

Against this background, Bulmer Hobson, who was not involved in preparations for the Rising as he had fallen out with Tom Clarke and Seán MacDiarmada some years previously, had learned that a rebellion was imminent and the IRB intended to use the Volunteers. Pearse, in his position as Volunteer Director for Operations, had issued orders on 20 April 1916 for manoeuvres the following week as a cover for rebellion, supported by MacDonagh, who wrote in *The Irish Volunteer* that 'at Easter there will be manoeuvres at every part of Ireland. Officers must insist on full equipment being carried.'[24] The pretext for MacDonagh's announcement was that the Volunteers would be celebrating the anniversary of the battle of Clontarf on 23 April 1014. Alerting MacNeill to the fact that a rebellion was by now imminent, Hobson accompanied him to Scoil Éanna at midnight on Holy Thursday, where MacNeill sought an urgent meeting with Pearse. A heated conference ensued at which Pearse admitted that a Rising was being planned for Easter Sunday and that orders had been given for the disruption of railway traffic. MacNeill implored Pearse to cancel the rebellion and when the latter refused, MacNeill announced 'he would use every means in [his] power to prevent it.'[25] Following his meeting with Pearse, MacNeill drafted countermanding orders and dispatched loyal supporters to the country to cancel Pearse's earlier mobilisation order. MacDonagh believed that central to gaining MacNeill's support for the rebellion was the removal of Bulmer Hobson, asserting to Éamonn Ceannt that 'Hobson is the evil genius of the Volunteers, and if we could separate MacNeill from his influence, all would be well.'[26] As MacDonagh had suggested, the Military Council moved swiftly against Hobson, and on Good Friday, 21 April, he was lured to 76 Cabra Park, where he was held under gunpoint in the home of IRB activist Martin Conlon.

With Hobson out of the way, MacDonagh met Mac-Neill several times in the build-up to the Easter Rising. It was evident that he was functioning as an intermediary between the Military Council and the Volunteer Chief of Staff. In one of these meetings, he visited MacNeill with

Plunkett at his home, where MacNeill doggedly remained by his earlier position, leaving MacDonagh and Plunkett 'a bit shaken'. After informing MacNeill they would have to 'consult their friends further'[27], a reference to the Military Council, MacDonagh later returned to MacNeill for a second time. This time MacDonagh was far more shaken, however, as the two friends locked horns in a heated debate about the merits of the planned rising. With tensions escalating, MacNeill described MacDonagh as 'obstinate.'[28] Recognising the danger which MacNeill posed, on Good Friday Seán MacDiarmada went with Pearse and MacDonagh to his home, where they informed him of the imminent arrival of German arms at Kerry. Understanding that this would force the hand of the British army, MacNeill reluctantly agreed to the rebellion. In this he was pressed particularly hard by MacDiarmada, who reminded MacNeill that he had told a meeting of the Volunteer executive that in the event of an arms landing, he would support an uprising in Ireland. MacNeill had also learned that Hobson had been kidnapped, but rather than press the issue with the IRB, he believed that the unity of the Volunteers was paramount when faced with an imminent British reaction against the movement. The Rising now seemed a *fait accompli*.

MacNeill's enthusiasm for revolution was lacklustre at best, however, and in conversation with Seán Fitzgibbon on the Saturday before the planned Rising, he learned that

Casement had been arrested and the weapons had been intercepted off the south coast of Kerry. Both Fitzgibbon and MacNeill believed that, like the kidnapping of Hobson, the former had actually been sent to Kerry to isolate the Volunteer Chief of Staff. MacNeill also began to doubt the validity of the Castle Document, as surely the capture of Casement and the interception of the German weapons should have been a catalyst for the British to suppress the Volunteers. Dublin Castle had not budged, however. Again determined to stop the Rising, MacNeill now summoned a number of individuals to an urgent meeting in the home of Dr Seamus O'Kelly at 53 Rathgar Road, including Arthur Griffith, Michael O'Rahilly, Seán Fitzgibbon and Seán T O'Kelly. According to Seamus O'Kelly, MacDonagh had been summoned to O'Kelly's house by a dispatch, but left before the conclusion of the meeting. His brother John, who had arrived with MacDonagh but waited outside, recalled that at this point MacDonagh was 'rather agitated.'[29] Telling John about the meeting, MacDonagh said MacNeill had welcomed him, and suggested that he could consult with the men present. Realising that the majority of men whom MacNeill had assembled were against the rebellion, Mac-Donagh bluntly answered 'I'm sorry but there is no one here I can consult with', [30] choosing instead to appeal to the 'authority of my council.'[31]

MacNeill decided to issue a countermanding order preventing Volunteer mobilisation on Easter Sunday. This order was to be hastily couriered to all Volunteer units and a stream of messengers left O'Kelly's house throughout Saturday night on bicycles, motorcars, taxicabs and by foot. Sometime after midnight, MacDonagh again visited 53 Rathgar Road. As he was introduced to MacNeill, the Volunteer Chief of Staff had been in conversation with Joseph Connolly, a senior Volunteer from Belfast. MacDonagh was given the counter-manding order and stood reading it in MacNeill's presence. With tension palpable, Connolly recalled that MacDonagh remarked, 'of course, you realise that your order may not be obeyed.' MacNeill replied equally tersely, 'the responsibility for disobedience will fall on those who disobey.'[32] Soon after MacDonagh left, MacNeill made for the offices of the *Irish Independent* at 1.30am. Here he gave the assistant editor his countermanding order and strongly urged its publication:

> Owing to the very critical position, all orders given to the Irish Volunteers for tomorrow, Easter Sunday, are hereby rescinded, and no parades, marches, or other movements of the Irish Volunteers will take place. Each individual Volun-teer will obey this order strictly in every particular.

As MacNeill was arriving at the offices of the *Irish Inde-pendent*, MacDonagh, Joseph Plunkett, Diarmuid Lynch and Seán MacDiarmada were gathering at 27 Hardwicke Street. Arranging this meeting was difficult, as the Military Council were so preoccupied with security that they were staying in safe houses for fear of arrest, making a quick response to the MacNeill difficulty problematic. On hearing what MacDonagh and Plunkett knew, MacDiarmada was enraged but considered MacNeill's countermanding order doomed to failure as it was too late in the day to cancel the rebellion. After their meeting concluding at 2.30am, Plunkett and MacDonagh left for O'Kelly's house, where they intended to speak to MacNeill. As it was late, O'Kelly was quite dismissive of them both, and, on learning that MacNeill was not there, MacDonagh commented, 'God help the poor man.'[33]

On Easter Sunday morning, news broke that MacNeill had published his countermanding order in the press, thereby throwing the Easter Rising into chaos and securing a controversial place for himself within Irish history. Most of the Volunteers were unaware of the preparation for a Rising anyway, and took the order at face value from the head of the movement. But there was major confusion within the ranks of those Volunteers who had been expecting a rebellion, while the Military Council was incensed. Meeting at Liberty Hall, the majority agreed, with the notable exception of Clarke, to postpone the rebellion for one day, until noon on Easter Monday. Postponing the rebellion would allow the Military Council to undo as much of the damage caused by MacNeill's orders as they could. It was also imperative that they do so before Dublin Castle decided to move against them. In this new plan, the Military Council intended to hold Dublin City in the hope that the country would follow soon afterwards. MacDonagh now instructed the Dublin Volunteers to stand down until new orders were issued for the following day. The Military Council, who did not want MacNeill to know of their plans, then dispatched MacDonagh to meet the Chief of Staff.

Arriving at MacNeill's home with his son Donagh and his brother John, MacDonagh found the Chief of Staff in the company of his brother James MacNeill, Seán Fitzgibbon and Seamus O'Connor, all members of the Volunteer executive. While waiting on MacDonagh, John played with his nephew. The two were sparring and O'Connor, passing them, noted how Donagh was as 'pugnacious' as his father.[34] Much to his discomfort, MacDonagh had been instructed by the Military Council to deceive his friend by telling MacNeill that on account of the countermanding order the Rising had been cancelled. This, it was speculated, could neutralise any further damage that MacNeill could still inflict on the Military Council's plans. Fitzgibbon remembered MacDonagh as 'most friendly,' in his assurances of the cancellation.[35] He recalled that MacDonagh justified the kidnapping of Hobson because he had broken his oath to the IRB, rather than as a means of keeping him away from the moderate MacNeill. That these lies weighed heavily on MacDonagh's mind is evident from a note he penned on returning home from MacNeill's house explaining why he had been so duplicitous. While he never sent this note to anyone, from examination it is evident that he felt obliged to write it so that in the event of his execution, he could justify to others why he behaved in such an underhanded fashion to a man he called a friend. With a heavy conscience, Thomas MacDonagh wrote:

I have now at 8pm returned from a visit to Eoin MacNeill at Woodtown Park, Ballyboden. I have had a long conversation with MacNeill and Seán Fitzgibbon upon many aspects of the present situation. I hope that I have made clear to them my loyalty to Ireland, my honour as an Irish Volunteer and also – a thing for which I could not for obvious reasons state definitely – my intention to act with my own council and the position of that council. My future conduct may be different from anything now anticipated by MacNeill and Fitzgibbon, two honest and sincere patriots, though I think wrong in their handling of the present situation and in their attitude to military action. They and my countrymen must judge me on my conduct. I have guarded secrets which I am bound to keep. I have, I think, acted honourably and fairly by all my associates. I have had only one motive in all my actions, namely the good of my country. I now pray to God for the gifts of counsel and fortitude and his blessing for the cause of my country. [Signed] Thomas MacDonagh[36]

Chapter Nine

24 April 1916

'Long live the Republic!'

On Easter Monday morning, members of the Volunteers and the ICA were mobilising throughout Dublin. As a result of MacNeill's countermanding order the previous day, there was mass confusion, with some brigades and companies assembling with less than an hour's notice. At Beresford Place, beside Liberty Hall, they had heard the call to fall in from Volunteer William Oman. Addressed by Connolly and Pearse, the combined forces marched toward the General Post Office on Sackville Street, where they intended to seize the commanding edifice and establish the headquarters of the new Irish Republic. The 1st Battalion of the Irish Volunteers, under Commandant Ned Daly, assembled at Blackhall Place in preparation for their march on the nearby Four Courts, while Eamon de Valera's 3rd Battalion occupied Boland's Mills in Ringsend, with its commanding position overlooking the River Liffey and Westland Row train station. Other positions to be occupied including St Stephen's Green Park, the Harcourt Street train station and City Hall beside Dublin Castle.

In command of the 2nd Battalion, MacDonagh had given orders that Volunteers under his command assemble at St Stephen's Green Park before twelve noon. They were to be joined by members of Cumann na mBan and Na Fianna Éireann. Michael Mallin and the ICA were already present within the Green. MacDonagh's instructions included orders that Volunteers arrived with three days worth of rations, and should not march in military formation, lest the British authorities should be alerted. In the days before, he had temporarily secured an office at 130 St Stephen's Green in a house owned by a sympathiser named Blánaid Salkeld. According to his brother John, Mrs Salkeld's house became a centre for the delivery and dispatch of messages as MacDonagh frantically tried to get word to as many of his battalion as possible. At Salkeld's house, MacDonagh informed Volunteer Tom Slater that the general plan for the insurrection was to seize a number of strategic and symbolic buildings throughout the city. The 2nd Battalion were to seize Jacob's Biscuit Factory, a domineering building on nearby Bishop Street turning into Aungier Street, and establish outposts in its vicinity, preventing British access into the city from the nearby Portobello Barracks. He had also decided to mount an attack on Trinity College, Dublin, an important strategic building within the heart of the city centre overlooking Grafton, Westmoreland and Sackville Streets.

By noon, around 150 men had arrived at St Stephen's Green, and they were informed that a rebellion was taking place to establish an Irish Republic and outposts were being commandeered throughout the city. According to two of those present, Tom Slater and Sean Murphy, MacDonagh said that they were to divide into three groups, with the main body establishing their headquarters at Jacob's Biscuit Factory, supported by outposts in Fumbally Lane and Camden Street.[1] MacDonagh abandoned his plan to seize Trinity College, as the assembled battalion was too small. Speculating that he could only spare twenty men, he concluded 'it would have meant a heavy loss of life with no hope of getting in.'[2] Present at MacDonagh's address was Peadar Kearney, who knew MacDonagh well and had abandoned an Abbey Theatre tour to play a role in the Easter Rising (he would later find fame as the author of the Irish national anthem). Also present was Major John MacBride, who was making his way to see his brother, Anthony, when he happened upon the Volunteers and, on learning the rebellion was taking place, decided to become involved. He had previously told Joseph Plunkett how he would not take part in the rebellion before the fighting started as he feared 'he would only bring discredit to the Volunteers'.[3] MacDonagh did not share this concern as he offered MacBride the role of his second-in-command in place of Michael O'Hanrahan. This appointment was a stroke of luck, for MacDonagh lacked the practical military experience of MacBride, which as the week progressed would become obvious to the Volunteers.

At twelve noon the combined forces of the Irish Volunteers and the Irish Citizen Army occupied the General Post Office. At the GPO, Pearse and Connolly were joined by three of the five remaining members of the provisional government of the Irish Republic: Joseph Plunkett, Thomas Clarke and Seán MacDiarmada (the other two members were MacDonagh himself and Éamonn Ceannt, who was commandant at the South Dublin Union). Pearse assumed the role of president while Connolly was commandant general of the rebel forces. In this role Connolly was theoretically in charge of all military operations; however, due to the nature of the rebellion and the number of scattered outposts, the individual commanders essentially acted independently of the GPO HQ. Later that afternoon Pearse read the Easter Proclamation to a bemused Dublin crowd. Throughout the city, the Volunteers had seized other strategic outposts, including the Four Courts, the South Dublin Union, Boland's Mills, the Mendicity Institute under Seán Heuston, Watkins Brewery under Con Colbert, and around Mount Street Bridge under Lieutenant Michael Malone, to name a few. There was also an attack planned on Dublin Castle, the administrative centre of British Rule in Ireland and a site of great symbolic importance; however, mistakenly believing that the Castle was heavily guarded (when in fact there were less than thirty soldiers inside), the rebels decided instead to consolidate their position in nearby City Hall and so missed this opportunity.

As MacDonagh prepared to lead his forces toward the biscuit factory, the ICA under Mallin had already taken up position within the park, and as the Volunteers marched towards Jacob's their ICA comrades could be heard shouting 'it's now or never, boys' after them.[4] It is often overlooked in the histories of the Rising just how strategically impor-tant Jacob's was, something that had been discussed by Mac-Donagh and Connolly in the weeks prior to the rebellion.[5] The building was a massive, almost fortress-like complex surrounded by four streets; at its tallest point it was five sto-ries high and housed two large towers offering a panoramic view of Dublin. It was within striking distance of Dublin Castle, and the view from the towers included Ship Street Barracks, attached to the Castle, and its Ship Street entrance, as well as Patrick's Street, St Patrick's Park and part of Dame Street. Jacob's was also within supporting distance of Michael Mallin at St Stephen's Green as well as the Volunteers in City Hall. The occupying of Jacob's and the outposts around City Hall, particularly at the offices of the *Daily Express and Irish Daily Mail* newspaper, made it clear that rebels sought to encircle the entrances to Dublin Castle. Another advantage possessed by Jacob's was that it was situated within a maze of streets and lanes occupying 'a controlling position across the route to the city and Dublin Castle by Camden and Aungier Streets, well stocked with food, and very difficult to take by direct assault. Its surroundings were in fact a death trap for all forces which might have the task of attacking it, and its strength made it formidable even against artillery.'[6] In the plan of the Rising, it is evident that another purpose of the Jacob's garrison, like Michael Mallin's forces at St Stephen's Green, was to prevent troops entering the city from the south.

Led by MacDonagh, his brother John, and MacBride, the Volunteers marched in military formation toward Mercer's Hospital and onwards to Aungier Street. As they marched, John MacDonagh remembered asking his brother who MacBride was, as the latter was well-dressed, sporting a cane and smoking a cigar. He also pointed out that they were being followed by G-Men, employees of Dublin Castle's intelligence division, including Detective Constable Daniel Hoey, and Detective Sergeant Johnny Barton, both of whom would be assassinated on the orders of Michael Collins in 1919 (allegedly for their role in picking out the leaders of the Rising from the vast mass of Volunteers interned after the rebels surrendered). The party were not worried by the detectives, however; of greater concern was the immediate threat presented by the ordinary citizens of Dublin. The area around Jacob's was strongly pro-British; in fact the factory, the main employer in the area, had seen its day-to-day operations noticeably affected by the enlistment of over 400 local men in the British army.[7] Marching through Cuffe and Mercier Streets, the Volunteers were met with abuse from separation widows (the wives of Irishmen serving in the British Army), the mildest being a heckle, recalled by John Mac-Donagh, recommending they go out and fight the Germans rather than annoy the British.[8]

Arriving at Jacob's, they found the main gate to the imposing institution locked. As some of the Volunteers entered through a window about six feet from the ground, Mick McDonnell was instructed to break down the gate using a large sledge. Eventually the Volunteers made their way inside and were met by a skeleton staff; as it was a bank holiday, the factory was closed and the only people on site were a few maintenance men, a watchman named Henry Fitzgerald, and the caretaker, Thomas Orr. Seeing the Volunteers entering the factory, Fitzgerald went straight to Orr, informing him the building was under siege. Orr rushed to the telephone room where he tried to call the chairman of the company, George Jacob, before the rebels cut the phone and telegraph lines. All the staff were rounded up and placed under armed guard. Orr, as the most senior staff member, pleaded for the release of his colleagues. MacDonagh allowed all non-combatants to leave, but Orr and the watchman refused to go, the caretaker explaining to MacDonagh how it was his duty to stay at the factory. Orr recalled that the rebels tried to convince him to leave, for when the British came he would be placed in danger.

Now in the custody of the rebels, Orr requested that MacDonagh firmly stress to his men an order forbidding smoking within the factory, with which MacDonagh complied. Orr next requested that fourteen horses, belonging to Jacob's, should be looked after for the duration of the occupation, but MacDonagh refused when he learned that the horses were stabled at a distance from the factory, thus placing his men at unnecessary risk, although he stated that if the horses were in danger he was willing to co-operate with the caretaker.[9] Orr and Fitzgerald remained together during the occupation but refused co-operation with the rebels. John McBride had initially seen them as potential recruits and, talking with Fitzgerald, asked him if he would like to join the Republican movement. To McBride's surprise, Fitzgerald answered that all he wanted was 'to go home to [my] wife and children.'[10]

Once inside the building, the battalion fortified their position, establishing solid barricades at points that were judged as weak and breaking the glass in the windows for fear of shrapnel when the British attacked. They then consolidated their position by placing bags of flour, of which the factory had an ample supply, against the windows. Shortly after

Right: Thomas MacDonagh reading in the garden of 29 Oakley Road, Ranelagh, Dublin, in 1915.

Below: MacDonagh was a strong supporter of women's suffrage. In this photograph, we see him with friends (he is seated second from the right) in front of a poster calling for votes for women.

DUBLIN BRIGADE ORDERS.

H.Q.

24th April, 1916.

1. The four city battalions will parade for inspection and route march at 10 a.m. to-day. Commandants will arrange centres.

2. Full arms and equipment n one day's rations.

Thomas Macdonagh.
Commandant.

Coy E 3 will Parade at Beresford Place at 10 a.m.

P. H. Pearse
Comdt.

Thomas MacDonagh mobilisation orders, countersigned by Patrick Pearse.

Above & right:
On 24 April 1916, Thomas MacDonagh and the 2nd Battalion of the Irish Volunteers seized Jacob's biscuit factory. The building was a fortress-like complex surrounded by four streets; it housed two large towers that offered a panoramic view of Dublin and Dublin Castle.

Above: Davy's Pub. **Below:** Surrender order, countersigned by Thomas MacDonagh.

In order to prevent the further slaughter of Dublin citizens, and in the hope of saving the lives of our followers now surrounded and hopelessly outnumbered, the members of the Provisional Government present at Head-Quarters have agreed to an unconditional surrender, and the Commandants of the various districts in the City and Country will order their commands to lay down arms.

P. H. Pearse

29th April 1916
3.45 p.m.

I agree to these conditions for the men only under my own Command in the Moore Street District and for the men in the Stephen's Green Command.

James Connolly

April 29/16

On consultation with Commandant Ceannt and other officers I have decided to agree to unconditional surrender also.

Thomas MacDonagh.

A list of demands from Richmond Prison, signed by
Thomas MacDonagh.

Above: Kilmainham Gaol, where Thomas MacDonagh was executed on 3 May 1916 along with Thomas Clarke and Patrick Pearse.
Below: Muriel MacDonagh, following the execution of her husband.

THOMAS MacDONAGH

(Commandant of Bishop Street Area),
EXECUTED 3rd MAY, 1916,
One of the Signatories of the " Irish Republic Proclamation."

Printed and Published by the Powell Press, 22 Parliament Street, Dublin. Price 2d.

Thomas MacDonagh in memoriam.

Left: Following the deaths of their parents, Donagh and Barbara were orphaned and became the centre of a legal battle between the MacDonaghs and Giffords.

Below: Father Albert Bibby with Barbara and Donagh.

taking the factory, the garrison engaged the British in their first encounter, when they successfully ambushed thirty British soldiers at Bishop Street and Redmond's Hill, wounding an officer and six men. After forcing a British retreat from the area, the Volunteers placed a ring of barbed wire around weak points of the building, then took biscuit tins and threw them out of the windows on to the road. They reasoned that if the British came during the night they would hit the tins and make noise, thus alerting the garrison of a potential attack. Unwilling to waste the contents of the tins, one volunteer recalled how 'he had a great time eating plenty of coca-chocolate and biscuits galore!'[11] MacDonagh, McBride and O'Hanrahan established a headquarters in the clerks' cloakroom and here they mulled over potential strategy. Recognising the importance of the towers, MacDonagh posted snipers who covered the area between Ship Street Barracks, Dublin Castle, St Patricks Park immediately behind St Patrick's Cathedral, part of Patrick Street, an entrance point into the city from the south, and Portobello Bridge. The factory was also 'less than three quarters of a mile from both Portobello and Richmond Barracks.'[12] In effect the garrison had succeeded in their intention of sealing several approaches to Dublin Castle for the British army, the most important of which was Portobello Bridge, which separated the city from a British military barracks. In anticipation of a British approach from Portobello, MacDonagh ordered some of the Volunteers to tunnel through the walls of the factory toward Kelly's public house, which adjoined Jacob's, as Kelly's dominated the corner of Camden Street. One Volunteer remembered how sledgehammers and steel bars were driven through walls, creating 'a scene of determined laborious activity in which danger was forgotten.'[13] Because Kelly's was a public house, MacDonagh only allowed a small party into the building through the tunnels, under the strict instruction that once inside no alcohol was consumed.

To facilitate the men, members of Cumann na mBan established a medical unit which was headed by Volunteer Patrick Cahill, a chemist. The medical unit was to be consolidated by regular sorties out of the factory seizing necessary chemical and surgical equipment, as the garrison was near the Adelaide Hospital. The garrison leaders predicted that in the event of any serious medical emergency, the hospital's doctors would be duty bound to assist the rebels. Apart from their duties in the medical unit, Cumann na mBan members acted as cooks and messengers. Michael O'Hanrahan's brother Henry set up a supply store and canteen for the benefit of the men, which provided the rebels with fresh clothing, boots, tobacco and food, greatly raising their spirits and later recalled as 'a boon to many.'[14] Several of those present were known to MacDonagh from his professional life: Máire Nic Shiubhlaigh from the Irish Theatre eventually took charge of the Cumann na mBan party in Jacob's, while Michael Hayes, a lecturer in UCD, also came to fight at the Jacob's factory after having been summoned by Mac-Donagh personally. Others who come did not belong to the 2nd Battalion, but had been in Dublin the previous day and had returned home when the countermanding order had appeared in the newspapers. One such individual was a young Derry Volunteer who, trying to get into town, came across the Jacob's garrison. He asked to be let in, but the garrison refused him entry as they did not know him. When he returned with a rifle, he was embraced by the rebels.

Outside the factory on Monday afternoon, a DMP officer stubbornly refused to leave the scene, and MacDonagh, increasingly losing his patience, threatened to have him shot. John MacDonagh eventually calmed down his brother, but was surprised to hear his suggestion that 'it might be necessary to shot some of these policemen and detectives to show our own men that we are at war.'[15] This suggestion was carried out early on in the occupation of Jacob's, when a plain-clothes police officer was noticed taking notes of the rebel positions and what they had done to the building. Instructing him to stop at once, they threatened that if he did not leave, he would be shot. When the police officer refused to do so, he was killed by a sniper. This was the exception to the rule, however. Throughout the course of the occupation, the Volunteers, who captured six police officers, treated them with great courtesy. John MacDonagh in particular was

211

a firm advocate in favour of sparing their lives and one of them profusely thanked him when the Rebellion was over for 'saving his life.'[16]

As the main party were settling into Jacob's, a smaller party of forty Volunteers marched on toward Kevin Street. Here four men broke from the party and formed a garrison in a building opposite Kevin Street Police Station. This move was intended to keep the police confined to their barracks. The remainder of the party moved further on to Malpas Street, where they occupied two tenement houses and seized Barmack's Distillery. Here they were met with great animosity from the tenement dwellers, including many separation widows, who were put out of their homes.[17] Strategically, Barmack's commanded the approach to Blackpits in Dublin's Liberties, and the rebels had seized the building for use as an outpost to intercept troops coming from nearby Wellington Barracks via Clanbrassil Street. Having seized the buildings, the Volunteers got supplies of water and facilitated observation and weapon discharge through narrow holes they bored in the walls. Here the Volunteers were addressed by Tom Hunter, MacDonagh's vice-commandant, who announced:

> Men! The Irish Republic has been proclaimed in Dublin today; we are in action; the headquarters of the Irish Republican Army is at the General Post Office, which has been taken possession of by the Republican troops. We are fighting to establish the Irish Republic.'[18]

A further group was moved to the corner of nearby Mill Street where a coachbuilder's yard was seized as the Volunteers took wood to build barricades. Here people had gathered to see what the Volunteers were doing, and many, particularly separation widows, continued to heap abuse on them, with some of these actually trying to tear down the barricades as the Volunteers built them. The apprehension of the curious and angry civilians was only increased when a Volunteer accidently dropped his gun, releasing a charge. Those who had gathered, however, quickly fell back when a rumour spread of an immediate British attack. Remaining units seized buildings on Camden Street and adjoining Wexford Street. They also seized outposts at Fumbally Lane and Ussher's Malthouse. This effectively meant that the main route for the British army stationed at Portobello was cut off. These outpost positions were later abandoned by the evening, however, as Volunteers were instructed to return to Jacob's. This was a strategic mistake and undermined the potential of the 2nd Battalion to actively engage with British forces.

On their return the Volunteers were again met by a barrage of abuse from separation widows, who had gathered outside the factory. Volunteer William James Stapleton, who was returning from Barmack's Distillery, recalled how rebels were regularly struck by locals and had their caps knocked off as they waited to be admitted into the factory. He found that this was a great test of discipline for the Volunteers, who despite provocation refused to retaliate against the unarmed crowd.[19] One of the Volunteers inside the factory, Martin Walton, recalled how the building was surrounded by 'a howling mob.'[20] Entering the factory, the newly arrived Volunteers, as Vinnie Byrne recalled, 'found a strenuous atmosphere ... the garrison had the appearance of a laborious day's toil. Barricades were raised on windows, doorways and other points of defence. Men were moving about covered with flour from head to toe, many hatless, some with coats off, actually engaged in the work of fortification. Others were in position awaiting the enemy.'[21] The command had even encouraged the manufacture of tin-can bombs to be thrown from the roof if necessary, and to this end an explosives department was fitted and established.

Throughout the day and into the evening, the garrison leaders had become increasingly concerned with the angry civilians who had gathered outside in support of the British. Some of the locals had tried to force their way into the factory, and the Volunteers who guarded the entrances to the building were regularly tested by the intensity of civilian anger. At one gate William James Stapleton was involved in preventing a charge on the building when a large mob attempted to burst through the factory gate. According to Stapleton, they 'kicked and barged [the gate] with some heavy implements, but seeing as it was of little effect they tried to set fire to it with old sacking which had been soaked in paraffin and pushed under the door and ignited.'[22] As the angry mob continued to try and force their way inside, MacDonagh ordered the men guarding the entrance to fire blanks at them. This had the desired effect of forcing the civilians to disperse, but locals, particularly the separation widows, remained a cause for concern throughout the occupation of the factory.

When the aggravation had calmed down, MacDonagh summoned the Volunteers together and explained in an address what they were fighting for. Declaring they were soldiers of the Irish Republican Army, he read them the Proclamation of the Irish Republic. Amongst great cheers and salutations, the commandant commended the Volunteers for their action and how well disciplined they were, particularly in relation to the hostile reaction from the local residents. One Volunteer recalled MacDonagh's speech:

> In picturesque language, of which he was a master, he gave an account of the Rising as it developed during the day, of the reinforcements marching to our aid from outlying districts, of allies landing on various parts of the coast, and of the reports that German submarines had formed a cordon around the country which effectually menaced any attempt on the part of the British to reinforce their garrisons with the aid of the British fleet. He also paid tribute to the magnificent qualities of soldierly discipline and energy displayed by the troops under his command.[23]

MacDonagh was followed by John McBride, who said amid cheers: 'Long live the Republic!'[24] However, despite their claims, the country had not risen up, nor had the Germans landed along the Irish coast. The rebels had seized several buildings throughout the city and declared an Irish Republic; it was now only a matter of time before the British responded.

Chapter Ten

• • • • • •

25 – 30 April 1916

'Boys, we must give in'

The question that haunted MacDonagh was how long the rebels could hold out. MacDonagh predicted that the First World War would soon come to an end and there would be a peace conference. Having declared an Irish Republic, Ireland would have to be recognised as a belligerent nation and permitted to attend.[1] This idea was not new to MacDonagh: as late as Easter Sunday morning he had exclaimed to Christopher Brady, a compositor of the Easter Proclamation, how 'we can hold out in this fight in order that Ireland's voice may be heard at the Peace Conference.'[2] Behind this idea was an agreement made by Roger Casement with Germany that if the rebellion could hold out for three days and the Germans won the war, they would grant legal recognition to the Republic.

On Monday evening the Volunteers were billeted in the factory engine room and boiler house, a section of the complex dominated by a large chimney. While the two rooms chosen were warm, they were not comfortable and many of the Volunteers found it difficult to sleep on the tiled floor. Expecting an attack at any time, many wondered as to the logic of placing them near a large chimney, as British artillery could strike it, forcing its collapse upon them. Volunteer Seosamh de Brun recalled how this worry left men feeling incredibly anxious.[3]

As Tuesday opened, the garrison were visited by a number of priests who offered them confession. During the day the Volunteers continued to barricade the building, and Mac-Donagh finally gave into Orr's demand to take care of the horses, ordering that they be removed from the stable and taken to a safe place in case of fire. MacDonagh also ordered that all flammable materials be removed as a precaution against incendiary shells causing a conflagration during a British attack. Following his orders, one Volunteer recalled how 'we worked as never we did before.'[4] MacDonagh and McBride had also come to the conclusion that lines of communications within the factory were too dangerous, as Volunteers had to cross exposed areas from one building to another, running the risk of unnecessary casualties in the event of a British assault. MacDonagh therefore ordered the breaking through of walls to enable tunnelling, so that Volunteers would not have to leave individual buildings or corridors to enter others. This ran parallel to further reinforcements of barbed wire around the yard of Jacob's Factory and by Wednesday 'the entire factory was in a state of perfect defence against a hand to hand attack from any exposed point.'[5]

While the Rising had taken the British by surprise, they quickly responded and actively sought to throw a line between the north and south side of Dublin City to isolate the rebel positions. They also set about defending the strategically important Trinity College, as Westland Row train station behind the college linked the city to Kingstown (Dún Laoghaire) Harbour and Dublin Castle. On Monday, fifty soldiers in the Royal Irish Rifles had been dispatched from Portobello Barracks to make for the Castle via Portobello Bridge. This route brought them directly into contact with Davy's pub, occupied by Volunteers under the command of a barman who worked there, James Joyce. They wasted their opportunity by opening fire on a lone British soldier, rather than the party of troops. Escaping from Davy's, the soldier made quickly to the barracks and warned his superior officers, who immediately advanced on the pub with machine guns, taking it from the rebels on Monday evening. This allowed the British army to take Portobello Bridge, and bypass Jacob's entirely.

By Tuesday, City Hall had fallen to the British and the most senior army officer in Ireland, Brigadier General William Lowe, arrived in Dublin from the Curragh camp in County

Kildare with a force of 5,000. Lowe immediately organised a series of cordons throughout Dublin, encircling the rebel positions and cutting their lines of communication. He recognised that once he isolated the rebels and consolidated the strength of the British army in the centre of Dublin, he could easily pick off their outposts one at a time. He concentrated assaults on buildings which he deemed strategically important, including the GPO and the Four Courts. Of particular interest to Lowe was the GPO: he predicted that if the headquarters of the rebellion fell, other outposts could not hold out. Overall Lowe's plan to undermine the Rising was reliant on heavy artillery, machine-gun fire and the British army's sheer force of numbers. By Tuesday evening the army had 6,627 soldiers in Dublin, and Michael Mallin in particular was involved in intense fighting at St Stephen's Green. The British army had undermined his position by placing soldiers with machine guns into the roof of the Shelbourne Hotel and the United Service Club, which both overlook the park. In urgent need of assistance, Mallin sent a messenger to MacDonagh, who was willing to dispatch twenty men to help him. The Stephen's Green garrison, however, was hopelessly outnumbered and outgunned, and was forced to abandon the park and retreat to the adjacent Royal College of Surgeons.

From Tuesday onwards, Jacob's Biscuit Factory remained in a state of preparation for a British assault which never

came. General Lowe had decided that it was too heavily fortified and not strategically important enough to risk an all-
out attack. He reasoned that once all the other garrisons had
fallen, it would have no choice but to surrender. One Volunteer recalled that the factory now resembled a fortress and
'presented the appearance of a well-organised military base.'[6]
MacDonagh could be seen regularly inspecting the garrison's defences with McBride. During the early part of the
rebellion he was regarded as 'very calm. He had an electric
lamp on a cord around his neck, which he used to consult
some papers.'[7] Despite the worry of an imminent British
attack, MacDonagh retained his warm personality and sense
of humour throughout; individual Volunteers recalled that
he made them feel at ease and this, coupled with McBride's
presence 'had a very reassuring effect.'[8] As the Rising progressed, however, MacDonagh gradually became more of a
figurehead, especially as he demonstratably lacked the military experience of MacBride. He developed a marked tendency towards indecisiveness and tended to countermand
his own orders, which caused general confusion amongst
the garrison and led the Volunteers to question his ability to
command. On one occasion, he ordered a group of Volunteers who had just gone to bed to make for the College of
Surgeons with food supplies and return to the factory with
rifles. Having done so, at great risk, the group returned to
find MacDonagh demanding bayonets. Asking the officer in

charge of the party who had returned from the college why he had not taken the bayonets, the officer pointed out that MacDonagh had not requested them. Peadar Kearney, who had been part of the contingent, recalled:

> The officer replied that he had heard nothing about them. MacDonagh then said that there were bayonets in the College of Surgeons to fit the rifles and that they would have to be brought over. He then told the officer that as the men present knew the way he had better take them back and get them.[9]

As a result of this, it was inevitable that McBride took more of an active military role within the garrison and actively supported excursions out of the factory, taking part in Volunteer operations and winning a great deal of respect amongst the rebel cadre.

While waiting on a predicted assault, snipers high up in the towers of Jacob's were regularly engaged in shooting at British forces in both Portobello Barracks and Dublin Castle. According to Seamus Pounch, a captain in Na Fianna Éireann, the snipers 'were constantly attacking troops from every angle and causing a lot of confusion to the enemy ... Portobello Bridge became a no man's land for British sentries and soldiers.'[10] Only at nightfall would the incessant sniping come to an end.

From Wednesday onwards, the rebels at Jacob's could

regularly hear the noise of British artillery and heavy shells battering their comrades in other outposts. This was hugely frustrating for the Jacob's garrison, many of whom were were itching to fight the British army and listened intently to the noise of 'improvised armoured cars as they raced around the side streets reconnoitring our position.'[11] However, although not involved in open combat, the garrison was important in providing assistance to nearby rebel positions. William Oman, who had escaped the fall of City Hall and joined with the Jacob's garrison, recalled how Mallin had sent Chris Caffery, disguised as a widow and wearing an emblem of the Royal Dublin Fusiliers to the factory in search of food. MacDon-agh dispatched fifteen men, including Oman, with sacks of flour, bread and cakes.[12] Other units were sent out to occupy positions in anticipation of a British attack from Portobello Barracks. Positions were established on Tuesday at a small shop called Byrne's Stores and Delahunt's pub in Camden Street. The intention was that the outposts could undermine the strength of the British army, which was consolidating at Portobello Bridge since the fall of Davy's pub.

That same day, MacDonagh instructed Sean Healy, a member of Na Fianna Éireann, to deliver a message to the Volunteers at Phibsboro Bridge. At fourteen years of age, Healy was quite young, but he lived in Phibsboro and knew the area quite well, so MacDonagh was desirous that he would go home after he had delivered the dispatch rather than return to the factory. Healy made for his mother's house, where he stayed briefly, but after leaving his house he was shot within minutes at the junction of Phibsboro and North Circular Roads by sniper fire. The first casualty from Jacob's, Healy died two days afterwards, and his last known words were 'God bless the Volunteers.'[13] On the same day that Healy was shot, Francis Sheehy Skeffington, who had been attempting to establish a citizens' group to prevent looting throughout the city, was arrested by a British soldier. Taken to Portobello Barracks, he was executed the following day, along with two journalists, Thomas Dickson and Patrick MacIntyre, on the orders of Captain Bowen Colthurst, who was later found to be insane. Although he had some sympathy for the rebels, Sheehy Skeffington had no connection with the Rising and his killing was totally unjustified.

As the week progressed, the rebels sought ways to relieve themselves of stress, even organising a ceílí. A tailor, Derry O'Connell, made an improvised Irish tricolour from materials he found in the factory and with MacDonagh's permission hoisted it over the factory to great applause. Others made their way to the machine shop where, waiting on the British assault, they passed the time by sharpening bayonets and knives against grindstones. On finding a piano in the building, some Volunteers regularly played the instrument, offering 'a contrast with the rifle fire.'[14] Others resorted to humour: on finding a gramophone player with only one record, the British national anthem 'God Save The King', they played it around MacDonagh and MacBride to get a friendly rise out of the leadership.[15] In another section of the factory, their comrades created a makeshift library by opening a bookcase and educating themselves on philosophy and history through a small study circle headed by Peader O'Cearnaigh, Frank Kearney, Mick Slater, Joe Thunder and Seamus Ó Maolfhainn. Others climbed to the roof of the towers and watched as the rebellion continued across Dublin. John MacDonagh recalled how, frustrated by the lack of a fight, he went to the top of the tower and looked across the skyline, where 'we could see towards the end of the week the glare in the sky from which the fires were raging in O'Connell Street. This heartened us, for it showed the magnitude of the Rising, which we knew would change the whole position of Ireland.'[16] Seosamh de Brun remembered looking through the windows in the direction of O'Connell Street, viewing the reflection of the burning city as if 'a red glare appeared in the sky.'[17] However, those in Jacob's had no way to confirm the progress of the Rising as there was little accurate news available to them. Peadar Kearney recollected how:

> Rumours circulated thick and plentiful, rumours of victory and rumours of annihilation. The Wexford men, having taken Kynoch's in Arklow, were marching to Dublin, the southern counties were in the hands of the Volunteers, and

Dublin Bay was full of German submarines. On the other hand, Dublin, north of the Liffey, was burned to the ground, all Volunteer positions were wiped out and the British were undermining Jacobs to blow it to the stars.[18]

According to Volunteer Padraig Ó Ceallaigh, however, the general feeling amongst those who debated the Rising was that it was 'a gallant and hopeless venture which could only end in early defeat.'[19]

By Wednesday the general feeling remained mixed. At 8am the British had sailed a gunship, the *Helga*, up the Liffey and started obliterating rebel positions on Sackville Street. Initially unaware of the use of heavy artillery missiles, Mac-Bride, who climbed to the tower with MacDonagh to witness the fighting, confirmed for the garrison that the British army were using shells against rebel positions, a counter strategy which the rebels had initially discounted. Later that day the garrison had received news of the Battle of Mount Street Bridge. Here a small force of Volunteers under the command of Michael Malone had routed an entire regiment of the British army, the Sherwood Forresters, who had only arrived from Liverpool that morning and were ill-prepared for urban combat. The Republican force, centred around 25 Northumberland Road and Clanwilliam House with support from de Valera's 3rd Battalion at Boland's Mills, were eventually defeated and Malone was killed, but the British army had suffered the death of four officers, while 216 soldiers were killed or wounded in the bloodiest encounter of the Rising. Despite raising their spirits, however, the rebels in Jacob's soon became concerned when a rumour rapidly spread that the nearby Adelaide Hospital was being evacuated in preparation for a British assault. This assault never came, though.

On Thursday, de Valera's 3rd Battalion were engaged in heavy fighting with the British army. They were running low on ammunition and de Valera had sent a messenger to MacDonagh requesting assistance. Studying the feasibility of getting ammunition to Boland's Mills, which was located at Ringsend, a great distance from Jacob's, MacDonagh had decided to authorise a small reconnaissance party. He intended to cause a diversion for the British army to take pressure off of Boland's Mills. MacDonagh asked for men to seize bicycles in the factory and surrounding area, and if Volunteers were willing they would be selected for action. Placing Volunteer Dan O'Riordan in charge of the sortie, a party of fifteen Volunteers were chosen to run British army lines. Before the sortie left, MacDonagh joined the chosen fifteen as they sat around and drank tea.[20] He warned how their mission was incredibly hazardous and there was a real possibility that they would be killed. Wishing them luck, MacDonagh explained:

> De Valera is very hard pressed at Westland Row Railway Station and Boland's Mills. I am sending out a party to

make a diversion and reinforce him. Doubtless you will meet with opposition. If you encounter the enemy and find your retreat cut off, take possession of the nearest houses and make the most of it. We must draw the attack off Boland's Mill.[21]

Leaving the factory from the Whitefriar Street entrance, the sortie cycled down toward St Stephen's Green, where they made for Leeson Street and onwards to Fitzwilliam Square. Despite the danger, Seosamh de Brun felt a great sense of exhilaration on having left the confines of the factory. One of the party, named O'Rourke, had stuffed feathers into his hat and de Brun imagined him as 'an Indian Brave.'[22] On reaching Merrion Square, they came under heavy fire when:

Khaki-clad men from Mount Street ran to the roadway dropt on their knees and blazed away, others from the corner of the Square fired through the railings. O'Riordan yelled 'take cover'. We jumped from our machines. There was little cover to take. I got possession of an electric tram standard in the middle of the road. Others got to railings and doorways, in fact there was precious little cover.[23]

Overwhelmed, the sortie was forced to return to Fitzwilliam Square and cycled back towards Jacob's. Reaching St Stephen's Green, they had to run a gauntlet of gunfire from Grafton Street and the Shelbourne Hotel as 'a blaze of bullets whizzed' by.[24] Turning into York Street, near the Royal College of Surgeons, one of the sortie, John O'Grady, was shot in the stomach and fell in open sight of snipers. The group were not prepared to leave a comrade behind and immediately fell back as a rear guard under heavy gunfire, covered by the ICA in the College of Surgeons. Returning to Jacob's, O'Grady, in great pain and bleeding badly, was taken to the medical unit and was examined by Patrick Cahill. Cahill, a chemist rather than a surgeon, warned MacDonagh that O'Grady was in urgent need of a doctor, and MacDonagh ordered a representative to go to the Adelaide Hospital. However, the hospital refused to provide one for the rebels, but stated that if O'Grady was brought to them he would receive care. MacDonagh flew into a rage and ordered that a doctor was to be forcibly taken from the hospital for the care of his dying comrade. A doctor was brought to the factory in armed custody; he examined O'Grady, but insisted he could not help him in the factory. O'Grady was taken on a stretcher to the Adelaide Hospital where he succumbed to his wounds, becoming the only active member of the garrison to have died during the Easter Rising.

On Friday 28 April, General Sir John Maxwell arrived in Ireland after being authorised by the British government to quell the violence in the country. Arriving at 2am, Maxwell wrote to his wife of how, approaching Ireland by sea, he saw a burning city, similar to 'the last days of Pompeii'[25] and could hear in the distance the crackle of musketry and heavy artillery as the British army continued to encroach upon rebel positions. Almost immediately on his arrival, Maxwell issued a military proclamation stating that he would use the most vigorous measures at his disposal to undermine the rebellion, including the destruction of buildings held by the rebels. While Maxwell was installed as military governor, his immediate junior, Brigadier General Lowe, still coordinated all British military forces in the city, which by now numbered almost 20,000 men, a measure of how seriously the authorities took the Rising.

From Jacob's the Volunteers could see the blazing GPO and hear the thundering noise of heavy artillery, with the Dublin skyline resembling 'a vivid picture of a huge inferno.'[26] Their means of communication, were, however, limited as the week came to an end and there were a number of unnerving rumours circulating amongst a garrison isolated from the wider rebellion. The rebels also noticed that there was an increasing consolidation of British soldiers in nearby St Patrick's Park. Against this background John MacDonagh recalled how 'we expected an attack at any moment … Rumours came thick and fast. Communications were becoming more difficult to maintain.'[27] Peadar Kearney recalled how the garrison was in the grip of constant anxiety, waiting in desperation for an attack that never came:

One never knew whether the flames were in the neighbourhood of a mile away, and according as the wind changed the ear-splitting crash of all sorts of arms gave the impression that the building was being attacked from front and rear. All this meant that nerves were taut as a violin at pitch, in addition to which physical exhaustion and lack of sleep had the men in such a nervous condition …[28]

Throughout Saturday, however, there was a noticeable cessation of gunfire and many began to wonder what had happened, with some fearing the rebellion had been defeated. Others suggested that a truce had been called, with a rumour quickly spreading throughout the garrison that William Walsh, the Archbishop of Dublin, had negotiated a cease-fire. With tension palpable, an unconfirmed rumour spread that the GPO garrison had issued an unconditional surrender. MacDonagh initially disbelieved it, until he received a memorandum from Pearse instructing immediate surrender as a way to 'prevent the further slaughter of Dublin citizens, and in the hope of saving the lives of our followers, now surrounded and hopelessly outnumbered.'[29] Nurse Elizabeth O'Farrell, who had accompanied Pearse when he surrendered to Lowe, delivered the message. Learning that Pearse was a prisoner, MacDonagh refused to accept the order and told O'Farrell that he would negotiate with Lowe personally. Frustrated by the defiant attitude of the Jacob's garrison, Lowe had made it his intention to force the rebels out of the factory, if necessary by using heavy artillery, even though he

was acutely aware that a major assault in such a densely populated area could lead to serious civilian casualties. Willing to
consider a final appeal, he approached Capuchin priests Fr
Augustine and Fr Aloysius to act as intermediaries. Recalling Lowe as 'a perfect gentleman,'[30] the brigadier general
provided them with a car and an assurance of safe passage.
Before they left, he entreated them to convince MacDonagh
of the necessity of unconditional surrender. The priests were
to stress to MacDonagh that if he did not agree to surrender,
Lowe 'would be obliged to attack and demolish the factory
with great loss of life.'[31]

Meeting with MacDonagh and MacBride, Frs Augustine
and Aloysius pleaded with the commandant to accept Lowe's
offer. MacDonagh is reported to have asked Fr Augustine if
there were any terms, to which he was told, 'I'm afraid there
is nothing for it but unconditional surrender.'[32] MacDonagh remained obstinate, refusing to accept the legitimacy of
Pearse's order. He stressed that Pearse was now a prisoner and
therefore invalided. As the most senior member of the provisional government still uncaptured, MacDonagh insisted
how he could not agree to nor recommend an unconditional surrender. He insisted that he would negotiate only
with Brigadier General Lowe and was willing to meet him
at Jacob's Factory or outside in the vicinity of his command.
MacDonagh further stressed to the Capuchin priests how
the Jacob's garrison 'had ample provisions and could hold

out for some weeks.'[33] It was apparent to Fr Aloysius that MacDonagh was deadly serious. Asking MacDonagh why he was so opposed to the idea of surrender, MacDonagh claimed that the war was coming to an end, and in the subsequent peace conference 'Ireland would command attention and a right to participate if it were a belligerent.'[34]

Leaving Jacob's, the intermediaries met with Lowe and conveyed MacDonagh's opposition to a surrender, but his willingness to meet. At Lowe's request, the priests accompanied him to visit General Maxwell, who authorised Lowe to meet with MacDonagh on condition that it not take place in Jacob's Factory, as this would grant legitimacy upon the rebel garrison. MacDonagh was to come to see Lowe in St Patrick's Park at 12 noon. The intermediaries were instructed to arrange the meeting and Lowe assured the two priests that MacDonagh would be allowed safe passage to and from the park without interference from the British army. Returning to Jacob's, the intermediaries explained Lowe's offer to meet MacDonagh, and after some discussion with MacBride and O'Hanrahan, MacDonagh insisted he would not go unless he was accompanied by another Volunteer. MacBride offered to accompany MacDonagh, but, due to his conduct in the Boer War, it was decided that he would be better served within the Factory, as his presence in the Park during delicate negotiations could unnerve the British. The priests agreed and MacDonagh, accompanied by one of the Volunteers, walked with them to the nearby St Patrick's Park. Fr Augustine recalled upon their arrival how 'at the hour that had been arranged General Lowe, leaving his car, advanced, and MacDonagh and he met, saluting each other in the usual military style.'[35]

MacDonagh presented himself as a member of the provisional government of the Irish Republic. He was recorded as looking worn down, lacking a commanding presence. The two spoke for quite some time in Lowe's car, but their discussion is lost to history, as neither MacDonagh nor Lowe left a record of the negotiations. However, it is beyond doubt that Lowe must have pointed out the loss of civilian life that would result from an all-out assault on the factory. As MacDonagh stepped out of Lowe's car, the intermediaries noticed a marked change in his demeanour, and he forlornly explained to the priests how 'he had decided to advise surrender.'[36] MacDonagh agreed to a truce with Lowe which would last until 3pm, and Lowe stressed that if he heard nothing by this time, he would have no choice but to attack. Lowe again offered the use of his car to the intermediaries and, according to Aloysius, 'begged us to see the whole thing through as any hitch might be fatal and he was anxious to avoid further bloodshed.'[37]

When MacDonagh arrived back to Jacob's, he entered into private discussion with MacBride and their senior staff, including Michael O'Hanrahan, Tom Hunter, John Mac-

Donagh, Seamus Hughes, Joseph Furlong and Eamon Price. Preparing himself to announce Pearse's order of unconditional surrender to the garrison, MacDonagh was visibly moved and, speaking in a broken voice, announced that:

> A splendid assertion of Irish independence had been gallantly made by the [Irish Republican] Army and its supporters; noble sacrifices had been made in the cause of Irish freedom ... Pearse was convinced that further sacrifice of life would be futile. With the welfare of the Irish people and the army at heart he had decided to cease hostilities. He had agreed with the commander of the British forces, General Maxwell, to surrender on the guarantee that the men of the Irish Republican Army would be treated as prisoners of war.[38]

MacDonagh again explained that as Pearse was a prisoner he did not have to be obeyed, and the garrison was warranted in disputing his orders. MacDonagh for his part recommended surrender and in this he was supported by MacBride, who asked his colleagues to consider his military reputation and whether they thought he would surrender if there was any chance of success. Seamus Hughes, horrified by what he heard, announced his opposition, citing how their leaders would be sacrificed to the British and it was 'better to die with guns in our hands than face the firing squad.'[39] MacDonagh agreed that the leaders would most likely be shot but he stressed that he had assurances from Lowe that the rank-and-file would be treated as prisoners of war. Some of those present poured scorn on Lowe's assurances, suggesting that the British could not be trusted. They argued that they could continue to fight by taking the Easter Rising to the streets and the hills. This idea was rejected as impractical, however, considering that the British had encircled the area and the Volunteers could only escape to the countryside in small groups. Michael O'Hanrahan urged his comrades to accept the decision to surrender; in this he was supported by Eamon Price, who argued that if the garrison did not surrender, they would be inviting destruction 'of the surrounding thickly populated area.'[40] MacDonagh, having listened to all the arguments made, finally stated: 'Boys, we must give in. We must leave some to carry on the struggle.'[41]

Tom Hunter was delegated to inform the Volunteers who were assembling outside of the decision. Outraged by the surrender, but duty bound as a soldier to follow the instructions of his senior officer, while descending to meet the assembled Volunteers he broke his sword in frustration. The news provoked uproar, with many Volunteers throwing their rifles on the floor or against the wall in shock, anger and frustration. William James Stapleton recalled how there was general disbelief 'and a lot of shouting.'[42] Some had concluded that 'a deal had been done behind their backs'[43], and many of the Volunteers advocated a British assault on the building 'crying fiercely and shouting, "Fight it out! Fight it out!"[44] As this chant echoed throughout the garrison, those who had not thrown their guns down held them in the air in defiance of the senior staff. Peadar Kearney recollected, 'fierce anger predominated, while the best of men collapsed and became temporary imbeciles.'[45] A Belfast Volunteer beside Kearney gave him his rifle, unbuttoned his tunic, and said, 'shoot me! I'm not going to surrender!' Another Volunteer, Thomas Burke, was in tears and approached by a comrade, Thomas Meldon, he lamented how he had 'come out to fight, not to surrender.'[46] Finally MacDonagh, looking 'very careworn and dishevelled,'[47] addressed those present and outlined the sacrifice which the garrison had made, arguing that they had succeeded in establishing an Irish Republic. Once more he commented on how the Volunteers assembled would be treated as prisoners of war and therefore could not be shot. MacDonagh insisted that 'the stand you have made this week has gone around the world and the enemy dare not shoot you; but let me impress on you all, the man who fires another shot in this building will incur a terrible responsibility.'[48] With great emotion in his voice, the unkempt Mac-Donagh announced:

> We have to give in. Those of you who are in civilian clothes, go home. Those of you in uniform, stay on; you cannot leave.[49]

With these final words, Thomas MacDonagh left the assembly. Fr Augustine, who witnessed his final remarks, noted how the commandant had 'burst into tears.'[50] He was asked if he wanted to see Muriel; he replied miserably, 'not like this.'[51] In his wake, many shouted how that the British could not be trusted and 'they have deceived us before.'[52] Others advocated evacuating the building at once without the recommendation of their commandant. This was perceived as mutiny by those in the officer class, and Hunter in particular argued that any man who left the garrison was guilty of desertion. Eventually MacBride restored some semblance of order and assisted many of the men in civilian clothes, and a few of those in uniform, to escape the building. Some of those who escaped were given civilian clothes by priests from the nearby Whitefriars Priory, which, it was hoped, would allow them to avoid arrest. As MacBride helped the men to escape, his final words to them were: 'Liberty is a sweet thing. If it ever happens again, take my advice, and don't get inside four walls.'[53] The Easter Rising in Jacob's Factory had come to an abrupt end.

Chapter Eleven

30 April – 3 May 1916

'A great and glorious thing'

Shortly after addressing the Jacob's garrison, MacDonagh made his way to the South Dublin Union under a white flag, accompanied by Fr Aloysius and Fr Augustine, to recommend surrender to a horrified Éamonn Ceannt. Ceannt wished to continue fighting through a guerrilla campaign, but decided that he would abide by the decision of his garrison. Leaving the commandant, MacDonagh and Fr Augustine made for Brigadier General Lowe's car, which due to a barricade could not drive toward the Union. As they did so, they were fired upon by a British soldier despite the agreed ceasefire. The soldier, who remains unknown, was immediately arrested by a British officer, who also apologised to MacDonagh. Fr Augustine was struck by MacDonagh's nonchalant attitude, as he claimed he did not notice he was being fired upon. Fr Augustine, for his part 'felt glad [the British soldier] was such a bad shot.'[1] Returning to Jacob's at 3pm,

MacDonagh left again for St Patrick's Park where he met with Lowe and confirmed the surrender. Lowe gave a guarantee that the British army would not enter the factory until 6pm, allowing the area to normalise. In recognition of the surrender, MacDonagh handed Lowe his belt and gun before travelling with Fr Augustine to the South Dublin Union for a second time, where he again met with Éamonn Ceannt. Fr Augustine recalled that MacDonagh was rather depressed:

> Walking back, he spoke more than usual. Amongst other things he pointed out to me the place where they had held a large Volunteer recruiting meeting some time previously, and a little later the spot near St. Catherine's Church where the scaffold was erected on which Robert Emmet was hanged. I could almost feel his thoughts.[2]

MacDonagh was then brought to Boland's Mills, as Éamon de Valera had initially thought Pearse's surrender order a trap as it had not been signed by MacDonagh, before being brought back to Jacob's. The garrison at Jacob's had organised itself into military formation and, led by MacDonagh at 4.30pm, they began marching toward nearby Bride Street, where the British army and a howling mob awaited them. The mob subjected the rebels to a tirade of abuse, shouting, throwing objects, and spitting at them. While the garrison despised the British army, many were privately pleased that they were there to keep the angry mob away.

As they left the factory, the Volunteers heard a loud bang within the complex, which some thought was an explosion, while a solitary sniper, not having learned of the surrender, continued firing from one of the towers. Immediately there were allegations of British duplicity, as many Volunteers questioned whether the British had begun an assault on the complex irrespective of the ceasefire. This suspicion was strengthened by the fact the British, despite their earlier assurance that they would not enter the factory before 6pm, had done so immediately upon the rebels' evacuation. Mac-Donagh was horrified and angrily announced that:

> Although his men had laid down their arms in order to surrender, the soldiers had opened fire on them, were throwing bombs and that the military had broken into the factory and were killing his men.[3]

Before the rebels had left, MacBride, fearful of the possibility of civilian entry to the complex, had taken Thomas Orr to the rebels' makeshift explosives depot and instructed him to protect them until the British army took charge of the factory. MacBride insisted that under no circumstances were the bombs to fall into civilian hands. However, when the rebels had occupied the building, they left a rope hanging from a high window, and looters had discovered it. Orr and some Jacob's staff members who had returned to the building following the surrender, grabbed a number of rifles left by the rebels and bravely fought them off. But when the British entered the complex, they saw the caretaker holding a rifle and shot at him. In doing so, they pierced a sprinkler and drenched the building. Orr recalled how:

> A volley of shots rang out all round about where I was standing, and the second sprinkler over my head was pierced through with a bullet, and that the hat was knocked off my head by a bomb fired through the open window. Luckily for me it passed through a window and exploded over a refrigerator outside. Well, I thought my last hour had come.[4]

Orr explained how he was the factory caretaker and pointed out the explosives. He recalled that the soldiers were more interested in the Republican flag flying over the factory and demanded that Orr show them how to get to it. Placing him at the point of a bayonet, he ushered them toward the tower. Tearing down the tricolour flag, Orr remembered how the officer in charge could not have been 'prouder if he was after taking the Empire of Germany.'[5]

It was only the intervention of Fr Aloysius that forced the British army to leave the complex, stressing how they had agreed not to enter the building until 6pm. This had the unfortunate side effect of further facilitating looters, who entered the complex in greater numbers, taking ammunition, guns, clothing and whatever food they could find. Fr

Aloysius waded through the drenched complex and helped Orr to secure the building. As he had done with the British army, he implored the looters to leave, and such was his influence within the community that some actually put back what they had stolen following his condemnation.

When the Volunteers had completely evacuated Jacob's, they were marched by the British army to nearby Bull Alley Street, parallel to St Patrick's Park, arriving at 5pm. Directed to lay down their arms, the Volunteers remained in military formation as the British army surrounded them. Instructions had been issued to take the rebels to Richmond Barracks in Inchicore, where they were to be held overnight. General Maxwell's plan was to contain all the male prisoners in one large barracks, with women prisoners taken to Ship Street Barracks adjoining Dublin Castle. MacDonagh and his staff were allowed to lead the Volunteers under their command to Inchicore. Arriving at Richmond Barracks, John Mac-Donagh recalled how soldiers' wives in the area continued the abuse they had earlier received as they were marched from Jacob's. Enclosed in the barracks, the verbal abuse from outside was incessant, adding with the frustration, anger and dejection the men felt now that the rebellion had ended in failure. Each internee knew what was coming next: they were either to be shot or imprisoned, while their superior officers almost certainly faced execution. Placed together into a large room, conditions were harsh: while they received tea and some hard biscuits, they were not provided with beds, blankets or toilets, and had to rest on a cold stone floor. On top of that, the prisoners were filthy, worn-out, and denied washing arrangements. MacDonagh tried to keep their spirits high. John recalled how MacDonagh made an effort to meet with each of his soldiers and shared concentrated food tablets with some of them. Noticing that John MacBride was cold, MacDonagh gave him his coat. As commandant of his garrison, MacDonagh sought better conditions for the men at Richmond and approached Fr Columbus OSFC to act as his intermediary with the barrack authorities. It was evident from his discussions with Fr Columbus that he hoped the men could receive the normal treatment afforded to prisoners of war, and in a note to the authorities, MacDonagh sought:

> 1. Visits to prisoners; 2. Treatment of officers; 3. Dependents and relations; 4. Blankets; 5. Books; 6. The wearing [of] Red Cross badge who were not combatants; 7. Washing arrangements.[6]

The British army did provide eventually provide washing facilities for the men, but they refused MacDonagh's other requests.

The following day, the Volunteers from Jacob's were paraded in the square of Richmond Barracks, where Mac-Donagh, MacBride and O'Hanrahan, who had all been identified by Dublin Castle as significant figures within the rising, were separated from the general group. The garrison was then taken to the barrack gymnasium and placed against the wall with those who had fought under Ceannt's command. Here G-Men arrived and identified more of the senior rebels, including Con Colbert and Tom Hunter. Following the identity parade, each individual rebel was questioned by G-Men, who took their names and inquired of the antecedents and addresses prior to the rebellion. As they were questioned, they were instructed to place any valuables they owned into a nearby large bath in the command of a temporary adjutant from Portobello Barracks, with the army stockpiling watches, rings, wallets and cash. Interviewing John MacDonagh, police learned that he was Thomas's younger brother and placed him under arrest. He was later sentenced to life imprisonment, first at Knutsford Gaol in England and then in the Frongoch internment camp in Wales. Escorted from the barracks, John glimpsed Thomas for the final time and remembered his brother gently waving his hand toward him as he said goodbye.[7]

The court-martial of Thomas MacDonagh, Prisoner No. 39, in front of a military tribunal began at Richmond Barracks on 2 May 1916, immediately after that of Patrick Pearse. He was not allowed legal defence. Similar to others court-martialled for their involvement in the Rising, MacDonagh's trial was largely procedural and quite short, with great discretion given to the military tribunal about procedure and judgement. After each court-martial the tribunal followed a formal procedure where the individual would be taken away and there would then be private deliberation as to his fate, his sentence being announced later while in custody. General Maxwell, who had authority over the establishment of the military tribunals, insisted that the proceedings be conducted in private, an order made with a view to the preservation of security. This decision, however, established a perception amongst the public that the trials were a sham and the British had already decided that there would be summary executions.

MacDonagh's trial was presided over by Brigadier General Charles Blackadder, while the prosecution was led by William Wylie. The tribunal charged him with treason, citing he had taken part in a rebellion for the purpose of assisting Germany. MacDonagh announced he was not guilty. With only one witness, Major James Armstrong, the evidence against MacDonagh was circumstantial at best. Armstrong asserted that he and other British soldiers based at St Patrick's Park had come under fire from the direction of Jacob's, injuring a number of his colleagues. In his evidence, Armstrong was clearly unsure as to where the gunfire was coming from and could not confirm it had emanated from the factory. Equally he testified that 'MacDonagh made several journeys through our lines'.[8] On no occasion did Armstrong mention that

MacDonagh had been in contact with Lowe, and the latter had authorised his presence as part of the negotiations prior to surrender. Finally, Armstrong blatantly lied to the tribunal and claimed that MacDonagh was carrying arms when he surrendered, which contradicts the recollection of Fr Aloysius that MacDonagh had handed over his weapons to Lowe prior to the garrison surrender.

Taking no part in his trial and offering no defence, Mac-Donagh called no witnesses to contradict the evidence. Offering a final statement to Blackadder, he announced 'I did everything I could to assist the officers in the matter of the surrender, telling them where the arms and ammunition were after the surrender was decided upon.'[9] In hindsight, writing to Muriel, this statement greatly troubled MacDonagh as it appeared he was seeking clemency for his actions, which was not the case. Wylie asserted that MacDonagh never spoke during the tribunal and was the only prisoner who said 'absolutely nothing'[10] However, the official transcript indicates that MacDonagh made a brief statement, which is corroborated by his final letter to his wife Muriel, written in Kilmainham Gaol.

Finding MacDonagh guilty of treason, the tribunal recommended his execution. General Maxwell concurred and, believing MacDonagh was active in Sinn Féin (which was not the case) as well as knowing that he was prominent within the Irish Volunteers and was in command of the Jacob's garrison, authorised his execution for 3 May 1916.[11] Perhaps the greatest justification for his execution, according to Maxwell, was the discovery of a letter on the person of John Mac-Bride, signed by Commandant Thomas MacDonagh, which not only described him as a member of the provisional government of the Irish Republic, but also indicated that he was a member of the Irish Republican Army (as the rebels had termed themselves).[12] With MacDonagh's fate sealed, Wylie lamented, 'I was always sorry MacDonagh was executed. It was particularly unnecessary in his case.'[13] Following his execution, a statement purporting to be his address to his court-martial was widely circulated in the press, reading:

> The Proclamation of the Irish Republic has been adduced in evidence against me as one of the signatories; you think it already a dead and buried letter, but it lives, it lives. From minds alight with Ireland's vivid intellect it sprang, in hearts aflame with Ireland's mighty love it was conceived. Such documents do not die. The British occupation of Ireland has never for more than 100 years been compelled to confront in the field of fight a Rising so formidable as that which overwhelming forces have for the moment succeeded in quelling. This Rising did not result from accidental circumstances. It came in due recurrent season as the necessary outcome of forces that are ever at work. The fierce pulsation of resurgent pride that disclaims servitude may one day cease to throb in the heart of Ireland – but

the heart of Ireland will that day be dead. While Ireland lives, the brains and brawn of her manhood will strive to destroy the last vestige of British rule in her territory. In this ceaseless struggle there will be, as there has been, and must be, an alternate ebb and flow. But let England make no mistake. The generous high-bred youth of Ireland will never fail to answer the call we pass upon them – will never fail to blaze forth in red rage of war to win their country's freedom. Other and tamer methods they will leave to other and tamer men; but they must do or die. It will be said that our movement was doomed to failure. It has proved so. Yet it might have been otherwise. There is always a chance of success for brave men who challenge fortune. That we had such a chance none knows so well as your statesmen and military experts. The mass of the people of Ireland will doubtless lull their consciences to sleep for another generation by the exploded fable that Ireland cannot successfully fight England. We do not profess to represent the mass of the people of Ireland. To Ireland's soul and intellect the inert mass, drugged and degenerate by ages of servitude, must in the distant day of resurrection, render homage and free service – receiving in return the vivifying impress of a free people. Gentlemen, you have sentenced me to death, and I accept your sentence with joy and pride, since it is for Ireland I am to die. I go to join the godly company of the men who died for Ireland, the least of whom was worthier far than I can claim to be, and that noble band are, them-selves, but a small section of the great unnumbered army of martyrs whose captain is the Christ who died on Calvary. Of every white-robed Knight in all that goodly company we are the spiritual kin. The forms of heroes flit before my vision, and there is one, the star of whose destiny sways my own; there is one the keynote of whose nature chimes harmoniously with the swansong of my soul. It is the great Florentine, whose weapon was not the sword but prayer and preaching. The seed he sowed fructifies to this day in God's Church. Take me away, and let my blood bedew the sacred soil of Ireland. I die in certainty that once more the seed will fructify.[14]

There is no record of this speech in the official transcript of MacDonagh's trial, and as a result there has been consider-able controversy over its authenticity. When first published, it was rumoured that an officer present at his court-martial was so moved by MacDonagh that he recorded his testimony in shorthand. Muriel and his family believed that the speech was not a forgery, with his brother John attesting how he believed it was 'genuine, being so characteristic of him, both in feeling and language.'[15] His son Donagh similarly believed in the validity of MacDonagh's court-martial address, hold-ing, like his uncle, that the speech had 'the impress of Mac-Donagh's mind.'[16] For Donagh it was evident that the speech had been made by his father because of the reference to 'the great Florentine', which he believed to be Girolamo Savonarola, a Renaissance preacher who taught civic virtue and freedom from tyranny. MacDonagh had mentioned Savonarola in *When The Dawn Is Come*, when his protagonist, Turlough, compares himself to the preacher. In the speech there is also a direct quote from Horace, a Roman lyric poet whom MacDonagh studied. However, Donagh MacDonagh grew to doubt its truthfulness and eventually decried it as a forgery, going so far as to appeal in 1966 to Taoiseach Seán Lemass that the Irish government seek access to the then closed court-martial records. Lemass ultimately declined for fear of undermining Anglo-Irish relations.

When the trial transcripts were finally made public in 1999, the absence of MacDonagh's speech from the official record indicates that it was indeed a forgery. Strong evidence of this is that MacDonagh states in his speech, 'Gentlemen, you have sentenced me to death' when it's beyond doubt that none of the men sentenced to death learned of the order at their court-martial. This is demonstrated by the experiences of Éamon de Valera, Piaras Béaslai and Seamus Brennan, among others, whose death sentences were not carried out for various reasons. MacDonagh may have known that he was going to be executed, but there is no reason to believe that his court-martial would have been different to anyone else's. Finally, the alleged speech contradicts MacDonagh's final letter to his wife Muriel, which specifically references that he had received sentence of death on the night of 2 May 1916 while at Kilmainham Gaol.

Whether or not the address was genuine, its publication after his execution unnerved the British, particularly considering the growing respect for the rebels amongst the Irish people. The supposed statement justified the rebellion and highlighted the significance of the Easter Rising as a demonstration that would inspire future generations of Irish people to rise up and demand independence. The image of MacDonagh defending the Easter Proclamation before a British court-martial was a powerful symbol, reminiscent of Robert Emmet considering his own imminent death and its ability to inspire future generations when before Lord Norbury in 1803. Recognising this, the British government quickly moved to suppress the alleged speech using the powers given to Dublin Castle through the Defence of the Realm Act, arresting four men they claimed were involved in its publication. The first, JM Butler, had previously worked for *The Freeman's Journal* and was a popular newsagent within the north inner city, based at Amiens Street. He had organised the printing of 10,000 copies of the statement, and had advertised it for sale from his shop window, selling 470. They were seized by an Inspector Mills of the DMP in preparation for a case against the newsagent, and on 30 June 1916 Butler was tried for selling what the British termed 'a false statement likely to cause disaffection to his Majesty.'[17] In citing the case against Butler, the Crown prosecutor referred to MacDonagh's alleged court-martial address as 'pure fiction, and no such statement, so far as he could gather, was made by [MacDonagh].'[18] The prosecution claimed that it was printed by a Republican movement who were intent 'on causing disloyalty and disaffection'[19] in Ireland. Butler was fined £20 and was bound over by the Court. Three print-ers, Peter Paul Curtis, Robert Latchford and WH West, were also arrested in Dublin under the powers of the Defence of the Realm Act and accused of producing seditious material likely to foment public disorder. Tried at the South Dublin police court, the prosecution tried to claim that the trio were the actual authors of the alleged speech; however this could not be established, with the printers claiming that they were completely apolitical and simply, according to their defence, printing the document in 'the ordinary course of business.'[20] The trio were eventually fined £5 on an assurance that they would not print the alleged speech again.

Following his court-martial on 2 May, MacDonagh was taken from Richmond Barracks to the west wing of nearby Kilmainham Gaol to await the verdict. Conditions were far from desirable: Kilmainham had not functioned as a prison since 1910, when the General Prison Board evacuated the complex. It was not occupied again until 1914, when on the outbreak of the war it was used by the British army as a billet and military prison. The army, however, only occupied the east wing, and as a result the older west wing had fallen into disrepair. The cell MacDonagh was placed into was damp and putrid. While there was glass in the windows, it had been shattered, allowing the cold air to seep in, and there was no bed, blanket, toilet, or washing facilities. Later that evening, MacDonagh would have to sleep on the floor. At midnight on 2 May, a soldier arrived at his prison cell to inform Mac-Donagh of the sentence of death, and that he was scheduled to be shot in a few hours, on the morning of 3 May.

Prior to their execution, both Pearse and MacDonagh had asked to see Fr Aloysius, who recalled that 'the preparation these two men made to meet death was simply inspiring and edifying.'[21] MacDonagh's sister Mary (Sr Francesca) was given permission to visit him in his cell in the company of Fr Aloysius, who left to give them privacy. Mary remembered meeting her brother as an 'awful moment.'[22] Taking her hand, MacDonagh explained to her how she needed to take care of Muriel and the children. He assured Mary that Muriel would become a Catholic and again asked her to 'guard and see after her and the children.'[23] MacDonagh suggested to his sister that her sole guardianship of his wife and children would be temporary and that when John was released from prison he would also help to look after them, explaining how knowing that his family would look after his wife and children gave him great comfort.[24] It was evident that the welfare of his family weighed greatly on his mind and Mary asked him if she could expect any help from Muriel's mother Isabella, but 'he said emphatically no. Never.'[25] MacDonagh explained that Isabella Gifford had effectively cut off all ties with her daughter. Doggedly sectarian, Isabella had even cancelled the allowance she had promised her daughter on the latter's wedding, as Muriel's failure to attend regular Protestant service led Isabella to suspect that her daughter had secretly become Catholic. Instructed by the prison guards that she had to leave, Mary gave her brother a family heirloom, her mother's rosary beads. MacDonagh was reluctant to take them for fear of damage, telling his sister, 'ah no … they will shoot it to bits.'[26] Mary assured him that she would get them back. Before she left, MacDonagh took two photographs of his children and Muriel from his pocket and kissed them.

Fr Aloysius had demanded that he attend the executions, desiring to be with MacDonagh and Pearse at the end; however, he was told that regulations forbade his presence. Forcing a British soldier to contact army headquarters, he received the same response and was bluntly told there would be no exceptions. Reluctantly he was forced to leave the prison and, despite feeling he had given Pearse and Mac-Donagh dispensations and pastoral care, he deeply regretted that he was not permitted to be by their side 'to the end.'[27]

A British soldier was sent to the MacDonagh family home on Oakley Road to inform Muriel of the impending execution. Seeing Donagh, the soldier told him his father was to be shot, sending the three-year-old into hysterics. Earlier, soldiers had been encamped outside the home and Donagh later recalled how they menaced the family 'with their guns sighted on our house.'[28] According to Muriel, he was left traumatised and fearful 'at the sight of a soldier'.[29] Muriel was informed by the British soldier that her husband was scheduled to be executed in Kilmainham Gaol, and while she was given permission to see him, the soldier failed to give her a permit enabling her to travel through the city. Following the Rising there was a military curfew in Dublin, and citizens needed permits to pass through army checkpoints. Tragically, she was stopped at such a checkpoint, and as she was unable to adequately provide evidence as to who she was, the soldiers refused to allow her pass. Despite her greatest efforts to see her husband, she never got the opportunity to say goodbye. MacDonagh was left unaware of all this and, having sent a request to see her, in his final statement he wrote, 'I do not know if she can come.'[30]

As the night drew to a close, MacDonagh wrote his final statement. Concerned with his family's welfare to the last, he recommended that Muriel should meet with David Houston, who would help her publish *Literature in Ireland*, MacDonagh's last book, to help with any financial difficulties. MacDonagh predicted that after his execution there would be a large demand for his work and he was desirous that royalties could be paid to Muriel for the benefit of his family. He wrote:

> To my son Don. My darling little boy, remember me kindly. Take my hope and purpose with my deed. For your sake and for the sake of your beloved mother and sister I would wish to live long, but you will recognise the thing I have done, and see this as a consequence. I think still I have done a great thing for Ireland, and with the defeat of her Army, won the first step of her freedom. God bless you, my son.
>
> My darling daughter, Barbara, God bless you. I loved you more than ever a child has been loved.
>
> My dearest love, Muriel, thank you a million times for all you have been to me. I have only one trouble in leaving life – leaving you so. Be brave, darling, God will assist and bless you … Goodbye, my love, till we meet again in Heaven. I have a sure faith of our union there. I kiss this paper that goes to you … God help and sustain you, my love. But for your suffering this would be all joy and glory.[31]

Seeking to justify his involvement in the Easter Rising, he clarified his earlier statement to the court-martial, holding:

> I made a statement as to the negotiations for surrender with General Lowe. On hearing it read after, it struck me that it might sound like an appeal. It was not such. I make no appeal, no recantation, no apology, for my acts. In what I said I merely claimed that I act honourably and thoroughly

in all that I set myself to do. My enemies have, in return, treated me in an unworthy manner. But that can pass. It is a great and glorious thing to die for Ireland and I can well forget all petty annoyances in the splendour of this. In all my acts I have been actuated by one motive only, the love of my country, the desire to make her a sovereign independent state. I still hope and pray that my acts may have for consummation her lasting freedom and happiness.[32]

On the morning of 3 May 1916, Thomas James Clarke, Patrick Pearse and Thomas MacDonagh were executed in Kilmainham Gaol. Taken from his cell after Clarke and Pearse had already been shot, MacDonagh was led down a dark corridor in the direction of the Catholic chapel, where that evening his friend Joseph Plunkett would marry his sister-in-law Grace Gifford. Entering the corridor prior to the chapel, he was ushered left through a small doorway leading to a dusty spiral staircase, which brought him out to a small exercise yard. Turning right he was ushered into the Stonebreakers' Yard, which had been chosen as it was the only enclosure in Kilmainham Gaol that had no windows, and as such was isolated from the wider prison body. As he entered, MacDonagh was greeted by a firing squad of twelve men commanded by Major Charles Harold Heathcote, a British officer, who had taken charge of the prisoners at Richmond and oversaw their removal to Kilmainham. The squad was composed of soldiers belonging to the Sherwood Foresters. That this regiment had been selected to carry out the executions was in deference to the fact that they had been overwhelmed at Mount Street Bridge by the rebels.

On the morning of 3 May, unlike the following executions, the firing squad was not changed with each separate shooting. Of the twelve, one man was given a blank round. Known as a conscience round, none of the squad knew who had been given the bullet, thus in theory each soldier could believe that he had not killed the prisoner. To MacDonagh's surprise, the squad which had been detailed to take his life were little older than boys, many of whom were terrified at the prospect of killing him and showed 'considerable nervousness.'[33] A personable individual to the last, he tried to put them at ease and shared cigarettes to the squad, handing to the officer in charge his silver cigerette case, commenting 'I won't be needing this, would you like to have it?'[34] As he was placed standing with his back to a wall of sandbags, he was reported to have said, 'I know this is a lousy job, but you're doing your duty – I do not hold this against you.'[35] A British officer next tied MacDonagh's hands behind his back and blindfolded him, and at 3.30am Thomas MacDonagh was executed. A British officer who witnessed the killing commented afterwards, 'they all died well, but MacDonagh died like a Prince.'[36]

Chapter Twelve
• • • • • • • •

May 1916 – July 1917

'A loss both to Ireland and to literature'

Thirteen other men were shot following Thomas Mac-Donagh. They included the seven signatories of the Easter Proclamation alongside all of the Dublin commandants, excluding Éamon de Valera, whose sentence of death was changed to imprisonment on account of the a cabinet decision that the executions should stop amidst growing public opposition. Outside of Dublin, the only men to be executed were Thomas Kent, who was shot in Cork Gaol, and Roger Casement, who was hanged in Pentonville Prison in London. Of the sixteen, it is arguable that three died for reasons other than their involvement in the Rising: Willie Pearse for who his brother was; John MacBride because of his military career, especially his actions in the Boer War; and Michael O'Hanrahan because he was quartermaster of the Volunteers.

Before these executions, few people had supported the Easter Rising. Nationalist Ireland was dominated by the demand for Home Rule, and the idea of an independent Irish republic was consigned to fringe politics. After them, however, there was growing sympathy for the rebels and their political goals. This was recognised by Winston Churchill, who wrote of how the executions had changed the course of Irish history; he later lamented how 'the position of the Irish Parliamentary Party was fatally undermined. The keys of Ireland passed into the keeping of those in whom hatred of England was the dominant and almost the only interest.' [1]

From a nationalist perspective, John Dillon, the deputy leader of the IPP, denounced the government's response to the rebellion, in what *The New York Times* described as 'a speech which for bitter denunciation has not been surpassed since Parnell's days.'[2] Dillon angrily condemned 'these horrible executions'[3] and stated that it was 'not murderers who were being executed; it is insurgents who fought a clean fight.'[4] He warned the British government of how 'you are washing out our whole life work in a sea of blood.'[5] MacDonagh's friend Francis Ledwidge graphically represented this change within the Irish people. Like MacDonagh, he had joined the Irish Volunteers as an advocate of Irish Home Rule. While initially opposing Redmond's call to join the British army, Ledwidge eventually enlisted as he genuinely believed that the First World War was a battle for civilisation against German barbarism. On learning of MacDonagh's untimely death while in Europe, he commented, 'If someone were to tell me now that the Germans were coming over our back wall, I wouldn't lift a finger to stop them. They could come!'[6] Ledwidge even penned a poem to his friend, 'A Lament for Thomas MacDonagh':

> He shall not hear the bittern cry
> In the wild sky, where he is lain,
> Nor voices of the sweeter birds
> Above the wailing of the rain.
> Nor shall he know when loud March blows
> Thro' slanting snows her fanfare shrill,
> Blowing to flame the golden cup
> Of many an upset daffodil.
> But when the dark cow leaves the moor,
> And pastures poor with greedy weeds,
> Perhaps he'll hear her low at morn
> Lifting her horn in pleasant meads.

This growing sympathy for the rebels brought attention to the work of the executed leaders, and of these, there were four who were in a position to explain the significance of the rebellion in the written word: Pearse, Connolly, Plunkett and MacDonagh.[7] This afforded them a recognisable status within the historiography of the rebellion and meant that they could be used to posthumously speak of the Rising and its ambitions. In the aftermath of the executions, many began

to see the Rising as an honourable battle between nationalists and British aggressors. However, there was also an
increasing tendency to identify the nationalism of the Easter
Rising with Catholicism as a means of tying the Republican
ethos of the rebellion to wider popular culture in Ireland,
which at the time was overwhelmingly Catholic (except in
the northeast).

This view of the Rising began to be expressed immediately after the rebellion. Following the executions, *The
Catholic Bulletin* carried an editorial with three blank pages
to signify their disgust at the executions, while elsewhere the
periodical spoke of the nation's martyrdom. In its July issue,
it included biographical notes of those rebels who were shot
or who had been killed during the fighting. In June 1917,
Studies: An Irish Quarterly Review, a Jesuit publication, carried an article entitled 'Pearse, MacDonagh and Plunkett, An
Appreciation', written by Arthur E Cleary, which described
MacDonagh as having 'the purity of the Irish Catholic', and
defined the rebellion as 'a Catholic revolution.'[8] Drawing on
MacDonagh's earlier studies with the Holy Ghost Fathers,
the author praised the order for instilling in the Irishman 'a
complete absence of affectation.'[9] This narrative ran counter to the historical reality: while Pearse and Plunkett were
deeply Catholic in their outlook, Connolly certainly wasn't,
and MacDonagh had wrestled with his faith and the Church's
teachings since his youth. Writing of MacDonagh in 1919,

The Irish Monthly (also published by the Jesuits) noted that MacDonagh was 'a little hard to understand.'[10] This was in reference to the difficulty which MacDonagh presented to early interpretations of the Rising within a religious narrative. Having conceded this point, however, the Jesuit publication went on to remark how:

> It has been hinted that Thomas MacDonagh fell away from his childhood's – the Catholic – faith but surely his poems refute this accusation. They reveal, it is true, a man tortured by religious difficulty; but they show no less a soul reconciled with the divine order, a will that no matter how rebellious against things of mans devising, yet bowed in childlike simplicity, to the law of God.[11]

Despite all the evidence to the contrary, *The Irish Monthly* asserted that MacDonagh was a beacon of Catholic virtue who had triumphed over his doubts and had become stronger in his faith from the experience. Much of this perception arose from the court-martial statement attributed to him after his execution, particularly his references to Christ and religion. Within this revised theme MacDonagh was a described as a man marked by 'devotion to art, a fineness of mind, an intellectual courage, which could look without trembling even on the throne of God, a greatness of conception, an elevation of spirit [and] a grandeur of passion undefiled.'[12]

MacDonagh posed similar difficulties to cultural interpretation of the Easter rebellion. One of the most important contributions to the foment of ideas surrounding the Rising, and one which has been greviously overlooked, is his posthumously published *Literature in Ireland*, which stood at odds with his earlier pronouncements on the Irish language and the importance of its preservation. His final book is divided between eight studies and includes an anthology of poetry. Defining what he earlier termed the Irish mode, *Literature in Ireland* was a detailed study of the development of language in Ireland. He contended the two dominant Irish literary customs, Gaelic and English were supplanted in the late nineteenth century by a new Anglo-Irish tradition, with literature written in English but maintaining a definite and unique Irish voice. As the Irish began to speak English, based on their understanding of the Irish language, the two traditions fused to form an Irish mode with 'the alien language' stirring 'to expression on the lips of the native people'.[13] Accordingly, it has been suggested that MacDonagh concluded Anglo-Irish was 'more vigorous, fresh and simple,'[14] than either the Irish or English languages. It is important to note that when MacDonagh used the term Anglo-Irish he specifically applied it to Irish literature written in English, and justifying his analysis he commented:

An Anglo-Irish literature, worthy of a special designation, could only come when English had become the language of the Irish people, mainly of Gaelic stock; and when the literature was from, by, of, to and for the Irish people ... That the ways of life and the ways of thought of the Irish people – the manners, customs, traditions and outlook, religious, social and moral – have important differences from the ways of life and of thought which have found expression in other English literature ... That the English language in Ireland has an individuality of its own, and the rhythm of Irish speech a distinct character. [15]

MacDonagh argued how Anglo-Irish literature should be recognised and valued for its cultural merit as 'a distinctly new literature.'[16] In effect, he rejected the assumption that a national literature could only be created within the Irish language, commenting:

[The] Irish race [is] now mostly English speaking. That life, those ways of thought expressed in the new literature, are the life and ways of the Gael, modified by the change of language from Gaelic to English and by the things that brought about that change, but still individually Gaelic, spiritually, morally, socially filled with memories of the old Gaelic literature moving to the rhythm of Irish music ...[17]

MacDonagh also speculated that the English language, as spoken in Ireland, was relatively young, and the literature it produced was affected by the impending death of the Irish language. This influence, he asserted, would make it the case that as Irish literature developed, it would intrinsically differ from its British counterparts as the mentality of the people of Ireland would continue to differ from their neighbours. With reference to the Irish language he concluded:

> Whatever the fate of the Gaelic language and literature now may be – whether its long sickness end now in death without issue, or as some of us confidently hope, in revival and vigorous life, with renewal of the same personality, a second youth, or in the birth of a new language to utter a new literature destined to take after its Gaelic mother only in some parts … whatever it is to be in the unknown future, it would be folly to deny the sickness, the decadence, of the immediate past.[18]

The fact that MacDonagh had written that the English language, as spoken in Ireland, was individual and not foreign, posthumously placed MacDonagh at odds with the supposed Gaelic aspirations of the Easter Rising, specifically with what Patrick Pearse had earlier termed an Ireland not merely free but Gaelic.[19] While MacDonagh had desired a revival of the Irish language, his final published work indicates that he was more pragmatic on the Irish language question than his contemporaries within the Irish-Ireland movement. It also suggests that he was willing to consider the formal death of the language. What MacDonagh was hinting at in his last book could be suggested to have been a recognition that the decline of the Irish language was not, as he had previously believed, disastrous to the cultural benefit of the nation, but could be seen as a natural, albeit regrettable, progression.

Literature in Ireland was well received. His points about the evolution of an Anglo-Irish language were ignored, however, by the broader nationalist movement, particularly by the new Irish state that followed the Irish revolution in the 1920s, with its emphasis on compulsory Irish and Irish literature. Recognising the controversial nature of his final book, *Studies: An Irish Quarterly Review*, noted that his posthumous work was 'likely to cause a clamour amongst Gaelic Leaguers.'[20] The journal argued that in his final work MacDonagh had excelled and produced stimulating research. Describing MacDonagh as having a fine sense of what is best in our native poetry,' it regarded *Literature in Ireland* as 'instructive both to the writer and critic of modern Irish.'[21] For critics of modern Irish, MacDonagh's final book was useful for their attacks on the Gaelic League and Irish nationalism: the Unionist-leaning newspaper *The Northern Whig* announced in this vein how MacDonagh had defended Anglo-Irish literature against 'Gaelic fanatics who would have it that nothing worth saying can be said by Irishmen in the English language.'[22] It is understandable that within the historiography of the Easter Rising it was difficult for nationalists to address a discussion on the issues that MacDonagh had raised within his final work, as to have done so would have challenged the very cultural ethos of the state and necessitated a more nuanced reappraisal of the relationship of the Easter Rising to the Irish language.

On a wider scale, removed from any debate in Ireland, the publication of *Literature in Ireland* after his untimely execution in Kilmainham Gaol meant that the world was introduced to Thomas MacDonagh the literary academic. The widespread attention that the Rising received encouraged many individuals to seriously study his work, and the recognition that he had craved with his earlier poetry was posthumously granted. Ezra Pound, the expatriate American poet, regarded MacDonagh's final book as 'very able and interesting.'[23] Pound paid tribute to MacDonagh as a man larded with common sense; decrying his execution, the poet contended that 'his loss is a loss both to Ireland and to literature, and it is a loss bound to be more felt as his work becomes more widely known'.[24]

While MacDonagh's loss to Ireland was openly noted, his loss to his family and friends was more poignant. Edward Martyn lamented to John MacDonagh how Thomas' untimely death was a great loss and he was a man of 'high ideals.' Reflecting on the executions, Martyn commented how they were 'abominable.'[25] James Stephens, referring to him as 'Tommy', mourned the loss of 'our poor friend.'[26] His students at UCD took the time to write a letter of condolence to Muriel, commenting:

[W]e beg to express our most sincere sympathy with you

on the loss of Mr MacDonagh. We too are very sorry to have lost him. Besides being an interesting lecturer, he was a kind friend – ever ready to help the students. We know he would always act nobly, and we are proud of him and the cause for which he died. [27]

Muriel, prone to depression, in regular ill-health, and caring for two small children, was devastated by the execution of her husband. As he had explained in his final letter to her, his finances were 'in a bad way.' Without any means of support and largely abandoned by her parents, she was unable to pay her mortgage and forced to leave the family home at 29 Oakley Road, staying first with the Plunketts at their Kimmage home and then in Thurles with her brother-in-law, Joseph. Returning to Dublin, she eventually settled at 50 Marlboro Road with the assistance of the Plunkett family, and was dependent on a fund administered by Tom Clarke's wife Kathleen, the Irish National Aid & Volunteer's Dependent Fund. Here her mother, Isabella, visited her and, while complaining about MacDonagh and his politics, offered Muriel £5. Muriel told her mother she was not going to accept any money from someone who spoke in a derogatory way about her husband.

Muriel's distress was further exasperated by MacDonagh's life insurance. Considering the circumstances of his death, the insurance company initially refused to pay out, and only after legal action was her claim successful. Taking MacDonagh's advice, Muriel, as his literary executor, had co-operated with David Houston on an anthology of his poetry. Published by Talbot Press, *The Poetical Works of Thomas MacDonagh* was introduced by James Stephens, who described his friend as 'a man in whom the instinct for friendship was so true, [and] one who was so prepared to use himself in the service of a friend'.[28] Stephens lauded MacDonagh's work as valuable, learned and worthwhile, noting:

> I will only say to his countrymen: here are the poems of a good man, and if outside of rebellion and violence, you wish to know what his thoughts were like, you will find all his thoughts here; and here more truly expressed than his public actions could tell it. You will find exactly what kind of man he was.[29]

As MacDonagh's final book was drawing a great deal of attention and helping to give Muriel a degree of normality in the aftermath of his execution, she decided to be baptised into Catholicism. This decision had largely come about through her friendship with her sister-in-law, Mary (Sr Francesca) and she converted from Anglicism in Easter 1917. This degree of normality was not to last, however.

In 1917 Muriel took Donagh and Barbara to Switzer's Department Store on Grafton Street. The National Aid Association had asked her if she would pose for a photograph with her children to be used as part of a pamphlet seeking to fundraise on behalf of dependents and prisoners. After the family had been photographed together, Donagh wandered away and fell down a flight of stairs, damaging his back. Rather than take him to hospital, Muriel cared for him in the family home. While he was recovering, Muriel was invited by the National Aid Association to go to Skerries in North County Dublin. Reluctant to leave Donagh, she was finally persuaded by her sister Grace to go. Eventually leaving Donagh in hospital, Muriel, Barbara, and Grace travelled to Skerries with Aine Ceannt, Lillie Connolly, her daughter Nora, and Nellie Gifford, among others. While there, she wrote to Fr Aloysius asking him to enquire about her son, and regularly sent postcards to Donagh in hospital.

On 9 July 1917 the ladies assembled on the south strand of Skerries Beach. Turning to Barbara, Muriel said, 'be a good girl now, Babbilly, and I'll be back soon.'[30] Getting undressed, Muriel entered the sea at 4.30pm. A champion swimmer, she set out to swim to Shenick Island, and when the group called for her to return she continued on and was pulled out by the strong tidal current. Barbara was taken away to a nearby house, while Grace and some of the women got several men together and found a boat, but it had no oars. They went its owner's house to commandeer them, but were refused by servants on account of their master not being home. Grace, however, speculated that they were refused help as they were known republicans, some of women wearing the emblem of

Cumann na mBan.

Muriel's body was found washed ashore the next day at 7.30am, less than a quarter of a mile from where she had gone swimming. According to an official examination, she had died of heart failure from exhaustion. As the body was taken away for a post-mortem to a nearby house, in the confusion Barbara went missing, and was later found crying outside the house where her mother lay.

Her death captured the public imagination. Nationalist Ireland had been unable to attend a funeral for the leaders of the Easter Rising, and Muriel MacDonagh's became a surrogate of sorts for those who wanted to express their detestation at the executions. Like the O'Donovan Rossa funeral in 1915, Muriel's service was organised by the IRB. Her coffin was draped in a tricolour flag and placed on an open hearse in advance of a public procession headed by a large body of Irish Volunteers. As the funeral party made its way from her home at Marlboro Road to the Pro-Cathedral on Marlborough Street, the hearse was followed by friends and family carrying wreaths. Arriving at the cathedral, Volunteers had assembled to marshal the crowd, which was estimated to have been in the thousands. Fred Allen of the IRB was in charge of the arrangements and had purchased a grave near to the resting place of Jeremiah O'Donovan Rossa in the Republican plot in Glasnevin.

Following the funeral mass, on 12 July 1917 Muriel was

removed to Glasnevin Cemetery. Tragically, Donagh was to unwell to attend his mother's funeral, but as the procession passed the hospital, he was picked up by a nurse who allowed him to look out the window. Looking down on the procession, the nurse told Donagh, 'That's your mammy going by.'[31] Donagh had lost both of his parents, and, compounding his tragedy, had been unable to say goodbye to either. In later life, both children were immensely proud of their parents' legacy: Barbara was a regular visitor to Cloughjordan and in 1966, on the fiftieth anniversary of the Rising, spoke of her father's great love for education, while Donagh wrote extensively about his father, even considering a biography about the man he was too young to have really known, saying of him:

> Thomas MacDonagh was a type which might be more common today had he lived, for he might have taught the young men of Ireland to bring, as he did, the wealth of classical study and the power of knowledge to their nationalism. A scholar, a poet, a musician, a dramatist, he was young and daring of mind, with the achievement of age still before him.[32]

NOTES

INTRODUCTION

1 Colum, Padraic, *Poems of the Irish Revolutionary Brotherhood* (Boston, 1916), p. xxviii.

2 Ibid, p. xxvi.

3 Ibid, p. xxvii.

4 The last statement of Thomas MacDonagh, written in Kilmainham Gaol, 2-3 May 1916, in MacLochlainn, Piaras F, *Last Words: Letters & Statements of the Leaders Executed After The Rising At Easter 1916* (Dublin, 1990), p. 60.

5 *The New York Times*, 7 May 1916.

6 Patsy McGarry, 'President reflects on 1916 Rising and its aftermath', *The Irish Times*, 9 April 2012.

CHAPTER 1

1 MacDonagh, Donagh, 'Thomas MacDonagh', *An Cosantóir*, 1945, p. 84.

2 'The Daily Life of a True Catholic – By a Convert', NLI Ms 10,858.

3 Williams, Roche, *In and Out of School: In The Home Of The MacDonaghs* (Tipperary, 1999), p. 60.

4 MacDonagh, Donagh, *Thomas MacDonagh* (undated), NLI Ms 33, 694/7.

5 Gifford, Sidney, *The Years Flew By* (Galway, 2000), p. 19.

6 TM, 'Knocknacree', quoted in Williams, Roche, *In and Out of School: In The Home Of The MacDonaghs* (Tipperary, 1999), p. 68.

7 TM, 'A Rule for Life', NLI MS 10,852.

8 Moody, TW, *Davitt and the Irish Revolution, (Oxford, 1982), p. 564.*

9 TM, *Literature in Ireland* (Dublin, 1916), p. 17.

10 Ibid.

11 TM to Dominick Hackett, 15 March 1909, NLI Ms, 22,934.

12 Wilson, Robert, *The Life and Times of Queen Victoria (London, 1900) p. 612.*

13 TM, *Literature in Ireland* (Dublin, 1916), p. 39.

14 Ibid, p. 17

15 Intermediate Education (Ireland) Commission: Final report of the commissioners, House of Commons Parliamentary paper, Vol. XXIII, c29060.

16 TM to Superior General Holy Ghost Fathers, May 1894, Blackrock College, Dublin.

17 'On Behalf of the Provisional Government', RTÉ TV programme, broadcast 1966.

18 TM, *Through the Ivory Gate* (Dublin, 1902), p. 10.

19 TM, 'Through The Night', *Through The Ivory Gate* (Dublin, 1902), p. 50.

20 Norstedt, Johann, *Thomas MacDonagh: A Critical Biography* (Virginia, USA, 1980), pp. 19-20.

21 TM, 'A Withered Flower', *Through The Ivory Gate* (Dublin, 1902), p. 40.

22 TM, 'De Mortuis', *Through The Ivory Gate* (Dublin, 1902), p. 32.

23 TM, 'Monody on Frederick Ransot', quoted in Norstedt, Johann, *Thomas MacDonagh: A Critical Biography* (Virginia, 1980), p. 21. There was no student called Frederick Ransot in Rockwell, so the name must be an invention.

24 TM to Superior General Holy Ghost Fathers, May 1894, Blackrock College, Dublin.

27 TM to Superior General Holy Ghost Fathers, 22 June 1901, Blackrock College, Dublin.

28 TM, 'The Parting', *Through The Ivory Gate* (Dublin, 1902), p. 107.

29 Parks, Edd Winfield and Aileen Wells, *Thomas MacDonagh: The Man, The Patriot, The Writer* (Georgia, USA, 1967), pp. 6-7.

CHAPTER 2

1 Rice, Gerald, 'Thomas MacDonagh *1878-1916*', *St Kieran's College Record 1966 (Kilkenny, 1966), p. 9.

2 Hyde, Douglas, 'The Necessity for De-Anglicising Ireland', delivered to the Irish National Literary Society in Dublin, 25 November 1892.

3 Ryan, Desmond, *Remembering Sion* (London, 1934), p. 95.

4 Norstedt, Johann, *Thomas MacDonagh: A Critical Biography* (Virginia, USA, 1980), p. 26.

5 *The Kilkenny Journal,* 24 January 1903.

6 Ibid.

7 Rice, Gerald, 'Thomas MacDonagh *1878-1916'*, *St Kieran's College Record 1966 (Kilk-enny, 1966), p.12.*

8 *The Kilkenny Journal*, 6 June 1903.

9 Rice, Gerald, ' Thomas MacDonagh 1878-1916', *St Kieran's College Record 1966 (Kilk-enny, 1966), p.13.*

10 TM to Dominick Hackett, 10 June 1903, NLI Ms, 22,934.

11 MacDonagh, Donagh, 'Thomas MacDonagh' in *An Cosantóir*, 1945, p. 527. 'Malbrouc se va t'en guerre' was a popular French folk song about the supposed death of the Duke of Marlborough after the Battle of Malplaquet in 1709.

12 *The Weekly Freeman*, 22 July 1916.

13 Parks, Edd Winfield and Aileen Wells, *Thomas MacDonagh: The Man, The Patriot, The Writer* (Georgia, USA, 1967), p. 76.

14 TM to Dominick Hackett, 23 September 1903, NLI Ms 22,934.

15 TM to Dominick Hackett, 2 August 1903, NLI Ms 22,934.

16 TM to Dominick Hackett, 24 December 1904, NLI Ms 22,934.

17 TM to Padraig MacSuibhne, 25 August 1905, UCC BL/P/TMC/4(1)

18 TM to Dominick Hackett, 5 February 1904, Ms 22,934.

19 TM, *The Golden Joy* (Dublin, 1906).

20 Clippings of newspaper reviews, NLI Ms 10, 857/1.

21 *The Freeman's Journal*, 25 May 1907.

22 Clippings of newspaper reviews, NLI Ms 10, 857/1.

23 Norstedt, Johann, *Thomas MacDonagh: A Critical Biography* (Virginia, USA, 1980), p. 51.

24 TM diary entry, 11 September 1904, quoted in Norstedt, Johann, *Thomas MacDonagh: A Critical Biography* (Virginia, 1980), p. 52.

25 TM to Dominick Hackett, 5 May 1908, NLI Ms 22,934.

26 Norstedt, Johann, *Thomas MacDonagh: A Critical Biography* (Virginia, 1980), p. 55.

27 TM to Dominick Hackett, 27 February 1908 NLI Ms 22,934.

28 WB Yeats to TM, 3 December 1907, NLI Ms 44,332/1

29 JM Synge to TM, 30 March 1908, quoted in Parks, Edd Winfield and Aileen Wells, *Thomas MacDonagh: The Man, The Patriot, The Writer* (Georgia, USA, 1967), p. 102.

30 TM to Dominick Hackett, 27 January 1908, NLI Ms 22,934.

CHAPTER 3

1 McGee, Owen, *The IRB: The Irish Republican Brotherhood from the Land League to Sinn Féin* (Dublin, 2005), p. 317.

2 Jackson, Alvin, *Home Rule: An Irish History 1800–2000* (London, 2003), p. 112.

3 TM to Dominick Hackett, 15 March 1909, NLI Ms 22,934.

4 Kelly, MJ, *The Fenian Ideal and Irish Nationalism 1882–1916 (Woodbridge, 2006), p. 15.*

5 Griffith, Arthur, *The Resurrection of Hungary* (Dublin, 1918), p. 139.

6 Griffith, Arthur, *The Resurrection of Hungary* (Dublin, 1918), p.161.

7 TM to Dominick Hackett, 4 May 1909, NLI Ms 22,934.

8 Ibid.

9 Ibid.

10 TM to Dominick Hackett, 15 March 1909, NLI Ms 22,934.

11 The evidence of John Cooke in *Report on housing conditions of the working classes in the City of Dublin, Parliamentary Papers 1914, Vol. 19 CD 7317, pp. 101-2.*

12 Sheehy Skeffington, Hannah, Irish Secondary Teachers, *The Irish Review*, Vol. 2. No. 20, October 1912, p. 397.

13 Farrell, Brian, 'Markievicz and the Women of the Revolution' in Martin, FX (ed.), *Leaders and Men of the Easter Rising: Dublin 1916* (London, 1967), p. 229.

14 Quoted in Levenson, Samuel, *Maud Gonne* (London, 1976), pp. 169-170.

15 Smith, Bonnie G, *Changing Lives: Women in European History since 1700* (Massachusetts, USA, 1989), p. 383.

16 F. Cruise O'Brien, *The Leader,* 13 March 1909.

17 TM to Dominick Hackett, 9 November 1908, NLI Ms 22,934.

18 *The Irish Times,* 31 January 1910.

19 *The Leader,* 13 March 1909.

20-27 Ibid.

28 TM to Padraig MacSuibine, 25 October 1908, UCC BL/P/TMD/13 (1).

29 An Claidheamh Soluis, quoted in Ruth Dudley Edwards, Patrick Pearse: The Triumph of Failure (Dublin, 2006), p. 115.

30 Scoil Éanna Prospectus 1908-1909, Pearse Museum PMSTE.

31 TM to Padraig MacSuibhne, 18 December 1908, BL/P/TMD/16 (1).

32 Ibid.

33 TM to Dominick Hackett, 4 May 1909, NLI Ms 22,934.

34 Milo McGarry, interviewed in RTÉ in On Behalf of the Provisional Government (1966).

35 Gifford, Sidney, *The Years Flew By* (Galway, 2000), pp. 19-20.

36 Sean Dowling, interviewed in This Man Kept a School, RTÉ Radio 1, 1978.

37 Quoted in This Man Kept a School, RTÉ Radio 1, 1978.

38 Ibid.

39 Gifford, Sidney, *The Years Flew By* (Galway, 2000), p. 26.

40 Ibid, p. 20.

41 Ibid, p. 19.

42 Sidney Gifford, interviewed in RTÉ in On Behalf of the Provisional Government (1966).

43 Ibid.

44 *The Irish Times*, 15 October 1908.

45 Quoted in Norstedt, Johann, *Thomas MacDonagh: A Critical Biography* (Virginia, USA, 1980), p. 58.

46 Unknown newspaper, NLI Ms 44,340/6.

47 Holloway, Joseph, Joseph Holloway's Abbey Theatre - A Selection of His Unpublished Journal 'Impressions of a Dublin Playgoer' (Illinois, USA, 1967), p. 168.

48 *The Irish Times*, 16 October 1908.

49 TM to Dominick Hackett, 5 November 1908, NLI Ms 22,934.

50 TM to Dominick Hackett, 9 November 1908, NLI Ms 22,934.

51 TM to Dominick Hackett, 5 November 1908, NLI Ms 22,934; see also TM to Padraig MacSuibhne, 20 October 1908, UCC BL/P/TMD/12 (1).

52 TM to Padraig MacSuibhne, 20 October 1908, BL/P/TMD/12(1).

53 TM to Dominick Hackett, 5 November 1908, NLI Ms 22,934.

54 TM to Padraig MacSuibhne, 20 November 1908, BL/P/TMD/14.

55 TM to Dominick Hackett, 9 November 1908, NLI Ms 22,934; see also TM to Padraig MacSuibhne, 8 December 1908, BL/P/TMD/15 (1).

56 TM to Padraig MacSuibhne, 8 November 1908, BL/P/TMD/15 (1).

57 TM to Dominick Hackett, 21 November 1908, NLI Ms 22,934.

58 TM to Dominick Hackett, 5 November 1908, NLI Ms 22,934.

59 WB Yeats, Autobiographies, quoted in Norstedt, Johann, TM: A Critical Biography (Virginia, USA, 1980), p. 66.

60 Ibid, pp. 66-7.

CHAPTER 4

1 Quoted in Parks, Edd Winfield and Aileen Wells, *Thomas MacDonagh: The Man, The Patriot, The Writer* (Georgia, USA, 1967), p. 23.

2 TP's Weekly, 9 April 1909.

3 Declan Kilberd 'Inventing Ireland', quoted in Ferriter, Diarmuid, *The Transformation of Ireland* (London, 2005), p. 95.

4 TM, *Literature in Ireland* (Dublin, 1916), p. 55.

5 *The Leader*, 8 January 1910.

6 Ibid.

7 Colum, Mary, *Life and The Dream* (New York, 1947), pp. 174-5.

8-10 Ibid.

11 Dillon, Geraldine Plunkett, *All In The Blood* (Dublin, 2006), p. 136

12 MacDonagh, Thomas, 'Year After Year', *The Poetical Works of Thomas MacDonagh* (Dublin, 1916), p. 8.

13 TM to Gertrude Bloomer, 17 June 1910, NLI Ms 8903.

14 TM to Dominick Hackett, 29 March 1911, NLI Ms 22,934.

15 Ibid.

16 MacDonagh, Donagh, 'Thomas MacDonagh' *An Cosantóir*, 1945, p. 527.

17 Ibid.

18 TM to Dominick Hackett, 29 March 1911, NLI Ms 22,934.

19 Ibid.

20 Norstedt, Johann, Thomas MacDonagh: A Critical Biography (Virginia, 1980), p. 80.

21 TM to Dominick Hackett, 29 March 1911, NLI Ms 22,934.

22 Ibid.

23 Ibid.

24 James Stephens, *The Poetical Works of Thomas MacDonagh* (Dublin, 1916), p. xi.

25 TM to Dominick Hackett, 29 March 1911 NLI Ms 22,934.

26 Ibid.

27 Ibid.

28 The Irish Times, 8 July 1911.

29 Aine Ceannt, BMH WS 264, p.5.

30 Irish Independent, 9 July 1911.

31 Sidney Gifford, BMH WS 909, p.7.

32 Irish Independent, 9 July 1911.

33 Ibid.

34 *The Irish Review*, February 1912, Vol. 1, No. 12, p. 585.

35 Norstedt, Johann, *Thomas MacDonagh: A Critical Biography* (Virginia, USA, 1980), p. 85.

36 TM to Dominick Hackett, 5 November 1911, NLI Ms, 22,934.

37 Ibid.

38 *The Irish Independent*, 19 April 1912.

39 Ibid.

40 Norstedt, Johann, *Thomas MacDonagh: A Critical Biography* (Virginia, USA, 1980), p. 88.

41 Dillon, Geraldine Plunkett, *All In The Blood* (Dublin, 2006), p. 107.

42 Quoted in Parks, Edd Winfield and Aileen Wells, *Thomas MacDonagh: The Man, The Patriot, The Writer* (Georgia, USA, 1967), p. 23.

43 TM, *Thomas Campion and the Art of English Poetry* (Dublin, 1913), p. vii.

44 TM to Dominick Hackett, 5 November 1911, NLI Ms 22,934.

45 Quoted in Parks, Edd Winfield and Aileen Wells, *Thomas MacDonagh: The Man, The Patriot, The Writer* (Athens, 1967), p. 89.

46 Norstedt, Johann, *Thomas MacDonagh: A Critical Biography* (Virginia, USA, 1980), p. 75.

47 TM, *Songs of Myself* (Dublin, 1910), p. 10.

48 *The Irish Times*, 16 December 1910.

49 Colum, Padraic, *The Irish Review,* Vol. 1, No. 1 (March 1911), p. 48.

50 TM, *Songs of Myself* (Dublin, 1910), pp. 51-2.

51 TM to Dominick Hackett, 5 November 1911, NLI Ms 22,934.

52 Recollection of Mary MacDonagh, undated, NLI Ms 44,336/2.

53 Muriel Gifford to TM, 3 October 1911, NLI Ms 44,320/2.

54 Muriel Gifford to TM, 13 October 1911, NLI Ms 44,320/2.

52 Muriel Gifford to TM, 8 October 1911, NLI Ms 44,320/2.

53 TM to Muriel Gifford, undated, 1911, NLI MS 44,319/7.

54 Muriel Gifford to TM, 25 October 1911, NLI Ms 44,320/2.

55 Muriel Gifford to TM, 23 November 1911, NLI Ms 44,320/3.

56 TM to Dominick Hackett, 5 November 1912, NLI Ms 22,934.

57 TM to Dominick Hackett, 8 January 1912, NLI Ms 22,934.

58 TM to Muriel Gifford, 2 January 1912, NLI Ms 44,318/3.

59 TM to Dominick Hackett, 5 November 1911, NLI Ms 22,934.

60 Parks, Edd Winfield and Aileen Wells, *Thomas MacDonagh: The Man, The Patriot, The Writer* (Georgia, USA, 1967), p. 30.

61 TM, 'The Song of Joy', *The Poetical Works of Thomas MacDonagh* (Dublin, 1916), p. 14.

62 TM, 'Wishes for My Son', *The Poetical Works of Thomas MacDonagh* (Dublin, 1916), p. 127.

63 Gifford, Sidney, *The Years Flew By* (Galway, 2000), p. 19.

CHAPTER 5

1 David Houston to TM, 19 June 1913, NLI Ms 10,854.

2 Padraic Colum to TM, 20 June 1913, NLI Ms 10,854.

3 *The Irish Review*, Vol. 3. No. 29, July 1913, p. 220.

4 Ibid, p. 224.

5 Ibid, p. 225.

6 Gifford, Sidney, *The Years Flew By* (Dublin, 2000), p. 63.

7 *The Irish Times*, 7 January 1914.

8 The evidence of TM to the Askwith Inquiry, *The Irish Times*, 7 January 1914.

9 Connolly, James, 'Labour in Dublin', *The Irish Review*, Vol. 3 No. 32, October 1913, p.

386.

10 Ibid, p. 391

11 Kettle, Thomas, 'The Agony of Dublin', *The Irish Review*, Vol. 3. No. 33, November 1913, p. 442.

12 *Irish Independent*, 8 October 1913.

13 Ibid.

14 TM, *The Freeman's Journal*, 18 October 1913.

15 James Bertram 'Liberty under Capitalism' in *The Irish Review*, Vol. 3, No. 32, October 1913, p. 395.

16 Forward, 7 February 1914.

17 TM 'Of My Poems', *Lyrical Poems*, (Dublin, 1913), p. 2.

18 Norstedt, Johann, *Thomas MacDonagh: A Critical Biography* (Virginia, USA, 1980), p. 107.

19 TM to Muriel Gifford, 3 February 1913, quoted in Norstedt, Johann, *Thomas MacDonagh: A Critical Biography* (Virginia, USA, 1980), p. 2.

20 TM 'Of My Poems', *Lyrical Poems*, (Dublin, 1913), p. 82.

21 *The Athenaeum*, 28 February 1914.

22 Ibid.

23 *The Expository Times*, April 1914.

24 *The Irish Homestead*, 20 December 1913.

25 *The Academy*, February 1914.

26 Ibid.

27 TM to Dominick Hackett, 15 January 1914, NLI Ms 22,934.

28 Ibid.

29 Dillon, Geraldine Plunkett, *All In The Blood* (Dublin, 2006), p. 172.

30 Martyn, Edward, 'A Plea for the Revival of The Irish Literary Theatre', *The Irish Review*, Vol. 4, No. 38, April 1914, p. 83.

31 Agreement for the Foundation and Maintenance of a Partnership for the Irish Theatre Company between Edward Martyn, TM and Joseph Plunkett, 30 June 1914, NLI Ms 17,301.

32 Ibid.

33 Parks, Edd Winfield and Aileen Wells, *Thomas MacDonagh: The Man, The Patriot, The Writer* (Georgia, USA, 1967), p. 30.

34 Feeney, William J, *Drama in Hardwicke Street* (London, 1984), p. 51.

35 Joseph Mary Plunkett to TM, 20 June 1912, NLI Ms 44,329/1.

36 Ibid.

37 *The Irish Times*, 2 November 1914.

38 Feeney, William J, *Drama in Hardwicke Street* (London, 1984), p. 61.

39 *The Freeman's Journal*, 3 November 1914.

40 *The Irish Times*, 3 November 1914.

41 Holloway, Joseph, *Joseph Holloway's Abbey Theatre: A Selection from his Unpublished Journal* 'Impressions of a Dublin Playgoer' (Illinois, 1967), p. 168.

42 Feeney, William J, *Drama in Hardwicke Street* (London, 1984), p. 67.

43 *The Irish Times*, 5 January 1915.

44 *Irish Independent*, 4 January 1915.

45 Ibid.

46 Feeney, William J, *Drama in Hardwicke Street* (London, 1984), p. 71.

47 Ibid, p. 97.

48 *The Freeman's Journal*, 29 June 1915.

49 – 52 Ibid.

53 *Irish Independent*, quoted in Feeney, William J, Drama in Hardwicke Street (London, 1984), p. 100.

54 RTÉ Documentary on One: The Turret Room – Edward Martyn (radio programme, broadcast April 1956).

CHAPTER 6

1 Cavendish, Richard, 'The House of Lords rejects the 1909 People's Budget', *History Today*, Vol. 59, No. 11, 2009.

2 TM to Dominick Hackett, 29 March 1911, NLI Ms 22,934.

3 Blake, Robert, *The Unknown Prime Minister* (London, 1955), p. 130.

4 Ibid.

5 *The Penny Illustrated Paper*, 22 March 1913.

6 *The Times*, 5 November 1913.

7 *The Times*, 6 October 1913.

8 'The North Began,' *An Claidheamh Soluis*, 1 November 1913.

9 *The Irish Times*, 26 November 1913.

10 TM to Dominick Hackett, 15 January 1914 NLI Ms 22,934.

11 TM 'Marching Song of The Volunteers,' *The Irish Review*, Vol. 3, No.34, December 1913, pp. 500- 502.

12 Quoted in Norstedt, Johann, *Thomas MacDonagh: A Critical Biography* (Virginia, USA, 1980), p. 120.

13 TM to Dominick Hackett, 15 January 1914, NLI Ms 22,934.

14 Quoted in Parks, Edd Winfield and Aileen Wells, *Thomas MacDonagh: The Man, The Patriot, The Writer* (Georgia, USA, 1967), p. 41.

15 *The Derry Journal*, 20 April 1914.

16 TM to Muriel MacDonagh, 19 April 1914, NLI Ms 44,319/4.

17 John Redmond to Eoin MacNeill, 21 May 1914, quoted in Joseph P Finnan, *John Redmond and Irish Unity: 1912 – 1918* (New York, 2004), p. 137.

18 Hobson, John Bulmer, *A Short History of The Irish Volunteers* (Dublin, 1918), p. 128.

19 TM, 'Clontarf 1914,' The Irish Review, Vol. 4, No. 41, July- August 1914, supplement unnumbered.

20 Ibid.

21 Hobson, John Bulmer, *A Short History of The Irish Volunteers* (Dublin, 1918), p. 155.

22 Martin, FX (ed.), 'The Howth Gun Running and the Kilcoole Gun Running, 1914,' *The Irish Volunteers 1913-1915: Recollections and Documents* (Dublin, 1964), pp. 156-57.

23 Dillon, Geraldine, 'The Howth Gun Running,' *The University Review*, Vol. 3 No. 4, Spring 1964, p. 49.

24 TM 'Clontarf 1914,' in *The Irish Review*, Vol. 4, No.41, July- August 1914, Supplement unnumbered.

25 Dillon, Geraldine, The Howth Gun Running,' in *The University Review*, Vol. 3, No. 4, Spring 1964, p. 50.

26 De Burca, Seamus, *The Soldier's Song: The Story of Peadar O Cearnaigh* (Dublin, 1957), p. 100.

27 *Irish Independent*, 29 July 1914.

28 *The Ulster Herald*, 1 August 1914.

29 *The Freeman's Journal*, 30 July 1914.

30 *The Irish Times*, 24 June 1914.

31 TM to Dominick Hackett, 19 May 1915, NLI Ms 22,934.

32 Gwynn, Stephen, *John Redmond's Last Years* (London, 1919), p. 94.

33 *The Irish Times*, 26 September 1914.

34 'Manifesto to the Irish Volunteers', Thursday 24 September 1914, *The Irish Review,* Vol. 4, No. 42, September–November 1914, p. 282.

35 Ibid.

36 *The Irish Volunteer*, 14 November 1914.

37 Ibid, 21 November 1914.

38 Ibid.

CHAPTER 7

1 TM to Dominick Hackett, 15 January 1914, NLI Ms 22,934.

2 *The Irish Volunteer*, 26 December 1914.

3 TM to Dominick Hackett, 19 May 1915, NLI Ms 22,934.

4 Donagh MacDonagh, TM, NLI Ms 33,694/F.

5 The Irish Volunteer, 17 April 1915.

6 Frank Henderson, BMH WS 249, p 21.

7 Ibid, p 20.

8 Ibid, p.21

9 Liam Tannan, BMH WS 242 p. 4.

10 Joseph Lawless, BMH WS 1043, P. 37.

11 *The Irish Volunteer*, 12 December 1914.

12 *The Irish Volunteer*, 10 April 1915.

13 *The Irish Volunteer*, 3 April 1915.

14 Thomas J Meldon, BMH WS 734, p. 5.

15 Norstedt, Johann, *Thomas MacDonagh: A Critical Biography* (Virginia, USA, 1980), p. 139.

16 MacDonagh, *Pagans* (Dublin, 1920), p.38.

17 Ibid, p. 40.

18 Norstedt, Johann, *Thomas MacDonagh: A Critical Biography* (Virginia, USA, 1980), p. 131.

19 *The Irish Citizen*, 22 May 1915.

20 – 30 Ibid.

31 Sheehy Skeffington, Francis, 'An Open Letter to Thomas MacDonagh, 22 May 1915', Hannah Sheehy Skeffington Collection, NLI Ms 33,623 (14).

32 – 34 Ibid.

35 TM to Dominick Hackett, 19 May 1915, NLI Ms 22,934.

36 Ibid.

37 Colum, Mary, *Life and The Dream* (New York, 1947), p. 238.

38 Devoy, John, *Recollections of an Irish Rebel* (New York, 1929), p. 323.

39 *The Irish Times*, 30 June 1915.

40 Devoy, John, *Recollections of an Irish Rebel* (New York, 1929), p. 319.

41 Ibid.

42 Connolly, James, 'Why The Citizen Army Honours Rossa,' O'Donovan Rossa Funeral Souvenir Handbook (Dublin, 1915), p. 6.

43 Griffith, Arthur, 'The Influence of Fenianism,' O'Donovan Rossa Funeral Souvenir Handbook (Dublin, 1915), p. 14.

44 Mrs Eileen O'Donovan Rossa McGowan to the editor of *The Straits Times*, 8 March 1956, NLI Ms 10,974 (iii).

45 Pearse, Patrick, 'A Character Study,' O'Donovan Rossa Funeral Souvenir Handbook (Dublin, 1915), p. 19.

46 Pearse, Patrick, 'Graveside Panegyric,' O'Donovan Rossa Funeral Souvenir Handbook (Dublin, 1915), p. 2.

47 TM, 'The Irish Volunteers in 1915,' O'Donovan Rossa Funeral Souvenir Handbook (Dublin, 1915), p. 9.

48 John MacDonagh, BMH WS 532, p. 2

49 Pearse, Patrick, 'Graveside Panegyric' in O'Donovan Rossa Funeral Souvenir Handbook (Dublin, 1915), p. 3.

50 *Irish Independent*, 2 August 1915.

CHAPTER 8

1 *Irish Independent*, 31 March 1916.

2 *The Irish Volunteer*, 29 January 1916.

3 Ibid.

4 *The Irish Volunteer*, 19 February 1916.

5 *The Irish Volunteer*, 26 February 1916.

6 Donal O'Hannigan, BMH WS 161, p. 8.

7 *The Irish Volunteer*, 15 April 1916.

8 Donal O'Hannigan, BMH WS 161, p. 34

9 Ibid, p. 33

10 *The Irish Volunteer*, 22 April 1916.

11 Ibid.

12 Aine Ceannt, BMH WS 264, p. 16.

13 Oscar Traynor, BMH WS 340, p. 3.

14 Secret information respecting the Sinn Féiners, TNA CO 904/23.

15 Clarke, Austin, *A Penny in the Clouds* (London, 1968), p. 25.

16 Kitty O'Doherty, BMH WS 355, p. 4.

17 Ibid.

18 Aine Ceannt, BMH WS 264, p. 17.

19 Michael Staines, BMH WS 284, p. 7.

20 Ibid.

21 Secret information respecting Sinn Féin Volunteers, Detective Department, 22 April 1916 TNA CO 904/23/3.

22 Undated memorandum by Eoin MacNeill, Eoin MacNeill papers, NLI Ms 43,228.

23 Martin, FX, 'Eoin MacNeill on the 1916 Rising', *Irish Historical Studies*, Vol. 12, No. 47, March 1961, p. 258.

24 *The Irish Volunteer*, 22 April 1916.

25 Undated memorandum by Eoin MacNeill, Eoin MacNeill papers, NLI Ms 43,228.

26 Aine Ceannt, BMH WS 264, p. 20.

27 Ibid.

28 Undated memorandum by Eoin MacNeill, Eoin MacNeill papers, NLI Ms 43,228.

29 John MacDonagh, BMH WS 532, p. 7

30 Ibid.

31 Martin, FX, 'Eoin MacNeill on the 1916 Rising', *Irish Historical Studies*, Vol. 12, No. 47, March 1961, p. 267.

32 Ibid.

33 Dr Seamus O'Kelly, BMH WS 471, p. 7.

34 John MacDonagh, BMH WS 532, p. 8.

35 Sean Fitzgibbon 'The Easter Rising from the Inside', *The Irish Times* 19 April 1949.

36 Copy, TM statement, written 23 April 1916, NLI MacNeill Papers, Ms 43,228.

CHAPTER 9

1 Tom Slater BMH WS 263, p. 5, and Seán Murphy, BMH WS 0263 pp. 13–14.

2 Tom Slater BMH WS 263, p. 15.

3 Dillon, Geraldine Plunkett, *All In The Blood* (Dublin, 2006), p. 223.

4 Vinnie Byrne, BMH WS 423, p. 2.

5 John MacDonagh in McGarry, Feargal, *Rebels: Voices from the Easter Rising* (London, 2011), p. 154.

6 Ryan, Desmond, *The Rising: The Complete Story of Easter Week*, 3rd ed. (Dublin, 1957), p. 164.

7 Foy, Michael and Barton Brian, *The Easter Rising 1916* (Sutton, 1999, Kindle DX edition]

8 John MacDonagh, BMH WS 532, p. 10.

9 Quoted in Ó Maitiú, Seamus, *W&R Jacob: Celebrating 150 Years of Irish Biscuit Making* (Dublin, 2001), p. 43.

10 Ibid, pp. 42–3.

11 Vinnie Byrne, BMH WS 423, p. 3.

12 Foy, Michael and Barton Brian, *The Easter Rising 1916* (Sutton, 1999), p. 40.

13 Seosamh de Brun, BMH WS 312, p. 7.

14 Ibid, p. 8.

15 John MacDonagh, BMH WS 532, p. 11.

16 John MacDonagh, BMH WS 532, p. 11.

17 Seamus Pounch, BMH WS 267, p. 11.

18 Seosamh de Brun, BMH WS 312, p. 3.

19 William James Stapleton BMH WS 822, p. 5.

20 Martin Walton, in Kenneth Griffith and Timothy O'Grady, *Curious Journey: An Oral History of Ireland's Unfinished Revolution* (Cork, 1998), p. 58.

21 Vinnie Byrne, BMH WS 423, p. 5.

22 William James Stapleton, BMH WS 822, p. 7.

23 Vinnie Byrne, BMH WS 423, p. 6.

24 Ibid.

CHAPTER 10

1 Fr Aloysius in McGarry, Feargal, *Rebels: Voices from the Easter Rising* (London, 2011), p. 355.

2 Christopher Brady BMH WS 705, p. 4.

3 Seosamh de Brun, BMH WS 312, pp. 6-7.

4 Ibid, p. 7.

5 Ibid, p. 7.

6 Ibid, p. 10.

7 William James Stapleton BMH WS 822, p. 6.

8 Ibid, p. 7.

9 Peader Kearney, TCD MS 3560.

10 Seamus Pounch, BMH WS 267, p. 15.

11 Seosamh de Brun, BMH WS 312, p. 11.

12 William Oman, BMH WS 421, P. 10.

13 Bateson, Ray, *They Died By Pearse's Side* (Dublin, 2010), p. 155.

14 Seosamh de Brun, BMH WS 312, p. 9.

15 John MacDonagh, BMH WS 532, p. 2.

16 Ibid, p. 13.

17 Seosamh de Brun, BMH WS 312, p. 11.

18 Kearney, Peadar, 'Personal Narrative of Easter Week,' in De Burca, Seamus, *The Soldier's Song: The Story of Peadar O Cearnaigh* (Dublin, 1957), p. 126.

19 Padraig Ó Ceallaigh, BMH WS 376, p. 4.

20 Seosamh de Brun, BMH WS 312, p.14.

21 Ibid, p.13.

22 – 24 Ibid.

25 De Burca, Seamus, *The Soldier's Song: The Story of Peadar O Cearnaigh* (Dublin, 1957), p. 108.

26 Kearney, Peadar, 'Personal Narrative of Easter Week,' in De Burca, Seamus, *The Soldier's Song: The Story of Peadar O Cearnaigh* (Dublin, 1957), p. 119.

27 John MacDonagh BMH WS 532, p. 16.

28 Kearney, Peadar, 'Personal Narrative of Easter Week,' in De Burca, Seamus, *The Soldier's Song: The Story of Peadar O Cearnaigh* (Dublin, 1957), p. 120.

29 Fr Aloysius, BMH WS 200, p. 6.

30 Liam Roache, BMH WS 1698, p. 146

31 Fr Aloysius, BMH WS 200, p. 7 and Fr Augustine BMH WS 920, p. 10.

32 Liam Roache, BMH WS 1698, p. 146.

33 Ibid.

34 Fr Aloysius, BMH WS 200, p. 7.

35 Fr Augustine, BMH WS 920, p. 12.

36 Fr Aloysius, BMH WS 200, p. 8.

37 Barton, Brian, *The Secret Court Martial Records of the 1916 Easter Rising* (Gloucestershire, 2014), p. 125

38 John MacDonagh, BMH WS 532, p. 18.

39 Joseph Furlong, BMH WS, 335 p. 8

40 Eamon Price, BMH WS 995, p. 10.

41 Ibid.

42 William James Stapleton, BMH WS 882, p. 9.

43 Quoted in Foy, Michael and Barton Brian, *The Easter Rising 1916* (Sutton, 1999.), p.

95.

44 Ibid.

45 Kearney, Peadar, 'Personal Narrative of Easter Week,' in De Burca, Seamus, *The Soldier's Song: The Story of Peadar O Cearnaigh* (Dublin, 1957), p. 127

46 Thomas J Meldon, BMH WS 7034, p. 28.

47 Ibid, p. 128.

48 Kearney, Peadar, 'Personal Narrative of Easter Week,' in De Burca, Seamus, *The Soldier's Song: The Story of Peadar O Cearnaigh* (Dublin, 1957), p. 128.

49 Quoted in Foy, Michael and Barton Brian, *The Easter Rising 1916* (Sutton, 1999.), p. 95.

50 Fr Augustine, BMH WS 920, p. 13.

51 Clare, Anne, *Unlikely Rebels: The Gifford Girls and the Fight for Irish Freedom* (Cork, 2011), p. 161.

52 Michael Walker, BMH WS 139, p. 7.

53 Thomas Pugh, BMH WS 397, p. 7.

CHAPTER 11

1 Fr Augustine, BMH WS 920, p. 14.

2 Ibid, p. 15.

3 Quoted in Foy, Michael and Barton Brian, *The Easter Rising 1916* (Sutton, 1999), p. 149.

4 Quoted in Ó Maitiú, Seamus, *W&R Jacob: Celebrating 150 Years of Irish Biscuit Making* (Dublin, 2001), p. 46.

5 Ibid.

6 List of demands made by TM whilst jailed in Richmond Barracks, 1 May 1916 CA/IR/1/2/2.

7 John MacDonagh BMH WS 532, p. 15.

8 TM, offence armed rebellion, prosecution witness statement, TNA WO 71/346.

9 Ibid.

10 Barton, Brian, *The Secret Court Martial Records of the 1916 Easter Rising* (Gloucester-shire, 2014), p. 127.

11 Ibid, p. 128.

12 Memorandum by General Sir Henry Maxwell, 11 May 1916, Asquith Papers, Bodleian Library, Oxford BL MS 43/26-33.

13 Wylie, William, quoted in Barton, Brian, *The Secret Court Martial Records of the 1916 Easter Rising* (Gloucestershire, 2014), pp. 128-29.

14 Extract copy taken from the printed sheet: 'Last and Inspiring Address of Thomas MacDonagh', UCC BL/P/TMD/26 (1-5).

15 John MacDonagh BMH WS 532, p. 15.

16 MacDonagh, Donagh, 'Thomas MacDonagh' in *An Cosantóir*, 1945, p. 533.

17 *The Freeman's Journal*, 30 June 1916.

18 Ibid.

19 Ibid.

20 *The Irish Times*, 1 July 1916.

21 Fr Aloysius, BMH WS 200, p. 13.

22 Statement of Mary MacDonagh, TM Papers, MS 44, 336/2.

23 – 25 Ibid.

26 Parks, Edd Winfield and Aileen Wells, Thomas MacDonagh: The Man, The Patriot, The Writer (Georgia, USA, 1967), p. 70.

27 Fr Aloysius, BMH WS 200, p. 14.

28 MacDonagh, Donagh, 'Thomas MacDonagh' in *An Cosantoir*, 1945, p. 534.

29 *The Irish Press*, 9 July 1969.

30 The last statement of Thomas MacDonagh, written in Kilmainham Gaol, 2 - 3 May 1916, in MacLochlainn, Piaras F., *Last Words: Letters & Statements of the Leaders Executed After The Rising At Easter 1916* (Dublin, 1990), p. 61.

31 Ibid, p. 62-3.

32 Ibid, p. 60.

33 BMH WS 189, p. 4.

34 Redmond, Lucille, quoted at http://heatseekers.blogspot.ie/2008/07/people-of-1916.html

35 Ibid.

36 Raybould, A, 'Thomas MacDonagh' in *The Irish Monthly*, Vol. 47. No 555, Sept. 1919.

CHAPTER 12

1 Churchill, Winston, *The World Crisis: The Aftermath* (London, 1929), p. 281.

2 *The New York Times*, 12 May 1916.

3–4 Ibid

5 John Dillon in the House of Commons, 11 May 1916, in *Great Irish Speeches* (Dublin, 1996).

6 Text of speech at wreathlaying and poetry reading in memory of Francis Ledwidge by Padraig Yeates, National War Memorial Gardens, Islandbridge, Dublin, August 4th, 2013.

7 Cooke, Pat, 'The Unrevised Stereotype: Thomas MacDonagh and the 1916 Rising' in *The Graph* 1996 Vol. 2 No. 2. p. 124.

8 Cleary, Arthur E. 'Pearse, MacDonagh and Plunkett, An Appreciation' in *The Irish Quarterly Review*, Vol. 6., No. 32, July 1917, p.215 and p. 220.

9 Ibid, p. 219.

10 Raybould, A, 'Thomas MacDonagh' in *The Irish Monthly*, Vol. 47, No. 555, September 1919, p. 476.

11 Ibid.

12 Ibid, p. 219.

13 TM, *Literature in Ireland* (Dublin, 1916), p. 39.

14 *The Irish Times*, 21 Jun 2005.

15 TM, *Literature in Ireland* (Dublin, 1916), p. viii (see also TM to Dominick Hackett, 19 January 1914, NLI Ms 10,854).

16 Ibid, p. 23.

17 Ibid.

18 Ibid, p. 38.

19 Pearse, Patrick, 'Graveside Panegyric' in O'Donovan Rossa Funeral Souvenir Handbook (Dublin, 1915), p. 4.

20 *Studies*, 7 September 1916, Vol. 5 No. 19, p. 464

21 Ibid, p. 465.

22 Cooke, Pat, 'The Unrevised Stereotype: Thomas MacDonagh and the 1916 Rising',

The Graph, Vol. 2 No. 2. 1996, p. 125.

23 Pound, Ezra, 'TM as a Critic in Poetry' Vol. 8, No. 6 September 1916, p. 309.

24 Ibid, p. 312.

25 MacDonagh, John, 'Edward Martyn', *Dublin* magazine (January 1924)

26 James Stephens to John MacDonagh, 24 August 1916, NLI Ms. 20,648/2.

27 Students of UCD to Muriel MacDonagh, 2 June 1916, NLI Ms 44,332/1.

28 TM, *The Poetical Works of Thomas MacDonagh* (Dublin, 1916) p. ix.

29 Ibid, p. xii.

30 Redmond, Lucille, 'The Lady Vanishes', *Skerries News*, October 2008.

31 Ibid.

32 MacDonagh, Donagh, 'Thomas MacDonagh' in *An Cosantóir*, 1945, p. 533.

BIBLIOGRAPHY

MANUSCRIPTS

Blackrock College

Private papers in the possession of Fr Seán Farrager.

Bodleian Library, Oxford

Asquith Papers.

Capuchin Archives, Dublin

Fr Aloysius Travers Papers.

Military Archives, Dublin

Bureau of Military History Witness Statements.

National Library, Dublin

Thomas MacDonagh Family Papers.

Geraldine Plunkett Dillon Papers.

Correspondence etc. of Patrick Pearse.

Eoin MacNeill Papers.

Hannah Sheehy Skeffington Papers.

The Pearse Museum, Dublin

St Enda's School Collection.

University College, Cork

Padraig MacSuibhne Papers.

University College, Dublin

Eamon de Valera Papers.

Eoin MacNeill Papers.

National Archives, London

War Office Papers.

NEWSPAPERS AND PERIODOCALS

The Academy

The Athenaeum

An Claidheamh Soluis

An Cosantóir

An Macaomh

The Expository Times

Irish Freedom

Skerries News

St Kieran's College Record

Studies

The Freeman's Journal

The Gaelic American

The Irish Citizen

The Irish Homestead

The Irish Independent

The Irish Monthly

The Irish Press

The Irish Review

The Irish Quarterly Review

The Irish Times

The Irish Volunteer

The Kilkenny Journal

The Leader

The New York Times

The Penny Illustrated Paper

The Times

The University Review

TP's Weekly

WORKS BY THOMAS MACDONAGH

POETRY

Through the Ivory Gate (Dublin, 1902).

The Golden Joy (Dublin, 1906).

Songs of Myself (Dublin, 1910).

Lyrical Poems (Dublin, 1913).

The Poetical Works of Thomas MacDonagh (Dublin, 1916).

ACADEMIC TEXTS

Thomas Campion and the Art of English Poetry (Dublin, 1913).

Literature in Ireland (Dublin, 1916).

THEATRICAL WORKS

The Exodus: A Sacred Cantata (with Benetto Palmieri)(London, 1904).

When The Dawn Is Come (first performed and published Dublin, 1908).

Metempsychosis (first performed and published, Dublin, 1912).

Pagans (first performed Dublin, 1915; first published Dublin, 1920).

BOOKS AND ARTICLES

Barton, Brian, *The Secret Court Martial Records of the 1916 Easter Rising* (Gloucestershire, 2014).

Bateson, Ray, *They Died By Pearse's Side* (Dublin, 2010).

Blake, Robert, *The Unknown Prime Minister* (London, 1955).

Churchill, Winston, *The World Crisis: The Aftermath* (London, 1929).

Clare, Anne, *Unlikely Rebels: The Gifford Girls and the Fight for Irish Freedom (Cork, 2011).*

Clarke, Austin, *A Penny in the Clouds* (London, 1968).

Colum, Mary, *Life and the Dream*, (New York, 1947).

Colum, Padraic, *Poems of the Irish Revolutionary Brotherhood* ((Boston, 1916).

Cooke, Pat, 'The Unrevised Stereotype: Thomas MacDonagh and the 1916 Rising' in *The Graph*, Vol. 2 No. 2. 1996.

De Burca, Seamus, *The Soldiers Song: The Story of Peadar O Cearnaigh* (Dublin, 1957).

Devoy, John, *Recollections of an Irish Rebel (New* York, 1929).

Dillon, Geraldine Plunkett, *All In The Blood* (Dublin, 2006).

Dugdale, Blanche Elizabeth, *Arthur James Balfour* (London, 1939).

Edwards, Ruth Dudley, *Patrick Pearse: The Triumph of Failure* (Dublin, 2006).

Farrell, Brian, 'Markievicz and the Women of the Revolution, in Martin, FX (ed), *Leaders and Men of the Easter Rising: Dublin 1916* (London, 1967).

Feeney, William J, *Drama in Hardwicke Street* (London, 1984).

Ferriter, Diarmuid, *The Transformation of Ireland* (London, 2005).

Foy, Michael and Barton Brian, *The Easter Rising 1916* (Sutton, 1999).

Gifford, Sidney, *The Years Flew By* (Galway, 2000).

Griffith, Arthur, *The Resurrection of Hungary* (Dublin, 1918).

Griffith, Kenneth and O'Grady, Timothy, *Curious Journey: An Oral History of Ireland's Unfinished Revolution* (Cork, 1998).

Gwynn, Stephen, *John Redmond's Last Years* (London, 1919).

Hobson, John Bulmer, *A Short History of The Irish Volunteers* (Dublin, 1918).

Holloway, Joseph, *Joseph Holloway's Abbey Theatre - A Selection of His Unpublished Journal 'Impressions of a Dublin Playgoer'* (Illinois, USA, 1967).

Hoppen, Theodore K, *Ireland since 1800: Conflict and Conformity* (New York, 1992).

Jackson, Alvin, *Home Rule: An Irish History 1800–2000* (London, 2003) p. 112.

Kelly, MJ, *The Fenian Ideal and Irish Nationalism 1882-1916* (Woodbridge, 2006).

Lowry, Donal, 'Thomas Michael Kettle' in *The Dictionary of Irish Biography* (Cambridge, 2009).

Martin, FX (ed), *The Irish Volunteers 1913-1915: Recollections and Documents* (Dublin, 1964).

McCormack, William, *Dublin 1916: The French Connection* (Dublin, 2012).

McGarry, Feargal, *Rebels: Voices from the Easter Rising* (London, 2011).

McGee, Owen, *The IRB from the Land League to Sinn Féin* (Dublin, 2005).

Moody, TW, *Davitt and the Irish Revolution*, (Oxford, 1982).

Nic Shiubhlaigh, Máire, *The Splendid Years* (Dublin, 1955).

O'Donovan Rossa Funeral Souvenir Handbook (Dublin, 1915).

Ó Maitiú, Seamus, *W&R Jacob: Celebrating 150 Years of Irish Biscuit Making* (Dublin, 2001).

Norstedt, Johann, *Thomas MacDonagh: A Critical Biography* (Virginia, USA, 1980).

MacLochlainn, Piaras F, *Last Words: Letters & Statements of the Leaders Executed After The Rising at Easter 1916* (Dublin, 1990).

Parks, Edd Winfield and Aileen Wells, *Thomas MacDonagh: The Man, The Patriot, The Writer* (Georgia, USA, 1967).

Ryan, Desmond, *Remembering Sion* (London, 1934).

Thompson, William Irwin, *The Imagination of Insurrection* (Oxford, 2007).

Williams, Roche, *In and Out of School: In the Home of the MacDonaghs* (Tipperary, 1999).

Wilson, Robert, *The Life and Times of Queen Victoria*, (London, 1900).

Index

A

Abbey Theatre 55-7, 81-2, 97,
126-9
Academy, The 124
Adelaide Hospital 229
Alexandra, Queen 39
Alfred Nutt (publisher) 53
Allen, Fred 273
Allgood, Sara 81
Aloysius, Fr 232-4, 239, 242-3,
247, 254-5, 272
Ancient Order of Hibernians
59
Anglo-Irish Treaty 27
April and May 49-50, 53, 122
Aran Islands 48-9, 51, 71-2
Armstrong, Major James 246-7
Arnold, Matthew 86, 91
Asgard 150-1
Ashe, Thomas 27
Askwith Inquiry 117
Asquith, Herbert 136-8
Association of Intermediate
and University Teachers 66
Association of Secondary
Teachers of Ireland 16, 66-7
Athenaeum 124
Augustine, Fr 232, 234, 238,
239-40
Austro-Hungarian Empire 62

B

Bachelors Walk massacre 154-5
Barrett, Michael 51
Barton, Detective Sergeant
Johnny 206
Bean na hEireann 68
Béaslaí, Piaras 150, 251
Bertram, James 121
Billington-Greig, Theresa
69-71
Bingham, Daniel 26
Bingham, Sir Richard 21
Blackadder, Brigadier General
Charles 246-7
Bloody Sunday 116, 183
Blythe, Ernest 181
Boland, James 144
Boland's Mills 201, 226-8, 240
Bonar Law, Andrew 140, 143

Brady, Christopher 217
Brennan, James 155-6
Brennan, Reverend Nicholas
32-3
Brennan, Seamus 251
Brian Boru 154
British Army
and Easter Rising 219-44
enlistment of Irishmen in 158-
9, 207, 243
occupies Kilmainham Gaol
253-4
Bulfin, William 73
Burke, Thomas 237
Butler, JM 252-3
Byrne, John 116

C

Caffery, Chris 223
Cahill, Patrick 210, 229
Campion, Thomas 99-100
Carre, JM 130
Carson, Edward 141-3, 157
Casement, Roger 111-13, 148,
150, 185-6, 196, 217, 260
Catholic Bulletin, The 263
Catholic Church 118
Catholic Truth Bulletin, The 22
Cavendish, Lord Frederick 31
Ceannt, Áine 187, 272
Ceannt, Éamonn 94-5, 150,
156, 163, 194, 204, 239-40,
245
Celtic Literary Society 50
Chalk (British spy) 188, 191
Charles Elkin Matthews
(publisher) 53
Chekhov, Anton 132-4
Childers, Erskine 150
Churchill, Winston 261
Citizen, The 69
Claidheamh Soluis, An 72-3,
144-6
Clan na Gael 31-3, 157-8,
176-7, 185
Clarke, Kathleen 270
Clarke, Tom 63, 163, 175, 177-
8, 190-1, 193, 198, 270
in Easter Rising 204, 258
Cleary, Arthur E 263
Cloughjordan 21-5, 30
Coghlan, Charles 120
Colbert, Con 150, 204, 245
Collins, Michael 206
Colthurst, Captain Bowen 224

Colum, Padraic 17-18, 55, 76,
85, 88-93, 102, 108-10
Columbus, Fr 244
Conan Doyle, Sir Arthur 111
Conlon, Martin 194
Connolly, James 118, 122, 156,
176, 183, 191-2, 263
in Easter Rising 201-38
writings 262
Connolly, Joseph 197
Connolly, Lillie 272
Connolly, Nora 272
Conradh na Gaeilge *see* Gaelic
League
Cook, John 86-7
court-martial 245-51, 253
Cousins, Margaret 68
Craig, James 142
Crehan, Reverend 49
Crimes Bill 31
Cruise O'Brien, Francis 70-1
Cúchulainn 73
Cumann na mBan 156, 189,
202, 210-11, 273
Curtis, Peter Paul 253

D

Daily Chronicle 54
Daly, Ned 201
Davitt, Michael 29
de Brun, Seosamh 218, 225,
228
de Valera, Eamon 189-90, 201,
226-8, 240, 251, 260
death sentence and execution
248, 252, 254-9
Defence of The Realm Act *see*
DORA
Devoy, John 176, 185
Dickson, Thomas 224
Dillon, John 261
DMP 95, 152, 183, 211, 252
Dolan, CJ 64
Dollard, Fr 46
Donovan, Professor Robert 99
DORA 181-3, 193, 252-3
Dowling, Sean 78
Dryhurst, Nora 68, 78
Dublin
MacDonagh settles in 57-8
slums 64-5
Dublin Castle 27, 29-30, 115,
136, 181, 183, 191-3, 196,
198
and Easter Rising 204-6, 209,

245, 252
Dublin Civic League 122
Dublin Corporation 94, 156, 193
Dublin Employers' Federation 114, 120-1
Dublin Industrial Peace Committee 16
Dublin Metropolitan Police *see* DMP
Dublin Trades' Council 120
Dublin United Tramways Company 114-15
Dudley, Yseult 176
Duffy, Mary 155-6
Dun Emer Guild 125
Dunsany, Lord 92

E

Easter Rising 201-38
aftermath 260-74
preparations for 184-9, 195, 198-9
Proclamation of the Irish Republic 204, 215, 217, 260
Edward VII, King 39, 127, 138
Egan, Patrick 30
Emmet, Robert 252
executions 254-9
Exodus, The: A Sacred Cantata 52
Expository Times, The 124

F

Farrell, Lord Mayor John J 94-6
Fay, Frank 129-30, 132
Feis Ceoil 52
Fenianism 60, 63, 175-6
Fermoy 50, 53, 57
Fianna Eireann, Na 144, 156, 202, 222, 223
Field, William 121
Figgis, Darrell 152-3
First World War *see* World War One
Fitzgerald, Henry 207-8
Fitzgibbon, John 150
Fitzgibbon, Seán 94-5, 156, 195-6, 199-200
Forster, William 29
Franz Josef, King of Hungary 62
Freeman's Journal, The 54, 121, 131, 134, 252

French, Percy 135
Furlong, Joseph 235

G

GAA 178
Gaelic League 16, 38, 42, 55, 67, 85, 98, 119, 192, 268
Fermoy branch 51-2
Johnswell branch 46
journal *An Claidheamh Soluis* 72-3, 144-6
Kilkenny branch 43-50
and *Na hAisteoirí* 72-3, 127
Garahan, Margaret 71
General Post Office *see* GPO
George V, King 94-5, 138
Gifford, Frederick 78-9
Gifford, Grace 79, 85, 95, 258, 272
Gifford, Isabella 78-9, 103-4, 255, 270
Gifford, Muriel 78-9, 81, 89, 95, 102-6
see also MacDonagh, Muriel
Gifford, Nellie 115-16, 272
Gifford, Sidney 78-80, 95, 103-4, 116
Gilligan, Peter 179
Gladstone, William Ewart 29, 50
Gleeson, Evelyn 125
Gogarty, Oliver St John 120
Golden Joy, The 53-4, 122
Gonne, Maud 68, 127
GPO 201-2, 220, 230-1
Gregory, Lady Augusta 56, 97, 126, 131
Gregory, Padraig 9
Griffith, Arthur 3, 50, 61-2, 63, 127, 176, 196
Griffith, DW 26
Gwynn, Stephen 73

H

Hackett, Dominick 48, 54-5, 83, 90-3, 99, 139, 146-8, 161, 175
Hague, The 171, 173
Haig, Major Alfred Edward 152
hAisteorí, Na 127
Harrell, William Vesey 152-4
Hayden, Mary 76
Hayes, Michael 211
Healy, Sean 223-4

Heathcote, Major Charles Harold 258
Henderson, Frank 166
Heuston, Seán 204
Higgins, President Michael D 19-20
Hitchcock, Alfred 81
Hobson, John Bulmer 60-3, 144-5, 149, 152-3, 162, 193
kidnapped 194-6, 199
Hoey, Detective Constable Daniel 206
Holloway, Joseph 82, 131, 133
Holy Ghost Fathers 32-8, 52
Home Rule 28, 30, 32, 59-60, 64, 71, 163, 192
and change of public opinion following executions 261
first Bill 31, 137
third Bill 136-7, 140-7, 157-8
Horace 251
Houston, David 91-2, 108-9, 256, 271
Howth gunrunning 150-5
Hughes, Seamus 235
Hunter, Tom 212-13, 234, 236, 238, 245
Hyde, Douglas 41-2, 76, 85

I

Ibsen, Henrik 135
Industrial Peace Committee 119-22
Inghinidhe na hÉireann 68
IPP 8, 32, 41-2, 58-61, 63-4, 94, 114, 119, 121
and third Home Rule Bill 137-9, 157
undermined by executions 261
IRB 15-16, 19, 22, 60-2, 144-5, 147-8, 157, 162-3
and funeral of O'Donovan Rossa 177-8
infiltrates Sinn Féin 62-3
MacDonagh in 175, 186, 188, 191
Military Council 163, 186, 188, 191-2, 194-5, 199
organises Muriel MacDonagh's funeral 273
preparations for rebellion 183-93, 195
Supreme Council 181
Irish Act of Union 62
Irish Citizen 172

Irish Citizen Army 156, 178, 183–4, 192
in Easter Rising 201, 229
Irish Homestead 124
Irish Independent 97, 114–15, 132–4, 155–6, 180, 197
Irish Literary Theatre 126–7
Irish Monthly, The 264
Irish National Aid & Volunteer's Dependent Fund 270
Irish National Foresters 156
Irish National Invincibles 31
Irish National Land League 28–30
Irish National Teachers' Organisation 66
Irish Parliamentary Party *see* IPP
Irish People, The 175
Irish Republican Army 215, 248
Irish Republican Brotherhood *see* IRB
Irish Review, The 93, 108–11, 118, 121, 123, 127–8, 151, 159–60
Irish suffragette movement 67–9
Irish Theatre 126–35, 164, 169
Irish Times, The 2, 10, 81, 125, 131, 176
Irish Transport and General Workers Union *see* ITGWU
Irish Volunteers 16, 18, 144–58, 164–8, 170–4, 178–84, 261
at Muriel MacDonagh's funeral 273
in Easter Rising 201–47
first convention 162–3
newspaper *The Irish Volunteer* 146, 160–1, 163–4, 167, 181–3, 186, 193–4
preparations for rebellion 184–9, 195, 198–9
split 160–1
Irish Women's Franchise League *see* IWFL
Irish Worker, The 113
ITGWU 16, 65–6, 113–15, 117, 120–2
IWFL 68–71

J

Jacob, George 207

Jacob's Biscuit Factory 17, 203, 205–34, 239–43, 247
Jeffs, Fred 131
Joyce, James (barman) 219
Judge, MJ 150

K

Kearney, Frank 225–6
Kearney, Peadar 203, 222, 230, 237
Kelly, Alderman Thomas 95, 193
Kelly, Matthew 60
Kennedy, PJ 67
Kent, Thomas 260
Kerrigan, Joseph Michaael 81
Kettle, Thomas 119, 121
Kilkenny 38–50
Kilmainham Gaol 17, 252–3, 258
King's Own Scottish Borderers 152, 154

L

Land Act 29
Land League *see* Irish National Land League
Land War 29–30, 60
Larkin, Jim 65–6, 114–17, 120
Latchford, Robert 253
Lawless, Joseph 166–7
Leader, The 69, 85
Ledwidge, Francis 92, 261–2
Lee, Edward 120
Lemass, Seán 251
Lenanne, Eoin 135
Liberty Hall 113
Literature In Ireland 16–17, 256, 265–9
Lloyd George, David 137
Lockout 16, 115–22, 183
Lonergan, Mick 144
Lowe, Brigadier General William 219–21, 230–4, 236, 239–40, 247, 257
Lynch, Diarmuid 197
Lyrical Poems 122–4

M

Mac an Bhaird, Art 132
Mac Guilla Ghunna, Cathal Buí 123
MacBride, Major John 203–9, 216, 221–2, 225–6, 232–5, 238, 241, 244, 248
execution 260
MacCaoilte, Seán 133
McCullough, Denis 60–3, 181
MacDiarmada, Seán 15, 61–3, 94–5, 150, 163, 190–1, 193, 195
in Easter Rising 204
in IRB 197–8
MacDonagh, Barbara (daughter) 90, 168–9, 271–4
MacDonagh, Donagh (son) 49, 106, 123, 125, 187, 199, 256–7, 271–4
writing about his father 165, 250–1
MacDonagh, Eleanor Louise (sister) 24, 26, 83
MacDonagh, James (brother) 24, 26
MacDonagh, John (brother) 24, 26, 128, 130, 132–3, 196, 199, 269
in Easter Rising 202, 206–12, 225, 230, 234–5, 243–5, 250, 254
MacDonagh, Joseph (brother) 24, 26–7, 270
MacDonagh, Joseph (father) 21–2, 32–3, 125
MacDonagh, Mary Josephine (sister) 24, 26, 102–3, 254–5, 271
MacDonagh, Mary Louise Parker (mother) 21–5, 32, 83
MacDonagh, Muriel (wife) 17, 123–5, 148, 168, 238, 247, 250–7
after MacDonagh's death 269–73
see also Gifford, Muriel
McDonnell, Mick 207
McGarrity, Joseph 63
McGarry, Milo 77
McGee, Owen 144
McGrath, Gussie 115–16
MacIntyre, Patrick 224
MacNeill, Eoin 42–3, 73, 76, 144–7, 156, 159, 162–3, 182
against Easter Rising 191–201
MacNeill, James 199
MacSuibhne, Padraig 51, 71
McSweeney, Councillor 47–8
Madame Rock's Little Theatre 130
Maguire, Mary 87–93, 103,

108-10, 124

Mallin, Michael 202, 205-6, 220, 223

Malone, Lieutenant Michael 204, 226

Markievicz, Countess Constance 95, 115-16, 127

Martin, Eamon 144, 150, 162

Martyn, Edward 126-31, 135, 269

Maxwell, General Sir John 229-30, 233, 235, 243, 246-8

Mayne, Rutherford 132

Meagher, J Anthony 133

Meldon, Thomas 237

Mellows, Liam 181

Metempsychosis 96-7

Mills, Inspector 252

Mitchelstown 51

Moloney, Fr Denis 23

Molony, Helena 68

Monaghan, Alfred 181

Moore, George 130-1

Munster Festival 52

Munster Training College 51

Murphy, Sean 203

Murphy, William Martin 114-15, 120

N

National Aid Association 272

National Literary Society 41-2

National Society for the Prevention of Cruelty to Children 65

National Volunteers 160-1, 173, 178

Nationalist, The 119

New Ireland Review 93

New York Times, The 19, 261

Nic Shiubhlaigh, Máire 129, 132, 133, 210

Nolan, Alderman James 47-8

Nolan, James (Bloody Sunday victim) 116

Norbury, Lord 252

Northern Whig, The 268

O

O'Brien, William 59

Ó Ceallaigh, Padraig 226

O'Cearnaigh, Peader 225

O'Connell, Derry 224

O'Connolly, Fr 182

O'Connor, Seamus 199

O'Connor, Una 129-30, 132

O'Doherty, Kitty 189

Ó Domhnaill, Liam 132

O'Donoghue and Company (publishers) 53

O'Donovan Rossa, Eileen 176-7, 178, 273

O'Donovan Rossa, Jeremiah 175-80

O'Duffy, Eimar 132

O'Farrell, Nurse Elizabeth 231

O'Grady, John 229

O'Grady, Standish 92, 93

O'Growney, Eugene 42

O'Hannigan, Donal 183-5, 187

O'Hanrahan, Henry 210

O'Hanrahan, Michael 163, 204, 209-10, 233-4, 236, 244, 260

O'Kelly, Dr Seamus 193, 196

O'Kelly, Seán T 196-8

O'Leary, John 179

Oman, William 201, 223

Ó Maolfhainn, Seamus 225

O'Rahilly, Michael ('The') 94, 146, 156, 162, 196

O'Reilly, Michael 30

O'Riain, Padraig 144

O'Riordan, Dan 227

O'Rourke 228

Orr, Thomas 207-8, 218, 241-2

Ó Seachain, Padraic 132

O'Shea, Katherine 32

O'Sullivan, Seamus 92

P

Pagans 169-70

Palmieri, Benetto 52

Paris 90-1

Parnell, Charles Stewart 28, 30, 32, 59, 64, 114

Pearse, Patrick 19, 71-8, 83, 90, 93-5, 105-6, 150, 177

court-martial 245

death sentence and execution 254-5, 259

in Easter Rising 201, 231-2, 235, 240, 263, 267

on executive of Irish Volunteers 162-3, 168, 170

graveside oration for O'Donovan Rossa 179-80

in IRB 162-3, 175, 186-7, 191-4

and Scoil Éanna 58, 72-8, 80,

83-4, 90-1

writings 262

Pearse, Willie 86, 133, 260

Penny Illustrated Paper, The 143

People's Protection Committee 127

Pim, Herbert Moore 181

Plunkett, Countess Mary Josephine 98, 125-6

Plunkett Dillon, Geraldine 89

Plunkett family 270

Plunkett, George 98

Plunkett, Geraldine 98-9, 126

Plunkett, Joseph 79, 98-9, 109, 111, 118, 120, 125-30, 162

in Easter Rising 203-4, 258, 263

in IRB 163, 175, 185-7, 191-3, 195, 197-8

writings 262

Poetical Works of Thomas MacDonagh, The 271

Pounch, Seamus 222

Pound, Ezra 269

Power, Ambrose 81

Price, Bob 163

Price, Eamon 235-6

Proclamation of the Irish Republic 204, 215, 217, 260

Protection of Person and Property Act 29

Q

Quinn, Patrick 155-6

R

Redmond, John 58-9, 139, 147, 149-50, 157-9, 162, 171, 174

RIC 183

Richardson, Sir George 142

Richmond Barracks 243-5

Roberts, George 109

Rockwell College 32-8

Rooney, William 50

Royal Irish Academy of Music 52

Russell, George William (AE) 92

Ryan, Desmond 78

Ryan, Fred 55

S

St Colman's College 50-1,

57, 66-7

St Kieran's Secondary School
40, 46-7, 50

St Mary's College, Dublin 52

Salkeld, Blánaid 133, 202

Savonarola, Girolamo 251

Scoil Éanna 58, 72-8, 80, 83-4,
90-1

Sheehy Skeffington, Francis 40,
68-9, 173-5, 224

Sheehy Skeffington, Hannah
66, 68

Sheridan, Richard 132

Sherlock, Lord Mayor Lorcan
156

Sherwood Forresters 226,
258-9

Sinn Féin 27, 61, 64, 94, 127,
139, 192, 247
infiltrated by IRB 62-3
newspaper 63, 79

Slater, Mick 225

Slater, Thomas 163

Slater, Tom 202-3

Smith, Eugene 192

Smith, FE 143

Society for the Preservation of
the Irish Language 41-2

Songs of Myself 100-2, 122

Spring Rice, Mary 150

Staines, Michael 90

Stapleton, William James 213-
14, 236-7

Stephens, James 92-3, 179,
269, 271

Stopford Green, Alice 109, 150

Strindberg, August 135

Stritch, James 144

*Studies: An Irish Quarterly
Review* 263, 268

Synge, JM 56-7, 86, 97

T

Tannan, Liam 166

Tenants' Defence League 28

Theatre of Ireland group 97

Through The Ivory Gate 35-6,
50, 53, 122

Thunder, Joe 225

TP's Weekly 86

Traynor, Oscar 188

Tribune, The 54

Triple Alliance 111

Triple Entente 110

U

UCD 85, 98-9, 105, 108, 125,
188, 269-70

Ulster Solemn League and
Covenant 141-2

Ulster Volunteer Force *see*
UVF

Unionism 139-42, 144, 151,
155, 157-9, 268

United Irishman, The 50

United National Societies
Committee 94-5

University College Dublin
see UCD

UVF 142-5, 182

V

Victoria, Queen 127

Villiers de L'Isle-Adam,
Auguste 132

W

Wall, James M 30

Walsh, Archbishop William 231

Weekly Freeman, The 49

West, WH 253

When The Dawn Is Come 55-6,
81-2, 96-8, 251

Whitman, Walt 100

Williams, Roche 23

Women's anti-war meeting
170-1

World War One 18, 157-9,
185, 217, 261-2

Wylie, William 246-8

Y

Yeats, WB 55-7, 76, 83-4, 93,
96-7, 126-8, 131